The Highlands of Ethiopia
Volume One

by

Sir William Cornwallis Harris

The Highlands of Ethiopia
Volume One
by Sir William Cornwallis Harris

ISBN: 978-93-62200-00-6

Published by

DOUBLE 9 BOOKS
2/13-B, Ansari Road
Daryaganj, New Delhi – 110002
info@double9books.com
www.double9books.com
Tel. 011-40042856

ABOUT THE AUTHOR

Major Sir William Cornwallis Harris was an English military engineer, artist, and hunter. He was the fourteen-year-old son of James Harris of Wittersham, Kent, and enrolled in Addiscombe Military Seminary. Two years later, in December 1823, he joined the East India Company's army as a second lieutenant in the Bombay Establishment of Engineers. Over the next thirteen years, he was deployed to several locations in India, allowing him to pursue his interests in outdoor sports and wildlife photography. He was promoted to first lieutenant in 1824, then captain ten years later. Harris landed in Cape Town in June 1836 on the 1467-ton Buckinghamshire, where he spent two years recovering from a fever. He was lucky to meet Dr. Andrew Smith, who had just returned from a voyage north where he had seen Mzilikazi in Mosega. From the Cape, he planned a hunting excursion to the Western Transvaal and Magaliesberg with William Richardson of the Bombay Civil Service, who had joined him on the voyage.

CONTENTS

Introduction

In putting forward a second edition of my "Highlands of Ethiopia," I have two very different duties to perform: first, to thank the press for the extremely liberal and generous manner in which it has received my work; secondly, to reply to certain objections which have been made by one or two periodicals, happily not of the first eminence, against both me and my travels. So numerous, however, are the publications that have evinced a favourable, I might almost say a friendly, disposition towards me, that I am unable to specify them. They will, therefore, I trust, accept in general terms my thanks to them one and all.

Their very flattering testimonies have induced me to revise carefully what I have written, in order, if possible, to render it worthy of their warm praise, and to justify their predilection in my behalf. On the other hand, *fas est et ab hoste doceri.* I have consequently turned to account even the animadversions of my enemies—for enemies unhappily I have, and those, too, of the most implacable and malignant character—mean persons to whom I have shown kindness, which they have apparently no means of repaying but by inveterate aversion. This circumstance I ought not perhaps to regret, except on their account. The parts we play are suitable to our respective characters; and I should even now abstain from prejudicing them in the estimation of the public, if I did not apprehend that my forbearance might be misconstrued.

The points of attack selected by my adversaries are not many in number. Ultimately, indeed, they resolve themselves into three: first, my style of composition, which they say is gorgeous and inflated, and therefore obscure; second, the inaccuracy of several of my details; and third, the absence of much new information, which it seems the public had a right to expect from me. On the subject of the first accusation it will not perhaps be requisite that I should say much. To any one who cannot understand what I write I must necessarily appear obscure; but it may sometimes, I think, be a question with which of us the fault lies. That my composition is generally intelligible may not unfairly, I think, be inferred from the number of persons who have understood and praised it; since it can scarcely be imagined that the majority of reviewers would warmly recommend to the public that in which they could discern no meaning. Besides, on the subject of style there is a great diversity of opinion, some thinking that very extraordinary scenes and objects should be delineated in forcible language, while others advocate a tame and formal phraseology which they would see employed on all occasions whatsoever. I may observe, moreover, that "style," as Gibbon remarks, "is the image of character," and it is quite possible that my fancy may have a natural aptitude to take fire at the prospect of unusual scenes and strange manners. Still I am far from defending obstinately my own idiosyncracies, and yet farther from setting them up as a rule to others. In describing what I saw, and endeavouring to explain what I felt, I may very possibly have used expressions too poetical and ornate; but the public will, I am convinced, do me the justice to believe that, in acting thus, my object was exactly to delineate, and not to delude. I called in to my aid the language which seemed to me best calculated to reflect upon the minds of others, those grand and stupendous objects of nature which had made so deep and lasting an impression on my own. At all events, I am not conscious of having had in this any sinister purpose to serve.

It is a far more serious charge, that I have presented the public with a false account of the Embassy to Shoa; that I have altered or suppressed facts; that I have been unjust to my predecessors and companions; and that I have at once misrepresented the country and its inhabitants. It has been already observed, that my accusers are few in number. Probably they do not exceed three individuals, two who affect to speak from their own knowledge, and one whom they have taken under their patronage as their cat's-paw. It may seem somewhat humiliating to answer such persons at all. I feel that it is so. But if dirt be cast at me, I must endeavour to shield myself from it, without enquiring whether the hands of the throwers be naturally filthy or not. That is their own affair. Mine is to avoid the pollution aimed at me. This must be my apology for entering into the explanations I am about to give.

When I undertook to lay before the public an account of my travels in Abyssinia, I had to choose between the inartificial and somewhat tedious form of a journal, and that of a more elaborate history, in which the exact order of dates should not be observed. I preferred the latter; whether wisely or unwisely remains to be seen, though hitherto public opinion seems to declare itself in favour of my choice. Having come to this determination, it was necessary that I should act in all things consistently with it. As I had abandoned the journal, it was no way incumbent on me to observe the laws which govern that form of composition. My business, as it appeared to me, was to produce a work with some pretensions to a literary character; that is, one in which the order of time is not regarded as a primary element, the principal object being the grouping of events and circumstances so as to produce a complete picture. I perfectly understood that I was to add nothing and to invent nothing, but that I was at liberty to throw aside all trivial details, and dwell only on such points as seemed calculated to place in their proper light the labours of the mission, with the institutions, customs, and type of civilisation found among the people to whom we had been sent. In conformity with this theory I wrote. One of the first consequences, however, of the view I had taken of my subject, was the sacrifice of all minute personal adventures, which scarcely appeared in any way compatible with my plan. I abandoned likewise the use of the first personal pronoun, and always spoke of myself and my companions collectively, thereby perhaps doing some little injustice to my own exertions, but certainly not arrogating to myself any credit properly due to others. Among my friends there are those who object to this manner of writing, and I submit my judgment to theirs. In this Second Edition, therefore, I have reconstructed the narrative so far as was necessary in order to convert the third person into the first. To the charge that I have not observed the strict chronology of a journal, I have already pleaded guilty. It seemed to me far better to arrange together under one head whatever belonged properly to one topic. For example, when recording the medical services rendered to the people of Shoa, high or low, I have not inserted in my work each individual instance as it occurred, but have placed the whole before the reader in a separate chapter. So likewise in other cases, that which appeared to elucidate the matter in hand, was introduced into what I thought its proper place, because there it might both receive and reflect light, whereas in any other part, perhaps, of the work, it might have been without significance, if not altogether absurd. Not being infallible, I may possibly have misinterpreted the laws of rhetoric which I adopted as my guide: of this let the public be judge. I have aimed, at all events, at drawing a correct outline of Shoa and the surrounding countries, as far as my materials would permit, and should I have sometimes fallen into error, I claim that indulgence which is always readily extended to authors similarly circumstanced. While in Abyssinia, my official position very greatly interfered with my predilections as a traveller. I could not move hither and thither freely. To enlarge the circle of science was not the principal object of my mission; but at the same time it must not be forgotten that I enjoyed some advantages which a traveller visiting the country under other auspices would scarcely have commanded. In drawing up my work, however, the character in which I travelled was of considerable disservice to me. Much of the information that I collected, it was not permitted me to impart, which I say, not by way of complaint against the regulations of the service in which I have the honour to be engaged, — on the contrary, I think it most just and proper that such should be the case — but that the reader, when he feels a deficiency in political or commercial information, may know that it has not been withheld through any negligence or disrespect of the public on my part.

I now come to consider more in detail the objections which have been urged against my travels. Some of these, it will at once be perceived, are so loose and indefinite as to be wholly incapable of being answered. For example, it is said, I have made no addition to the information already existing respecting the southern provinces of Abyssinia. How can I reply to this? Must I reprint all the works which had been previously published, and point out the additions I have made? The process, it will be acknowledged, is an unusual one. Besides, the scientific world has not hitherto been averse to look at several views of the same country, to compare them for itself, and to derive from the very comparison both pleasure and information. Some additions, moreover, to geographical science I undoubtedly have made, and there are those who have not been ashamed to borrow them. I have ascertained, for example, that the Gochob does not flow into the Nile, as it is made to do in a map which I have seen, constructed by one of the reviewer's greatest authorities. The inquiries I instituted render it probable that the Gochob is the same river with the Juba. And, above all, the longitude of Ankóber was, under my directions, and by a laborious series of operations, correctly determined. The importance of this to travellers who may not possess the ability or the means of resolving it themselves, I need scarcely point out. Previously, every position in the maps of Southern Abyssinia was calculated from a false position, and therefore of necessity wrong. But I shall not here enter upon an inventory of my humble services to science. I could wish they were more numerous, but such as they are I trust they will be found not wholly without their value.

In "ethnography," or rather perhaps "ethnology," the critic discovers my ideas to be all wrong; and he accounts for the circumstance by supposing in me some innate aversion to the "savage." I certainly dislike that particular variety of our species whether at home or abroad, but it does not necessarily follow that I have been therefore guilty of misrepresentation. These things, nevertheless, I leave to be determined by public opinion, which, so far as I can perceive, is little, if at all, influenced by the bitter and self-interested censures of my enemies.

When I determined on making some reply to the "slashing" Aristarchus who has assailed my work—I would say publicly, but that the thing is so obscure that few persons have even heard of it—my design was to attempt something like order, that I might not by a multiplicity of disjointed remarks confound the memory of my readers. But the impossibility of following any rational plan soon became apparent. The reviewer with whom I have to deal is a man who scorns all order and regularity. His only rule is that of *hysteron proteron*, or putting the cart before the horse. Not possibly that he considers such a method of writing best in itself, but that by introducing perfect anarchy into his critique, and returning a dozen times to each objection urged, my faults might in appearance be so multiplied that they would suffice to fill a whole encyclopaedia. Now if in my reply I followed any other than his fragmentary system, I might perhaps seem to many not to answer all his objections, whereas my intention is to demolish every one of them. I resolved therefore to begin *ab ovo*, and giving quarter to no impertinence or absurdity by the way, to clear the ground completely, and leave a perfect *rase campagne* behind me. That in so doing I shall not prove tedious, is more than I can hope. My adversary is insipidity personified. But if the controversy be unamusing, it shall, at least as far as I can render it so, be brief.

The critic whose vagaries I have undertaken to expose, though affecting not to be hypercritical, first dwells with a puerile pertinacity on the title of my book, which he pronounces to be a misnomer, because, forsooth, the territories of Shoa are not high lands, but a high land! Possibly he figures to himself the whole of Abyssinia as one single vast plateau, whose surface presents neither elevation nor depression, otherwise the reader will see no reason why it should be spoken of in the singular.

In describing the contents of the second volume, my reviewer speaks of "a slaving expedition among the Galla, *in which the Embassy*," he affirms, "*took part.*" The assertion, however, is incorrect, not to apply to it a harsher epithet; for the spectator who looks on a play can with no propriety be said to take part in the acting of it. The mission was sent to Sáhela Selássie, not to the city of Ankóber. It was consequently my business to attend the king, to watch his movements, and study his character, just as the Embassy under Sir John McNeil attended the Shah of Persia to Herát, though instead of taking part in the siege, he laboured earnestly to put a stop to it.

The contents of the third volume are next wilfully misrepresented, the critic desiring to make it appear that a very small portion indeed has reference to the country or people of Abyssinia, though at least two-thirds treat expressly of those subjects, whilst the remainder is strictly connected with them.

But it is not merely in the third volume that the critic is unable to discover any information respecting Shoa. He takes courage as he proceeds, advances from particulars to generals, and contends that the book contains no information at all in any part of it, that no account is given of the geography of the country, no sketch of its history, in short no account of it in any way whatsoever. Afterwards, indeed, an exception is made in favour of religion. Taking no interest in this, however, he treats it as a twice-told tale with which he was previously familiar. Considering the modes of thinking prevalent in the quarter, it may, without much uncharitableness, be permitted one to doubt this. Not to insist, however, on a point which may be disagreeable to the reviewer, I hasten to compliment him on his sagacity, which, through the table of contents, has made the discovery, that the political history of Abyssinia for the last thirty years is not given. I acknowledge the omission, and may perhaps have been to blame for suffering any consideration connected with the size of the volumes to weigh with me in such a matter. The historical sketch in question, however, was actually written, though the critic would probably not have derived from it any more satisfaction than from the rest of the book. He objected to its absence because it was not there. Had I introduced it, he would have said it was a twice-told tale, and absolutely good for nothing.

My adversary now and then qualifies, as he proceeds, his absolute affirmations. Having again and again maintained that there is no account, "historical or otherwise," given of the country, he afterwards admits his error, but says the account is "confused and unintelligible." I think it was Mr Coleridge who made the remark, when persons complained that they could not understand his work, that it was their fault, since all he had to do was to bring the book, and that it was their duty to bring the understanding. I make the same reply to the critic. Other people understand my account of Abyssinia; and if he really does not, I am sorry for him, but can offer him no assistance. However, there is an old proverb, I believe, which says, "There are none so blind as those who won't see."

The argument by which I am proved to have read Mr Salt, though I make no allusion to him, is curious; but I either profited by my reading, or I did not. If I profited, the consequences must be visible in my work; if I derived nothing from Mr Salt, then my work can contain no proof that I did. But it does, according to the critic, contain such proof; *ergo*, I have profited by Mr Salt's labours. It would have been well, however, if the critic had pointed out where and how much; for until he does so, my word will probably be thought as good as his, especially as he is anonymous, and I am not. One proof of my careless reading of Mr Salt is, I own, very remarkable. It seems, had I been well versed in his production, I should have known that Oubié is "still alive and ruler of Tigré;" Mr Salt having, of course, been careful to relate that circumstance. It so happens, however, that at the period I was engaged in writing my work, Oubié was a prisoner, and another prince seated on his throne—a fact, I believe, not preserved in Salt.

Next comes on the tapis the orthography of Ethiopia; *apropos* of which, the critic takes occasion to call in question my classical acquirements. I was not, however, aware that, by preferring one orthography to another, I was laying claim to profound erudition, or setting myself up for "an authority among scholars." On the contrary, I followed those who appeared to me very sufficient guides. Gibbon and Dr Johnson, — authors who may perhaps, even by the reviewer himself, be permitted to claim a humble niche among our classics. But they wrote, it may be said, in the last century. I therefore refer to a perfectly new publication, on a classical subject, if not the work of a classic, — I mean Mr Saint John's "History of the Manners and Customs of Ancient Greece," in which the orthography I have adopted is likewise made use of. If then I have been affected, I have at all events indulged my affectation in very good company. But the reviewer does not stop here. He thinks the orthography involves a mystery, and he goes about the unveiling of it in a very mysterious way. It is a proof he thinks that I am indebted to Mr Krapf for what little proficiency I may have made in the art of spelling; nay more, that I have derived from that gentleman all my knowledge of Abyssinia of every kind!

Before I make any other remark on this part of the subject, I will take occasion to compliment myself on my simplicity; for if I had desired to conceal my obligations to Dr Krapf, and have been conscious of any which I have not frankly stated, I should have been careful to spell Ethiopia *classically*, that is, as the reviewer does, in order to conceal the source from which I had drawn. I should thus clearly have put him on a very wrong scent, since a single letter suffices to lead him by the nose. But the most curious view of this question remains yet to be taken. Dr Krapf, he says, possesses the most complete knowledge of Abyssinia, its geography, language, and literature. He then goes on to maintain that Dr Krapf imparted his knowledge to me, and I that same knowledge to the public. But, no! the reviewer stops short here, and affirms that I envied the public the possession of Dr Krapf's knowledge, and withheld it all; since he everywhere asserts that there is no information whatever in my book. Verily, I have been taking a lesson from that ancient Briton who is represented as having plundered a naked Scotchman:

> "A painted vest Prince Vorti ern had on,
> Which from a naked Pict his grandsire won!"

Because, if I tell nothing new, and owe all I do tell to Dr Krapf, who also imparted to me all he knew, his knowledge must clearly have been very limited. I have acknowledged, however, and I repeat the acknowledgment, that Dr Krapf was of essential service to me in various ways; that he freely imparted to me the valuable information he possessed, and gave me to understand that I was at liberty to make use of it. I did make use of it, having previously however been careful to publish my obligations to him. In fact, there is no man who would be more ready than Dr Krapf, were he now in England, to express his perfect satisfaction with what I have done. He has, indeed, expressed it publicly in his "Journal," where he acknowledges himself to be under obligations to me; and the Church Missionary Society, in its preface, makes the same admission.

I am next blamed for not giving a connected history of the mission; the proper answer to which is, that I never undertook to give it. I have not entitled my book "the History of an Eighteen Months' Residence in Shoa," but have said that my observations were collected *during* an eighteen months' residence there. They are not all my observations, nor have I arranged them chronologically; therefore, though the reviewer feels disappointed, he has no right to quarrel with me. He expected one thing—I published another; simply because I did not write for him, or such as he, but for the public. As it is, however, I am not sorry that he is "tantalised," which he would not be if he possessed one-tenth of the knowledge to which he obliquely lays claim. On most points he is profoundly ignorant, and it suits my purpose to leave him so. Any information that I can impart, without prejudice to the public service, it is doubtless my duty to give; and accordingly, in this second edition, I have stated some facts not recorded in the first. In most cases, indeed, men publish a first edition as an *experiment*, to ascertain how far their views of what information the public needs are correct, that they may afterwards diligently, and to the best of their power, supply it.

The Mission, it is said, has been "a complete failure." But how is this proved? By a scrap extracted from some anonymous correspondent to a newspaper, who writes, not from Angollála or Ankóber, but from Caïro, which is nearly as though a person residing in Saint Petersburgh were to write authoritatively to China respecting what is going on in Lisbon. But it does not follow that the Mission has been a failure, because some Cairo gossip chooses to say so, or because all the fruits of it have not yet been reaped. A treaty has been concluded, friendly relations have been established, and upon this basis commerce will proceed, slowly perhaps, but surely, to erect its structure. It will be for the next generation to determine whether or not the mission was "a complete failure." A reviewer residing in the purlieus of High Holborn is not competent to do it.

On the subject of "German crowns," the critic may, for aught I know, be a great authority; or, as he says on another matter, may know somebody that is. But the quarrel which he seeks to pick with me is so utterly puerile, that I will not engage in it. His positiveness, however, is as usual proportioned to his ignorance, for even on so infinitesimal a point as this he contrives to be wrong, since the marks are not *three*, as he supposes, but *seventeen*, on the coronet and shoulder-clasp. However, supposing I had here been wrong, would it therefore have been fair to infer that on every other point I must be wrong also? An usurer would be a better authority on the aspect of a gold coin·than the Chancellor of the Exchequer, yet in finance the Jew might not be a match for the Chancellor. Let it not, however, be supposed that I desire to compare myself with Mr Goulburn, or the critic to a Jew; I merely mention these things by way of illustration. At any rate, my censor's blunder must be obvious to every one who has seen a German dollar, and to adopt his own phrase, "*Ex pede Herculem.*"

On the practice observed by the Mohammadans in slaughtering animals, the reviewer displays a vast deal of erudition, and quotes the treatise of Mr Lane, on the "Manners of the Modern Egyptians." It happens, however, that there are variations in the practices of the Moslems; and he might as well have argued, that because there are pyramids in Egypt, there must also be pyramids in Abyssinia, as that because the Egyptians do not make use of certain words on particular occasions, therefore, the Danákil and the Somauli cannot possibly employ them. My narrative does not touch on the customs of Egypt, on which Mr Lane writes but on those of a different part of Africa, in which, so far as I can discover, that author has never been. What I relate, however, is matter of fact, and the critic only exhibits his profound ignorance of human nature by supposing that Mohammadanism is stereotyped in any part of the world, since there are as many differences in the customs of the Mohammadan nations, as in those of Christendom. For example, — the practice of "bundling," so common in Wales, does not, I believe, prevail in Egypt; but if our critic were to infer that it is, therefore, altogether anti-Islamite, he would be as completely wrong as he is in the present instance; for that which the Egyptian Mussulman detests, is the established custom in certain parts of Afghanistan. So, likewise, is the invocation of the name of God during the slaughter of animals. The Egyptians, it seems, invoke the sacred name without coupling with it "the Compassionate, the Merciful," which they think would sound like mockery; but what proof is the reviewer prepared to advance in his wisdom, that this rule is observed in India and every other part of the East?

The Mohammadans, again, he says, never drink blood; and why? because it is forbidden them by the Korán. But stealing is no less peremptorily prohibited. Will he, therefore, argue, that there is no such thing as a Mohammadan thief? The question is not as to what is forbidden or ordained, but as to a simple matter of fact. I state what I saw with my own eyes. The critic, who was never in the country, who cannot possibly know what I saw or did not see, contradicts me. I leave it to the public to judge between us; asserting, however, that he is fully as ignorant of the people whose customs he so glibly writes about, as he is of the rules of common decency.

For verbal criticism I entertain no contempt, though I think that a strict application of its rules to a book of travels, is scarcely called for. However, let us see how the critic succeeds in his task. I relate that the Arabs call the cove *Mirsa good Ali*, the "source of the sea;" from which he immediately infers my utter ignorance of Arabic. The only thing, however, that is really clear from the remark he has made is, that he does not understand English when it happens to be in the slightest degree inverted. A Biblical critic. Dr Parr, if I remember rightly, objected to a passage in the English version of the Bible upon much the same grounds. "Thus," says the Scripture, "he giveth his beloved sleep." Now the doctor maintains "beloved" to be an epithet bestowed on sleep, although the real sense is, that sleep is given to the "beloved." Still, in my opinion, the meaning is so obvious, that it required some ingenuity to mistake it. In my own case, the meaning I think is equally obvious; at least, what I intended to say was, that the Adaïel bestow on Mirsa good Ali cove, the additional name of "the source of the sea."

Upon the remarks on "mafeesh," I scarcely know what to say; but if he were to ask me,—is there any point or sense in them? I should reply "*mafeesh*, there is none"—an idiom well understood in English. Let the critic try again at Richardson's dictionary, and if he really can make out the Arabic characters, I think he will be able to discover a meaning which would come in very properly where I have placed it. "It is of no consequence," exclaimed the young assassin, "none," which is precisely the answer sometimes given to the insatiate "beggars" that we are told "surround the traveller" in certain countries, "there is no money in my pocket—none." Nevertheless, as I have passed public examinations, and obtained certificates of superior proficiency in no more than four oriental tongues, I cannot be deemed so competent to offer an opinion on this subject as the reviewer and his accomplices.

With regard to the critiques on the Amháric expressions found in my work, it may be sufficient to say, that by his own confession "the reviewer does not understand one syllable of the language," but hazards his remarks on the strength of knowing somebody who does. This appears to me a very poor qualification. It is as though I should set up as a critic in Sanscrit because I have shaken hands with Professor Wilson. However, let us examine the notions of this man who is so learned by proxy. One of the greatest triumphs of his erudition is his explanation of the Amháric word "Shoolada," which, strengthened by Salt, and others, he determines to signify exclusively a "rump-steak." That it has this signification there can be no doubt, but if the critic be disposed to defer on this, as on other occasions, to Dr Krapf's Amháric scholarship, he may yet, as he expresses it, "live and learn." In a copy of manuscript notes in Dr Krapf's handwriting, still in my possession, occurs the following passage, which I quote *verbatim et literatim*:—"In one point the Abyssinian practices agree remarkably with those of the Jews, we mean the practice mentioned in Genesis chapter xxxii, where we find that the Israelites did not eat the nerve, since Jacob had been lamed in consequence of his earnest supplication to the Almighty, before he met his brother Esau. This nerve is called in Amháric 'Shoolada.' I cannot determine how far the abstinence from this kind of meat is kept in the other parts of Abyssinia, but it is a fact in Shoa, that many people, particularly those of royal blood (called Negassian), do not eat it, as they believe that by eating it they would lose their teeth, the Shoolada being prohibited and unlawful food. Therefore, if anybody has lost his teeth, he is abused with the reproach of having eaten prohibited meat, as that of vultures, dogs, mules, donkeys, horses, and particularly of man, the meat of whom is said to prove particularly destructive for the teeth."

From the above passage, if the reviewer be disposed to accept Dr Krapf for his teacher, he may clearly learn one or two particulars not hitherto comprehended within the wide circle of his knowledge. For example, he will perceive that the idea of eating man's flesh is not yet entirely exploded from that part of Africa. On the contrary, the forbidden luxury would appear sometimes to be indulged in even by those who are one step at least, advanced before the polite Danákil, whom, at the sacrifice of my reputation for charity, I have denominated "vagabonds and savages."

The critic's observations on the pronunciation of Amháric and Galla words are so elaborate a specie men of trifling, that it would be wholly lost labour to wade through them. Of the Galla language he knows nothing, and had the case been different, still I might be permitted to judge by my own ear in the case of a tongue absolutely unwritten. Those acquainted with the works of travellers in the East are aware that almost every one has adopted a peculiar system of orthography. All, therefore, but one, might, by a disingenuous critic, be accused of ignorance. But the reviewer goes on to inform the public that "the *vulgar* mistakes of English pronunciation— which are not participated in by Germans—are the wrong insertion or omission of the aspirate." This is designed as a death-blow to me for writing *Etagainya* without an initial A, which highly culpable omission he presently afterwards takes occasion to rectify. Under this charge of vulgarity it is some consolation to me to quote as my authority Isenberg's Amháric Dictionary, more especially since that gentleman *is* a German; but had he even been otherwise, I think his views on this subject of the aspirate might perhaps be preferred to those of any cockney.

The elaborate disquisition on *larva* and *boudak* (For *boudak* read *boudah*. It ought to have been translated *sorcerer*, but all artisans, blacksmiths especially, are regarded as *boudahs*. Vide Isenberg's Amháric Dictionary. For *larva* read *lava*.) proves the critic to be qualified for the reading of proof-sheets, which appears to be the highest praise he can justly lay claim to. He can detect a misprint in other men's works, and when his passions are unexcited, may possibly be able to correct it. But in the matters of ear or style, I would just as soon defer to the judgment of the great "Arqueem Nobba," whoever that may be, (Vide Anti-Slavery Reporter, November 29th, 1843, page 222. For the information of my readers, it may be proper to explain that "Arqueem nobba" is believed to be doing duty for "Hakim nabaroo," "You were the doctor") from whom he seems to have obtained so much of his Oriental learning. He well knows to whom I allude, if no one else does. I shall turn his weapons against himself, and take occasion to question the classical attainments of a reviewer who translates "*suum cuique*" — "be it for good or ill;" and shall direct the public indignation to the fact of his having aroused curiosity "without gratifying it," by the statement that I "studiously laboured to keep out of sight *a very* special service performed by the members of the Embassy." What was it? He must surely be thinking of *his reporters*, not of *my assistants*. Be this as it may, he will not attempt to screen himself behind the printer's devil, it being clear that no typical errors can be admissible in his forty pages of letter-press, if two are to be held inexcusable in my twelve hundred!

It will by this time, I think, be apparent that an extremely peculiar system of criticism has been adopted in reviewing my book. Here the diction is attacked, there the want of information; now we have complaints that information is given, but that it was obtained through the instrumentality of Dr Krapf; then the reviewer wanders into political and other considerations, and attacks my conduct as leader of the Mission. Occasionally he appears to be overwhelmed by a painful sympathy, an intense philanthropy, extreme sorrow for the dead, which betrays him into persevering rancour towards the living. In discussing, for example, the melancholy catastrophe at Goongoonteh, which, if credit be given me for the smallest particle of human feeling, I must be supposed to have regretted as much as any man, especially since Sergeant Walpole and Corporal Wilson were under my command, and both highly useful to me as soldiers and artisans, the critic suffers his compassion so powerfully to disturb his intellect, that he literally knows not what he says. He may, therefore, if such be his object, be thought extremely amiable by some people, but, upon the whole, I apprehend, he will appear to be infinitely more absurd: because, to obtain credit for a generous and expansive humanity, it is necessary, at least, to bear the semblance of an unwillingness to wound men's reputations, living or dead. A genuine sympathy is always most active in proportion to the capacity of feeling possessed by the object of it. Thus we sympathise with our contemporaries more than with generations passed away; with Christians more than with Turks and Pagans; with Englishmen more than with Chinese; with our relations and friends more than with persons whom we never saw. But my critic reverses this order of things. His benevolence clings to individuals whose names he never heard, and urges him to inflict injury at all events, and pain if he can, upon persons whose sensibilities, he supposes, lay them open to his attacks. In one publication it seems to be intimated that I killed the men myself, whilst in the other I am conjectured to have been standing sentry, and to have dropped asleep at my post. The former charge I shall leave the Government of my country to answer; for if I be guilty and still at large. Government has made itself my accomplice. Shall I on the second point enlighten the critic, or shall I not? The fact is, I was not asleep, though with the greatest propriety I might have been, but at the very moment of the perpetration of the murder, I was leaning in bed upon my elbow, conversing with Captain Graham. Nevertheless, from the form of the *wady*, I could not command a view of every part of the encampment, or discern in the dark the approach of the assassins, at the distant point which they selected for their noiseless attack.

As to the manner in which I have related the circumstance, that is another affair, and the critic is at liberty to judge of it as he pleases. I claim, however, the same liberty for myself, and will venture to observe, that this part of his review is more lumbering, heavy, and absurd than ordinary; that in attempting to display feeling, he is only betrayed into lugubrious affectation; and that however I may be able to wield our mother tongue, he manages it so unskilfully that he wounds no one but himself.

The next charge is based, like the former, on the critic's sympathy. I relate that at the village of Fárri the gentleman entrusted with the command of the watch, "worn out by incessant vigils," fell asleep. The apology, it will be perceived, precedes the statement of the fact. But this new knight of La Mancha is not satisfied. Putting his redoubtable quill in rest, he tilts most chivalrously at my narrative; and, the operation over, chuckles with delight at my supposed discomfiture. He may, perhaps, have learned from some prying visitor to what particular officer I allude in the above passage. But most assuredly the public has not, and therefore no evil consequence can arise from what I say. All our critic's ideas, however, are peculiar. He considers it criminal to hint indistinctly in a published work at a "breach of discipline," but thinks I might with propriety have reported the circumstance officially to Government! My theory of propriety is different. I made no report to

Government; but when there were so many broad shoulders to share the blame between them, I thought it quite safe to touch upon it in my volumes.

Having waded through the above tedious list of charges, we arrive, so the reader may be tempted to imagine, at something new. But that is not the critic's plan. On the contrary, we find Monsieur Tonson on the stage again. Well might Dr Krapf exclaim, "Deliver me from my friends!" if the reviewer in question be really one among the number. Secretly, however, it is not the Missionary that is aggrieved, but another individual whose name I will not be provoked to print in my pages. This person, we are told, came down to Dinómali, in company with Mr Krapf, "to welcome the Embassy." What he came down to do is not, however, the question. Come he certainly did; and I should have made honourable mention of him had I, during my stay in Shoa, found no reason to be dissatisfied with his conduct. The reverse was the case; and as I did not choose to be at the trouble of writing in his dispraise, I thought it better to say nothing. Let the reviewer be satisfied with that, for, if I should say anything further, I am sure his satisfaction would not be augmented. He is perfectly right in supposing, that I have not imparted to the public all the knowledge I acquired in Shoa, and that I have not related all the piquant comic anecdotes which were often at my pen's point, struggling to see the light. But who knows? The time for telling them with effect is not yet passed, and it is quite possible that, under certain combinations of circumstances, I may yet return to this part of my subject, especially if the anonymous system be persevered in, and attempts be made to wound me from behind the friendly figure of the Missionary.

I may here, however, mention by the way, that, besides the learned Theban alluded to, the critic has two other authorities. Dr Krapf and M. Rochet D'Héricourt. Upon them he relies with equal and entire confidence. But I would beg to suggest, that there exist some slight discrepancies between the statements of those two writers, and that weight can be laid on the testimony of the one only in proportion as you mistrust the other. Yet the critic appears to discover nothing of this, never perceives that their testimonies are inter-destructive, but is perfectly satisfied to play off each in his turn against me. These authorities, in fact, are the legs on which his whole accusation appears to stand, though there be in reality an anonymous authority, which, like the third leg in the riddle, helps to support the tottering figure. To Mr Krapf, it is said, the Embassy owed whatever influence it possessed in Shoa. The officers of the Mission were nothing; the presents were nothing; the expectation of assistance and support from the Indian Government, in which Sáhela Selássie indulged, were nothing: — the reverend missionary was the "life and soul of the Embassy." I know not whether, as Dr Krapf is a minister of the Gospel, this be meant as a compliment or as a sneer; but so it is. I am said to have had no influence with the king, save through him who was literally all-powerful at court. This being borne in mind, turn we now to the critic's other authority, M. Rochet D'Héricourt, who is said to have been equally influential. But here comes the difficulty, which the critic either perceived or did not perceive. In the latter case he is criminally ignorant of what he ought to have known before he ventured to attack me; and if he did perceive it, then he is still more criminal for having suppressed the truth, and made that suppression serve the purpose of its contrary. It will be seen that I abstain from harsh language, and rather extenuate than otherwise the unworthiness of my adversary. The circumstance, however, to which I allude, is this: the critic maintains that Dr Krapf was all-powerful with Sáhela Selássie; M. Rochet D'Héricourt, on the other hand, asserts that Dr Krapf possessed so little influence, that it was only through *his* special interference, and at *his* earnest entreaty, that the king suffered him to proceed towards the Galla frontier with the army. Nay, not only had the missionary, according to this traveller, (Rochet D'Héricourt, Voyage dans le Pays D'Adel, et le Royaume de Choa, pages 224-233.) no influence, but the king displayed the strongest possible repugnance for him, and made him feel the effects of his dislike throughout the whole campaign. Consult the "Journal" (Journal of the Rev. Messrs Isenberg and Krapf, page 187) of the worthy missionary himself; and we find that both he and M. Rochet D'Héricourt were, without solicitation or entreaty, on his part at least, "ordered to accompany the king." I am not pretending to dictate to the public as to which of these authorities it shall prefer. I only state facts, and leave others to draw the proper inference. The authority of Dr Krapf, however, at the court of Shoa to me seems to be strangely and wilfully exaggerated. It was a reflected authority, if I may so speak, that he exercised during the residence of the Mission in the country; an authority based upon the influence of the British Government, represented there for the time by me. The amount of his personal influence was such that the slightest accident sufficed to overthrow it. Had it been greater, his application to return would have been listened to. It may no doubt be observed in reply, that neither could my influence, which was fully exerted in his behalf, have been very considerable. But the caprices of despotism are not always to be accounted for, and they will serve to explain both the missionary's want of success, and my own.

This subject has been artfully connected with the return of the Mission from Shoa. It is said, that had we not retired, we should have been forcibly expelled. I can certainly offer no proof that we should not; but the probability is, that the king of Shoa would have been in no hurry to dry up a constant source of profit to himself. It may, in fact, be laid down as a general rule, that no Oriental despot ever expels the giver of presents. It is the receiver of presents that he regards as an eyesore, the man who is dependent on him for his daily bread. The critic, however, has been "assured," that had we not retired, we should "probably ere long" have been expelled. But to this I reply, that probably we should not; and I call on him to state his proofs of the "disrepute" into which he asserts we had fallen. I have been "assured," that "probably" he has none to give, and "probably" this assurance is correct; otherwise, I think he would have been too glad to offer them. Be this as it may, the fact is, that we were not expelled, but recalled by our own government, when it considered that the duties for which I had been deputed, were fully accomplished.

The next attack upon me is based on certain "strange stories," which the critic says he has heard. For myself, considering the strange people with whom he associates, I entertain not the slightest doubt in the world that he has been crammed with "strange stories," and that he firmly believes them. In fact, he reminds me strongly of an anecdote related by Vossius, who, as Charles the Second observed, would believe anything but the Gospel. So this critic, who has no appetite whatever for plain truth, will swallow "strange stories" by the bushel. For example, with an earnestness which does great credit to his simplicity, he believes that the British officers in Shoa, with the few rank and file under their command, assisted the king in making prisoners among the Gallas. He believes, too, of course, that the field-piece, which had been presented to the king, and was therefore no longer under the control of the embassy, was employed to batter down villages, and, in one word, to effect the triumph of Sáhela Selássie over his refractory subjects and heathen neighbours. I feel for the distress his humanity must have suffered, and all through the "strange stories" to which he lends so greedy an ear! But let him be re-assured. The slaughter was not perpetrated by means of the galloper gun, which went not on the expedition at all, but was left by the king at his palace newly erected near Yeolo, the place of rendezvous. (N.B. This is not meant as a translation.) There were no "rounds of *artillery*" in the case, and the escort of British soldiers was taken with us, not to join in the foray, but to protect our own tents. Neither is this "memorable circumstance." "omitted in my volumes," as asserted by the veracious critic. It is distinctly stated for the information of those who are able to read, and the conduct of one of the privates stands specially recorded, who was urged by the Amhára to destroy a Galla.

(As a military man, and an Engineer officer to boot, I may perhaps be permitted to suggest, although with the utmost deference to the reviewer and his anonymous authorities, that the term "ammunition" might here have been employed with advantage. But perhaps he may consider "rounds of *artillery*" to be a more *classical* expression!)

The critic's persevering patronage of Dr Krapf is so chivalrous, that I almost regret to show that it has been exerted in vain. Truth, however, requires that I should do so. Perhaps, indeed, the reviewer's purpose may be less benevolent than it appears at first sight. His object may not be so much to exalt the clergyman, as to depress me, by creating, as far as he is able, in the public mind, the belief of what he asserts so positively, namely, that the Embassy fell into utter "disrepute" after the departure of the missionary, that so far from being able to exercise any influence, it would have been forcibly expelled, had it not beaten a hasty retreat. My opponent is a man of dates, and parades them in a manner truly pathetic. But how on these points did he happen to remain so much in the dark? Had he not all the great Abyssinian authorities at his elbow? Was he not acquainted with those who knew everything about the country—Arabic and Amháric scholars, who, by the help of Isenberg's Dictionary, could translate *boudah*, and with the aid of Richardson, plunge into the mysteries of *mafeesh*? Where was the erudite individual who weighed my classical attainments in the balance, and found them wanting? Where was his *fidus Achates*, the "Arqueem Nobba?" How happens it that his oracles grew suddenly dumb when he consulted them on the subject of dates? The reader will scarcely credit the reason of all this when it is stated; but the fact is, that the reviewer had no other object in view than to misrepresent and injure me, though of course aware that it was in my power fully to refute him. I shall do so now, and, as I think, so satisfactorily, that he will not return to the charge.

I state in my travels, that through the interference of the British Embassy, four thousand seven hundred persons, reduced by an arbitrary edict of the king to bondage, were liberated; upon which the critic, full of the "strange stories" which his strange associates had related to him, immediately concludes that Dr Krapf might have had some hand in that transaction. At all events he must contrive to make it appear so, otherwise what would become of his primary thesis, that the Embassy "fell into such disrepute?" Montaigne, the reader will doubtless remember, observes somewhere in his essays, that in order to catch his critics napping, he often put forth the opinions of the greatest writers of antiquity, without making the least allusion to the author, in order that, if these should be turned into ridicule, as was not unlikely, he might show that it was not himself that they had attacked, but Seneca, or Cicero, or Plato. Without having any such intention, I have caught my critic in a similar trap. Believing he could attribute the honour to Dr Krapf, he does not call in question the issuing of the edict or the liberation of the slaves, but inquires knowingly, "had *he*, the missionary, nothing to do with their deliverance?" Next, with a skill which does him much credit, he connects the liberation of the princes with this other transaction, so that if the reader believes his unfounded assertion that it was Dr Krapf, not the Embassy, whose influence prevailed with the king in the one case, he may be led to suppose that it was so in the other. This, it must be acknowledged, is a very ingenious piece of workmanship, and has, I doubt not, earned its author much credit. Nevertheless, it will not bear the touch of examination. The simplest statement of facts in the world will suffice to destroy it, together with the critic's main theory on the subject of my loss of influence at the court of Shoa. Dr Krapf quitted Angollála on the 12th of March, 1842, and during May of the same year, left Massowah for Aden. His active influence, it may fairly be inferred, terminated at this date. The forlorn Embassy was now abandoned to its own resources. There was no one to interest the king in its behalf; no one to perform great and benevolent actions, in order that I might obtain the credit of them. While we were in this state of torpor, the proclamation in question was published by the herald. Before Dr Krapf quitted Massowah? Alas! no. For that event took place in May, whereas the royal edict was only promulgated on the 3rd of August. It was by me, therefore, and not by Dr Krapf, that the remonstrance was forwarded to Sáhela Selássie, which produced the liberation of the slaves. This fact is known to every member of the Mission, and it ought to have been within the recollection of some of those infallible authorities who at once supplied the critic with facts and with learning, who remembered for him, understood languages for him, and when need was, invented for him.

The statement that the parents of the four thousand seven hundred individuals liberated, were slaves, is not true. I have said that their fathers were bondsmen, and their mothers free women, and this position I maintain. To the question who delivered the petition, I reply, "my dragoman of course." Upon his boasted maxim of "giving honour to whom honour is due," the conscientious reviewer will doubtless award the sole credit of the success attending this remonstrance, not to myself, but to the party who presented it, and his doing so will be quite as reasonable as the decision that I collected no geographical information, because my assistant. Dr Kirk, was entrusted by me with the department of survey. In equity he ought surely to have taken the case of Dollond into consideration, since *he* made the satellite glass and the sextant used in determining the longitude of Ankóber, upon which every recent addition to the geography of southern Abyssinia is indebted for whatever value it does possess.

Next comes the deliverance of the princes, which took place little more than three months before my return to India. These facts, known to every person in Abyssinia, the correctness of which will be vouched for by every member of the Mission, and the whole particulars of which were laid at the time before the Indian and British governments, may, perhaps, suffice to show in what spirit I have been criticised, and how totally unscrupulous my assailants have been. The gross misstatements disseminated anonymously through some of the public journals, and repeated by the candid reviewer, I have already publicly contradicted with my name. I here also contradict the assertion, that the king remained silent during my sojourn on the frontier. What object the sage reviewer would propose by my going back to take *a second* leave of His Majesty, when such is the etiquette of no country in the whole world, and my public duties imperatively required my presence at Fárri, the reader will be, as I am, at some loss to comprehend.

The treaty concluded with the king of Shoa having now been placed by Parliament before the country, I should have thought it unnecessary to notice the remarks which have been made on that subject, but for one or two considerations connected with it. First, it is said, that the ancient practice of detaining strangers had in usage been previously abolished, and it seems that, notwithstanding the treaty, it was afterwards, in one particular case, revived. Clearly the critic does not perceive the force of his own statements; for if, in spite of the most solemn engagements that a prince can enter into, Sáhela Selássie denied a British subject ingress to his country, does it not follow that distinct stipulations on this point were necessary? What does it signify, that practically Sáhela Selássie had in many instances permitted Europeans to enter his country? Were they not all, whilst there, legally subject to his caprice, and was it not prudent to endeavour to emancipate them from that caprice? But Sáhela Selássie, it is said, shortly violated the treaty, and his act is made the subject of accusation against me. Had I broken it myself, the circumstance would have been somewhat more germane to the matter. At present, all that can be said is, that Sáhela Selássie is a novice in European diplomacy.

The case of hardship alluded to, is that of Dr Krapf, who, having quitted Shoa on urgent private business, was denied re-admission. On this subject I might enter into a long explanation, which, because of the peculiarity of my position, could never be complete. I therefore judge it more satisfactory to refer to the testimony of the Church Missionary Society, which, as well as Dr Krapf himself, has put on record its entire satisfaction with my proceedings. If, therefore, the parties most deeply concerned be content because they understand the whole state of the case, I may safely despise the reproaches of a critic who neither knows nor cares any thing about the matter, further than as it may enable him to prejudice me in public opinion.

In every page of the criticism the sophisms and fallacies of which I have undertaken to expose, there is some fresh proof that the reviewer does not see his own way, and that he is perpetually at contradiction with himself. For example, he insists on nothing more incessantly than the all-powerful influence of Dr Krapf over the king of Shoa, to which, he says, the Embassy owed whatever success it met with. No sooner, however, does the missionary quit the precincts of the court, than he is arrested and plundered, evidently, the reviewer insinuates, with the knowledge and connivance of his fast friend Sáhela Selássie. What then becomes of his prodigious influence, since it did not suffice for his own protection? But if Dr Krapf was powerless, so likewise, argues the critic, was the Embassy; "for we read of no remonstrances, no applications made to the king on behalf of the missionary, and surely there are no political considerations to restrain communicativeness upon a subject like this." He is perfectly mistaken. For although it may, without compromising any one, be stated that remonstrances were made, there are reasons, and those public ones too, which forbid me to explain why those remonstrances were ineffectual. Had the critic, or his Amháric philosopher, possessed one atom of sagacity, they would have divined those reasons; but as the case is otherwise, I leave them in the darkness which encompasses the whole coterie.

As to my having no right to use information expressly collected for me by the Political Agent at Aden, and by Lieutenant Christopher, in reference to the Eastern Coast, that is really a point upon which the reviewer can hardly be reckoned a competent judge. Lieutenant Barker, like Dr Kirk and the rest of my assistants, was under my orders, and sent with me for the express purpose of taking share, as I might see fit, in the duties allotted to me. The authorities quoted by the reviewer, as having been first in the field with every particular respecting slavery and the slave-trade in Shoa, do not bear out his assertion. Not to go any farther, where does he find the fact, which is rather an important one, that the king claims one out of every ten slaves that pass through his dominions? Like most other points which bear materially upon the subject, this is omitted in the "reports" which are so confidently advanced, in order to throw dust in the eyes of those who will take the Reviewer's word for whatever he has the effrontery to assert.

Next comes the question of the royal arms of Shoa, which I have stated to be the Holy Trinity. Here the critic, as he thinks, has me clearly at disadvantage. He denounces me, accordingly, to be in the wrong, by showing, not what the arms of Shoa are, but what are the arms of the Ethiopic empire; which is exactly the same as if a traveller in Flanders, having described the royal arms of that country, were to be taken to task because the arms of the Austrian Emperor were different. I make a statement on one subject, and he refutes me by making a different statement on a different subject, which is somewhat comic, to say the least of it. But the arms of Abyssinia are, it seems, the "Lion of the Tribe of Judah," to which the Catholic missionaries have added a cross. M. le Grand, in speaking of Abyssinian coronations, says: "The escutcheon is a lion holding a cross, with this motto: *Vicit leo de tribu Judah.*" But all this has nothing to do with the king of Shoa, who employs a device of his own, and that device is exactly what I have represented.

The ignorance of the reviewer and his anonymous authorities is again conspicuous in the remarks offered relative to the signet. Why has he not followed the rule he has laid down for my guidance, and "said openly," who these mysterious informants are, in order that, by their calibre, the public might have been enabled to judge whether on any, and on what subject, their opinion or their assertion is likely to be better than my own? As it is, the reader might really be tempted to believe that there existed a penny post in the kingdom of Shoa, and that every subject was in the daily habit of corresponding through it with all his acquaintance. But with exception of a few letters indited by His Majesty, or by the Queen, there are, perhaps, not half a dozen penned during the year, and those are upon scraps of parchment the size of a visiting card, and have neither signature nor superscription, much less device to adorn them. More than ignorance is displayed in the sneers cast upon my ability to use the pencil and the rifle. These qualifications, however incompatible their exercise may be with the dignity to which the critic has been pleased to elevate me, are far from being lightly estimated in Abyssinia; and that foreigner who can neither draw portraits, nor ride, nor slay wild beasts, is not likely to hold a very high place in the estimation of Sáhela Selássie, whatever may be thought of him by a learned reviewer.

The speculations indulged in as to the success or failure of my Embassy, are artfully spread over the whole article, a little here and a little there; so that the reader, should a reader be found, must always of necessity have doubts unanswered in his mind. There is some skill in this, and I give the writer credit for it; but though he manages his matter well, the matter itself is good for nothing. He puts himself in the place of the public, and demands certain explanations which I am not permitted to give. Parliament alone has it in its power to satisfy my critic, and to Parliament I refer him. Everybody else will feel that an imperfect explanation would be worse than none at all; a complete one I cannot furnish, though it may hereafter be permitted me to clear up the whole matter, which I am fully able to do.

It appears to me that I have now answered every objection worthy of notice that has been made against my work on Shoa. Not improbably, I shall be thought by some to have been too minute and circumstantial in my reply—to have exposed too seriously misrepresentations originating in ignorance or wanton malice—to have expended argument on that which deserved only contempt. But, respecting the public as I do, I judged it to be incumbent on me completely to disprove the assertion that I had imposed upon it. I trust I have established my own veracity, which I have been far more solicitous to do than to defend the plan adopted in the composition of my narrative. Much more might have been said, to show that the truth is neither in the reviewer, nor his "private informants," but it is not worth my while to trouble myself further with such people. The public, I am convinced, will agree with me in thinking that I have left no just cause for cavil, and if, therefore, the system of abuse should be persevered in, it can only be because I happen to have enemies who will make a point of pursuing me as long as I am above ground, and perhaps much longer. I wish they could discover some better and more profitable employment, and with that wish I leave them.

W.C. Harris.

London, March 31, 1844.

Extract of Instructions Addressed by the Secretary to the Government of Bombay to Captain W.C. Harris.

Bombay Castle, 24th April, 1841.

Sir,

I am directed to inform you, that the Honourable the Governor in Council having formed a very high estimate of your talents and acquirements, and of the spirit of enterprise and decision, united with prudence and discretion, exhibited in your recently published Travels "through the territories of the chief Moselekatse to the tropic of Capricorn," has been pleased to select you to conduct a Mission which the British Government has resolved to send to Sáhela Selássie, the King of Shoa in Southern Abyssinia, whose capital, Ankóber, is computed to be about four hundred miles inland from the port of Tajúra on the African coast.

The Mission will be conveyed to Aden in the Honourable Company's steam frigate Auckland, now under orders to leave Bombay on the 27th instant; and it has been arranged that one of the Honourable Company's vessels of war, at present in the Red Sea, shall be in readiness to convey the Mission thence to Tajúra, at which latter place it should immediately disembark, and commence its journey to Ankóber.

(Signed) J.P. Willoughby, Secretary to Government.

To Captain W.C. Harris, Corps of Engineers.

The Embassy was thus Composed:

Captain W.C. Harris, Bombay Engineers.

Captain Douglas Graham, Bombay Army. Principal Assistant.

Assistant-Surgeon Rupert Kirk, Bombay Medical Service.

Dr J.R. Roth, Natural Historian.

Lieutenant Sydney Horton, H.M. 49th Foot,—as a Volunteer.

Lieutenant W.C. Barker, Indian Navy.

Assistant-Surgeon Impey, Bombay Medical Service.

Mr Martin Bernatz, Artist.

Mr Robert Scott, Surveyor and Draftsman.

Mr J. Hatchatoor, British Agent at Tajúra.

Escort and Establishment:—

Two sergeants and fifteen rank and file; volunteers from H.M. 6th Foot, and from the Bombay Artillery.

An Assistant Apothecary.

Carpenter.

Smith.

Two Tent Lascars.

Introduction

Written in the heart of Abyssinia, amidst manifold interruptions and disadvantages, the following pages will, in many respects, be found imperfect. Their chief recommendation must be sought in the fact of their embodying a detail of efforts zealously directed, under the auspices of a liberal Government, towards the establishment of a more intimate connexion with a Christian people, who know even less of the world than the world knows of them,—towards the extension of the bounds of geographical and scientific knowledge, the advancement of the best interests of commerce, and the amelioration of the lot of some of the least favoured portions of the human race.

An obvious necessity for the introduction of the foregoing extract from his instructions will exonerate the Author from an intention to appropriate as his due the very gratifying encomium passed upon his previous exertions in Southern Africa. As a public servant, the freedom of his pen has now in some measure been curtailed; but his official position and resources, added to the able assistance placed at his command, have, on the other hand, extended more than commensurate advantages.

To Captain Douglas Graham, his accomplished and early friend, and principal assistant, he acknowledges himself most especially indebted, for the aid of a head and of a pen, such as are not often to be found united.

The exertions of Assistant-Surgeon Kirk alleviated incalculable human suffering; and his perseverance, although long opposed by an unfavourable climate, carried through a series of magnetic and astronomical observations of the highest importance to Abyssinian geography.

An indefatigable devotion to the cause of science, added to the experience gained during previous wanderings in Palestine, eminently adapted the learned Dr Roth to discharge the arduous functions of natural historian to the Mission; and the splendid collection realised, together with the researches embodied in the various appendices to these volumes, will afford the fullest evidence of his industry and success.

To all who were associated with himself, in view to the better attainment of the objects contemplated, the Author here offers his warm acknowledgments for the cheerfulness displayed under trials and privations. Of the able assistance of some he was unavoidably deprived during an early period of the service. The disappointment thus involved in his own person has been fully equal to that experienced by themselves; but they must be sensible that their hardships have not been undergone in vain, and that they too have accomplished their share in the undertaking, so far as fortune permitted.

To the Reverend Dr Krapf the thanks of Government have already been conveyed, for the valuable co-operation derived from his extended acquaintance with the languages of Abyssinia. But the Author gladly avails himself of this opportunity publicly to record his personal sense of obligation to the active and pious Missionary of the Church of England, whose kindness from the first arrival of the Embassy on the frontiers of Shoa, to the date of his own departure for Cairo, was unremitting.

By no tribute of his own could the writer of these volumes extend the well-deserved reputation of McQueen's Geographical Survey. It will nevertheless be satisfactory to one who takes rank among the foremost benefactors of the oppressed "children of the sun," to receive the additional testimony which is due to the undeviating accuracy of theories and conclusions founded upon years of patient and honest investigation; and this the Author unhesitatingly records, in so far as the north-eastern portions of Africa have come within the observation of the Embassy which he has the honour to conduct.

Ankóber, 1st January, 1843.

Postscriptum

The length of time that has unavoidably elapsed between the preparation and the appearance of these volumes, needs no apology, neither is it proposed to offer any for their termination in the country of which they treat, and wherein they were written. But the work must not now be suffered to go forth without the expression of the Author's gratitude for the assistance derived during its progress through the press, from the talents and literary taste of his friend Major Franklin Lushington, C.B.

VOLUME ONE

Chapter One
Departure of the British Embassy
from the Shores of india

It was late on the afternoon of a sultry day in April, which had been passed amid active preparations, when a dark column of smoke, streaming over the tall shipping in the crowded harbour of Bombay, proclaimed the necessity of a hurried adieu to a concourse of friends who still thronged the deck; and scarcely was the last wish for success expressed to the parties that had embarked, before the paddles performed their first revolution, and the Honourable East India Company's steam frigate "Auckland," bound upon her maiden voyage, shot through the still blue water.

A turbaned multitude of manifold religions had lined the pier and the ramparts of the saluting battery, to pay a parting tribute of respect to their late governor. Sir James Rivett Carnac, who, with his lady and family, was now returning to his native land. On board also were the officers and gentlemen composing an Embassy organised under instructions by the government of India. More than a fortnight had been diligently passed in the equipment of this mission; but its objects, no less than the destination of its innumerable bales and boxes, still served as puzzles to public curiosity; and many a sapient conjecture on the subject was doubtless launched after the bounding frigate as she disappeared amid the haze of the closing day.

Immortal Watt! sordid is the man who places his foot behind the Titanic engines which owe their birth to thee, and who would withhold, as an offering to the altar of thy memory, a mite, according to his worldly means, wherewith to erect a fabric colossal as the power enthralled by thy transcendent genius! Strange are the revolutions undergone in affairs nautical since the introduction of the marine steam-engine upon the Indian seas. The creaking of yards has given place to the coughing and sobbing of machinery, as it heaves in convulsive throes. Tacking and wearing have become terms obsolete, and through the clang of the fire-doors, and the ceaseless stroke of paddle-wheels, the voice of the pilot is rarely heard, save in conjunction with "Stop her," or "Turn a-head."

Marked by a broad ploughed wake, the undeviating course pursued through the trackless main was demonstrated midway of the voyage by a tall pillar of smoke from the funnel of the "Cleopatra," rising against the clear hot horizon, like a genie liberated from his sealed bottle, to proclaim the advent of the English mails. The deep blue sea was glassy smooth. Each passing zephyr set from Araby's shores; but, heedless alike of wind and opposing current, the good ship steadily pursued her arrow-like flight, — passed the bold outline of Socotra, redolent of spicy odours, — and before sunset of the ninth day was within sight of her destined haven, one thousand six hundred and eighty miles from the port she had left.

Cape Aden was the bold promontory in view, and it had borrowed an aspect even more sombre and dismal from a canopy of heavy clouds which stole across the naked and shattered peaks, to invest the castle-capped mountain with a funereal shroud. Crossed by horizontal ledges, and seamed with gaps and fissures, Jebel Shemshán rears its turreted crags nearly eighteen hundred feet above the ocean, into which dip numerous bare and rugged buttresses, of width only sufficient to afford footing to a cony, and each terminating in a bluff inaccessible scarp. Sand and shingle strew the cheerless valleys by which these spurs are divided, and save where a stunted balsam, or a sallow clump of senna, has struggled through the gaping fissure, hollow as well as hill is destitute of even the semblance of vegetation.

> "How hideously
> Its shapes are heap'd around, rude, bare, and high.
> Ghastly, and scarr'd, and riven! Is this the scene
> Where the old earthquake's demon taught her young
> Ruin? Were these their toys? - or did a sea
> Of fire envelope once this dismal cape?"

Rounding the stern peninsula, within stone's cast of the frowning headlands, the magnificent western bay developed its broad expanse as the evening closed. Here, with colliers and merchantmen, were riding the vessels of war composing the Red Sea squadron. Among the isolated denizens of British Arabia, the unexpected arrival of a steam frigate created no small sensation. Exiles on a barren and dreary soil, which is precluded from all intercourse with the fruitful, but barbarous interior, there is nothing to alleviate a positive imprisonment, save the periodical flying visits of the packets that pass and repass betwixt Suez and Bombay. In the dead of night the sudden glare of a blue light in the offing is answered by the illumination of the blockship, heretofore veiled behind a curtain of darkness. The double thunder of artillery next peals from her decks; and as the labouring of paddle-wheels, at first faint and distant, and heard only at broken intervals, comes booming more heavily over the still waters, the spectral lantern at the mast-head is followed by a red glow under the stem, as the witch, buffeting a cascade of snowy spray, vibrates to every stroke of the engine, and leaving a phosphoric train to mark her even course, glides, hissing and boiling, towards her anchorage. Warped alongside the blockship, the dingy hulls lean over like affectionate sisters that have been long parted; and, flinging their arms together, remain fast locked in each other's embrace.

And who are these swart children of the sun, that, like a May-day band of chimney-sweeps, are springing with wild whoops and yells over the bulwarks of the new arrival? 'tis a gang of brawny Seedies, enfranchised negroes from the coast of Zanzibar, whose pleasure consists in the transhipment of yonder mountain of coal, lying heaped in tons upon the groaning deck. To the dissonant tones of a rude tambourine, thumped with the thighbone of a calf, their labour has already commenced. Increasing the vehemence of their savage dance, they heave the ponderous sacks like giants busied at pitch and toss, and begrimed from head to foot, roll at intervals upon the blackened planks, to stanch the streaming perspiration. Thus stamping and howling with increased fury, while the harsh notes of the drum peal louder and louder to the deafening vehemence of the frantic musician, they pursue their task, night as well as day, amid clamour and fiendish vociferations, such as might suggest the idea of furies engaged in unearthly orgies. In the first burst of their revelry, the spectator is happy to escape from the suffocating atmosphere of impalpable coal-dust; and rarely does it happen that for every hundred tons of fuel received, fewer than one life is forfeited by the actors in the wild scene described—some doomed victim, swollen with copious draughts, and exhausted by the frenzy of excitement, invariably casting himself down when his Herculean task is done, to rally and rise up no more.

Chapter Two
Disembarkation at Cape Aden

Quitting the boisterous deck of the steamer, and pulling towards the shores of Arabia, a cluster of barren rocks, which might fitly be likened to heaps of fused coal out of a glass furnace, present an appearance very far from inviting or prepossessing. They are little relieved by a few straggling cadjan buildings, temporarily occupied by those whose avocations enable them, during the summer months, to fly the intolerable heat of the oven-like town. But under the roof of Captain Stafford Haines, who fills the honourable and responsible post of Political Agent, there awaited the embassy, on its landing, a hospitality of no ordinary stamp. It literally knew no bounds, and could not fail to obliterate at once any unfavourable first impression arising out of the desolate aspect bestowed by Dame Nature upon "Steamer Point."

A volunteer escort of European artillerymen was yet to be obtained from the garrison of Aden; horses, too, were to be purchased, and sundry other indispensable preparations made for the coming journey into the interior of Africa. During a full week there seemed no termination to the influx of bags containing dates, rice, and juwarree, and scarcely a shorter period was occupied in the selection from the government treasury of many thousand star-dollars of the reign of Maria Theresa, displaying, each in its turn, all the multifarious marks and tokens most esteemed by the capricious savage. Neither was the bustle one whit diminished by the remote position of the town, which, unless through the kindness of friends, is only to be attained on the back of one of the many diminutive donkeys stationed along the beach for the convenience of the stranger. Encumbered with a straw-stuffed pack-saddle far exceeding its own dimensions, the wretched quadruped is zealously bastinadoed into a painful amble by the heavy club of some juvenile Israelite with flowing auburn ringlets, whose chubby freckled cheeks, influenced by the sultry sun no less than by the incessant manual labour employed, are wont to assume a strangely excited appearance ere the journey be at an end.

Along the entire coast of Southern Arabia, there is not a more remarkable feature than the lofty promontory of Aden, which has been flung up from the bed of the ocean, and in its formation is altogether volcanic. The Arab historian (Masudi) of the tenth century, after speaking of the volcanoes of Sicily and in the kingdom of the Maha Raj, alludes to it as existing in the desert of Barhut, adjacent to the province of Nasafan and Hadramaut, in the country of Shaher. "Its sound, like the rumbling of thunder, might then be heard many miles, and from its entrails were vomited forth red-hot stones with a flood of liquid fire." The skeleton of the long-exhausted crater, once, in all probability, a nearly perfect circle, now exhibits a horse-shoe-shaped crescent, hemmed in by splintered crags, which, viewed from the turreted summit of Jebel Shemshán especially, whence the eye ranges over the entire peninsula, presents the wildest chaos of rock, ruin, and desolation.

From the landing-place at Ras Marbut, a tortuous track of five miles conducts past the coal-depôt and Seedie location, along various curvatures of the arid coast, to the cantonment and town of Aden. "Sublime in barrenness," the rugged and lofty cliffs pile themselves upward in masses of the most fantastic shape, now bare and bald, shooting into perpendicular spires, and now leaning over the caravan of heavily-laden camels that toil along the path. The sunshine of perpetual summer reigns throughout the scene. Glittering sand-hills slumber in breezy dimness around the land-locked harbour, and over the faint peaks of Yemen's distant mountains the unclouded sky floats bright and blue. The sparkling waters leap against the dark base of the naked islets; but the wide glassy surface beyond, reposing like a broad lake, is only ruffled by the circling eddy which follows the sportive plash of the bottle-nosed porpoise, or the pluming of a fleet of silver-winged terns, riding quietly at anchor on its tranquil bosom. As the road retires from the beach, the honey-combed cliff's assume the similitude of massive wads and battlements, every where pierced with loopholes and embrasures. A gradual ascent leads through a craggy portal, bristling with cannon, and guarded by the pacing sentinel. One narrow rift in the solid rock, to the foot of which the sun rarely penetrates, forms an abrupt division in the chain, and beyond it the eye suddenly embraces the basin-like valley wherein stands the decayed capital of Arabia Felix.

"Aden," saith old Ibn Batuta of Tangiers, "is situate upon the sea-shore—a large city, without either seed, water, or tree." Five hundred years have elapsed since this graphic account was penned, and the vegetation has in nowise improved. An amphitheatre of dimensions sufficient for the Devil's punch-bowl is formed by two volcanic ranges, once in connection, but obviously rent asunder, heaved outwards, and canted in opposite directions by some violent eruption that has forced an opening to the ocean. A sterility which is not to be surpassed invests the scene with an aspect most repulsive and forbidding. No tree varies the dreary prospect, no shrub relieves the eye, not even a flower lends its aid to enliven the wild and gloomy hollow, the fittest refuge that the imagination could picture for the lawless and the desperate. Fortifications are to be traced on every point either liable to assault or eligible for defence: ruined castles and watch-towers perched on the highest elevations of the precipitous hills stand the now inaccessible guardians of other days; and even the limited view to seaward, where the passing white sail of a small coasting craft, or the catamaran of the amphibious fisherman may occasionally be seen, is partially screened by a triangular rock, which frowns like a great spectre over the inner harbour. Seerah, "the fortified black islet," is said to have been the residence of Cain, "the first born of a woman," after the murder of his brother Abel; and, verily, it would be difficult to devise a more appropriate exile for the banished fratricide. Hurled into the sea by a convulsive shock, it is surrounded by pumice and by currents of obsidian, the products of volcanic emission, strewed among vast undulating waves of cavernous lava, or mingled with black masses of porous rock, which bear evidence of fusion, and yield to the touch a metallic sound.

Sterility has indeed claimed this dreary region as her own; and even in the more productive portions of the peninsula, little verdure is derived from the almost leafless Beshám, the *Balsamodendron Opobalsamum*, a dwarf shrub, which, according to the Arab tradition, formed a part of the present carried to King Solomon by the Queen of Sheba from the aromatic regions of myrrh and frankincense. Where incisions are made in its stem, the far-famed Balm of Mecca flows copiously, but the volatile oil quickly evaporating, leaves a tasteless insipid gum. Nursed by no periodical shower and by no hidden spring, the precious plant, scorched by a withering blast, derives its only moisture from the mists which envelope the mountain-top, when all is sunshine below.

Among the most singular features of the Cape is the supply of water, which is found only in the valley of Aden, close under the cliffs, and at the openings of the fissures from the steppes above. Here, piercing to a great depth through the solid rock, are upwards of one hundred wells; many dilapidated and choked up, but others yielding an abundant and unfailing supply. Whence or in what manner they are fed it is extremely difficult to conjecture. All near the beach are bad, and more or less brackish; some are sensibly affected by the tides, and very saline; whilst of those which afford sweet water, one only is visibly acted upon by some lower spring. It is excavated at the entrance of a dark gorge rent by some violent convulsion in the rugged bosom of Shemshán, and the surface, which is in a state of constant commotion, remains at the same level, although daily drawn upon from morning till night for the supply of thousands.

The almost total absence of the vegetable kingdom considered, it is not surprising that there should exist also a palpable deficiency in the animal creation. In perhaps no other quarter of the universe are the sparrow and the crow such perfect strangers. The pigeon, the fox, and the rat, divide the sovereignty of the rocky cleft; and the serrated heights are held without a rival by a garrison of monkeys. With these long-tailed occupants of the tower-capped pinnacles are connected wondrous superstitions, and an Aden tradition, extant throughout Southern Arabia, would exalt them into the remnant of the once-powerful tribe of Ad, "a people great, and strong, and tall," who are believed to have been metamorphosed into apes, in token of the displeasure of Heaven, when Sheddád, "the king of the world," illustrious in the annals of the East, impiously sought, in defiance of the prophet Hûd, to create unto himself a garden which should rival the Celestial Paradise. The Bostán el Irem, with its gorgeous palaces and shining domes, the similitude whereof had never been constructed on the regions of the earth, is said to be yet standing in the solitary deserts of Aden, although miraculously concealed from mortal ken. Within the silent walls of its lofty towers did Abdállah ibn Aboo Kelâba pass his night of wonder during the reign of Moâwiyeh, Prince of the Faithful; and it is believed by every good Moslem that this marvellous fabric of human skill and impiety, which finds a record in the sacred Korán, will endure until the Last Day, an imperishable, but rarely revealed monument of Divine retribution.

Note 1. Lieutenant J.C. Cruttenden, assistant to the Political Agent at Aden, heard the same version repeated at Saana, the capital of Yemen, which far-famed city he has been the first European to visit, since the days of Niebuhr.

Chapter Three
A Stroll through the Infant
Metropolis of British Arabia

A uniform system of architecture pervades the houses of Aden, nearly all of which would appear to have arisen out of the ruins of former more extensive edifices, now buried far below the surface of the accumulated soil. Tiers of loose undressed stone are interlaid, instead of mortar, with horizontal bands of timber; the walls thus traversed being perforated with pigeon-holes to serve as windows, and surmounted by a low parapet concealing the terraced roof. Many, occupied by the more wealthy, have attained to a third story; but nearly all are destitute of ornament. This is now restricted to the decayed palace of the sultáns of Yemen, where

"In proud state
Each robber chief upheld his armed halls,
Doing his evil will."

In the thick coating of cement with which the shattered edifice is still partially encrusted, are the remains of various raised devices; and a profusion of open fretwork in wood is still observable, interspersed with latticed cornices, comprising choice sentences from the Korán.

The shops of Parsee and Mohammadan merchants already extend an assortment of European commodities to the notice of the visitor; and in a bazaar, infested like other fish-markets by a legion of cats, are exposed sharks and a variety of the finny tribe. Water from the sweetest well is hawked about in dirty skins, instead of the lemonade and sherbet of large oriental towns; and piles of fruit, drugs, dates, molasses, and other abominations, present the same amount of flies, and no abatement of the compound of villainous smells, by which the booth of the shrewd and avaricious Gentoo is so invariably distinguished.

In the suburbs, the frail cadjan wigwam of the Arab and Somauli population impart the undeviating aspect of the portable encampment of the nomade hordes. The tattered goat-hair awning of the bare-footed pilgrim to the shrine at El Medina is here; and low crazy cabins of matting or yellow reeds are so slenderly covered in with the leaves of the palm as to form but a scanty shelter against the intolerable heat and dust occasioned by periodical blasts of the fiery Shimál.

During his diurnal reign, the sun has shone fiercely over the extinct crater of Aden, and the relentless shower of dust and pebbles has kept the inhabitants within their rude dwellings. But as the declining rays cast a lengthened shadow across the narrow alleys, and the hot puffs, abating in violence, are succeeded by a suffocating calm, the hitherto torpid population is to be seen abroad. That bronzed and sun-burnt visage, surrounded by long matted locks of raven hair—that slender, but wiry and active frame—and that energetic gait and manner, proclaim the untameable descendant of Ishmaël. He nimbly mounts the crupper of his now unladen dromedary, and at a trot moves down the bazaar on his way back to the town of Lahedge. A checked kerchief around his brows, and a kilt of dark blue calico about his loins, comprise his slender costume. His arms have been deposited outside the Turkish wall, which stretches its barrier across the isthmus from sea to sea, where flying parties of the Foudthli still infest the plain; and as he looks back, his meagre ferocious aspect, flanked by that tangled web of hair, stamps him the roving tenant of the desert.

The Arab has changed neither his character nor his habits since the days of the patriarchs, and he affords a standing evidence of the truth of the scriptural prophecy. He regards with disdain and with proud indifference every other portion of mankind, for who can produce so ancient monuments of liberty as he who, with little intermission, has preserved it from the very Deluge? Is the land of his ancestors invaded? A branch torn by the priest from the venerated *Nebek* (A tree bearing a fruit like the Siberian crab), having been thrust into the fire, is quenched in hot blood welling from the divided throat of a ram which has only the moment before been slaughtered in the name of God the one omnipotent. Dripping with the crimson tide, the emblem is solemnly delivered to the nearest warrior, who hies him forth with this his summons for the gathering of the wild dans. Down from their rocky fastnesses pour the old and the young, the untried stripling, and the stern veteran with a thousand scars. On, on speeds the messenger with the alarum of coming strife. Transferred from hand to hand, it rests not in the grasp of any; and in a few brief hours, thousands of wild spirits, calling upon Allah for victory, and thirsting for the blood of the foe, have mustered around the unfurled standard of their prophet.

Thus it was that the numerous hill-forts and strongholds studding the rich province of Assyr, which borders on the Holy Land of the Moslem, last poured forth their hordes to meet the invader of her fair plains, and the despoiler of her countless flocks. Sixteen thousand warriors, composing one of the most ancient as well as bravest of the Arab tribes, cast aside spear and falchion, and, armed only with the deadly creese, stole during the night upon the camp of the insatiate Egyptian, and slaughtering the greater number, drove Ibrahim Pacha, with the wreck of his army, to seek safety in precipitate flight to Hodeïda.

In yonder fat and sensual money-changer from the city of Surat is presented the very antipodes to the posterity of Hagar. In drowsy indolence, see him emerge from his treasures of ghee and groceries, among which, scales in hand, he has been patiently squatted since earliest dawn at the terrace of his booth, registering his gains in the daily ledger. Not one spark of animation is there. A dark slouching turban, and ample folds of snowy drapery, envelope the sleek person of the crafty Hindoo, and his lethargic motions render it difficult to comprehend how he should have contrived to exile himself from his native soil, and in such a forbidding spot, even in pursuit of his idol, Mammon.

Ajan and Berbera, famous for their early connection with the Greek kings of Egypt, have both contributed largely to the population that now throngs the street. The regular and finely-turned features of those Somauli emigrants from the opposite coast are at once selected from the group, although some have disguised their hair under a thick plaster of quick-lime, and others are rendered hideous by a wig of fiery red curls; whilst the dyed ringlets of a third have faded to the complexion of a housemaid's mop, and a fourth, forsooth, is shaven because his locks have been pulled in anger. (It is the practice of the Somauli to shave the head when thus insulted, and to make a vow that the hair shall not grow again until they have had their revenge.) All present a curious contrast to the jet black skin and woolly pate of the Suhaïli, who, in his turn, is destitute of the thick pouting lip which adorns that stalwart Nubian, swaggering like a great bully by his side. At the door of those cadjan cabins, which resemble higglers crates, not less in size than in form and appearance, groups of withered Somauli crones are diligently weaving mats, baskets, and fans, of the pliant date-leaf; and their laughing daughters, yon tall, slim, and erect damsels with the earthen pitchers above their plaited tresses, present, on their way up from the well, some of the comeliest specimens of the ebon race.

"Honesty," saith the Arab proverb, "is found only amongst poor fools." The Bedouin has for ages been celebrated for his ingenuity and daring, and the African offset is nothing behind the parent stock. A Somauli thief is perhaps "the cunningest knave in the universe." He has been known to cut away a pile of tobacco so as to leave to the merchant who reposed thereon, naught but the effigy of his own figure: and after entering through the roof of a house, the burglar has taken his exit through the door with chests of treasure, from the top of which the sleeping proprietor has been first hoisted, with his bed, by a tackle lowered through the aperture, and so left hanging until the morning!

Muffled in a Spanish mantilla, see the spouse of the bigoted Islám taking the air upon the crupper of a donkey, her fat face so scrupulously concealed, that nothing of it is visible save two sloe black eyes which glitter through perforations in the white veil, and impart a similitude to the horned owl. On the rude steps of the clustering habitations that she has passed, surrounded by rosy-cheeked urchins, are seated numerous dark-eyed and well-dressed Jewesses. Rachel, although discreet, and preserving the strictest decorum, is unveiled. Were it possible to prevail upon her to have recourse to daily ablution, in lieu of the hebdomadal immersion which celebrates her sabbath eve, her complexion would not be less fair than that of the native of Southern Europe; and in the well-chiselled features and aquiline profile of the brunette, are preserved all those marked peculiarities which in every part of the world distinguish the scattered daughters of Israël.

The children of the tribe of Judah are most completely identified with the soil of Aden, and may be regarded as the artisans and manufacturing population. Victims heretofore of the tyranny and intolerant persecution which the infidel has ever to expect at the hand of the true believer, they toiled and accumulated, but feared lest a display of the fruits of their labour should excite the cupidity of a rapacious master. Now their prospect has brightened, and the remnant of a mighty though fallen and dispersed people, no longer exists here in poverty and oppression, insulted and despised as they have always been in every part of the Eastern world; but in uninterrupted security ply their industrious occupation, and under British protection fearlessly practise those rites which have been religiously preserved from the time that their priests bore aloft the ark of the covenant. Stone slabs with Hebrew inscriptions mark the resting-place of the departed; schools witness the education of the rising generation; and men and women, arrayed in their holiday apparel, sit apart in the synagogue, to listen at each return of their sabbath to the law which had been read since "by way of the wilderness of the Red Sea" their fathers "went up harnessed out of the land of Egypt."

Chapter Four
The Gibraltar of the East

Aden, in its history and reverses, presents the type of many a mighty nation,—it flourished and has fallen. As it once stood, it was the maritime bulwark of Arabia Felix. So early as the reign of Constantine the Great, it was celebrated for its impregnable fortifications, its extended traffic, and its attractive ports. Here the camels of the Koreishites were laden with a precious cargo of aromatics. Here commerce first dawned; and little more than two centuries and a half have rolled away since the decayed city ranked among the most opulent emporia of the East. Its decline is only dated from the close of the illustrious reign of Suleïman the Magnificent; but the spider has since "weaved her web in the imperial palace, and the owl has stood sentinel upon the watch-tower."

In the eyes of the true believer, the Cape is hallowed by the tradition that it was honoured with the preaching in person of that arch impostor, "the last of all the prophets," who, with the sword in one hand and the Korán in the other, became the lawgiver of the Arabians, and the founder of an empire which in less than a century had spread itself from the Pyrenees to the Indus. Three hundred and sixty mosques once reared their proud heads, and eighty thousand inhabitants poured into the field, an army which accomplished the subjugation of El Yemen. This latter, famous from all antiquity for the happiness of its climate, its fertility and surpassing riches, became an independent kingdom at the period that Constantinople fell into the hands of Mahomet the Second. Aden frequently cast off its allegiance; and when the Turks, by means of their fleet built at Suez, rendered themselves masters of the northern coast of the Red Sea, they found the peninsula independent, under the Sultan of Foudthli. Turkey and Portugal, struggling for supremacy in the East, hotly contested its possession; but, being unable longer to maintain their rivalry, it finally reverted into the grasp of its ancient masters.

Great natural strength, improved by the substantial fortifications which had been carried by Sultán Selim completely round the zone of hills that engirds the town, now rendered it the fittest of all retreats for the piratical hordes of the desert; and the lawless sons of Ishmaël, scouring the adjacent waters, loaded their stronghold with booty. But after the loss of government, Aden could not be expected to retain its opulence. Its trade passed into the rival port of Mocha, and grinding oppression caused the removal of the wealthy. At the period of the British occupation, ninety dilapidated houses, giving shelter to six hundred impoverished souls, were all that remained to attest its ancient glories. The town lay spread out in ruin and desolation, and heaps of stone, mingled with bricks and rubbish, sternly pointed to the grave of the mosque and tall minaret.

Few fragments now survive the general decay, to record the high estate of the once populous metropolis, or reveal the magnificence it could formerly boast in works of public utility. The chief buildings are believed to have been situated ten miles inland, and to have been swallowed up by the ever rising, never ebbing, tide of the desert. The red brick conduit of Abd el Waháb can still be traced from the Durab el Horaïbi, whence it stretches to Bir Omheit, upwards of eight miles, across a now dilapidated bridge. Here are numerous wells, which supplied the reservoirs; but, "like the baseless fabric of a vision," every vestige of an edifice has vanished.

Among the most perfect and conspicuous relics of the past are the laborious and costly means adopted to insure in so arid and burning a climate, a plentiful supply of water. In addition to the wells, three hundred in number, the remains of basins of great magnitude are found in various directions; and in the Valley of Tanks are a succession of hanging cisterns, formed by excavations in the limestone rock. These are lined with flights of steps, and supported by lofty buttresses of imperishable masonry, forming deep reservoirs of semi-elliptical form, which still blockade every channel in the mountain side, and once served to collect the precious drops from heaven, when showers doubtless fell more abundantly than at the present day.

In the extensive repositories for the dead, too, may be found assurances of the former population of Aden. Many of the countless tombs in the Turkish cemetery were of white marble, and bore on jasper tablets elaborately-sculptured inscriptions surmounted by the cap and turban; but the greater number of these pillared monuments have either disappeared or been overthrown. Of the evidences of Mohammadanism that once graced the city, nearly all lie buried from sight beneath heaps of accumulated rubbish and débris, the removal of portions of which has disclosed many curious coins of remote date. The minaret of Menáleh, and a tottering octagon of red brick, attached to the Jama el Musjid, lone survivors of the wreck, still point to the sky; and of the few mosques that have been spared by the destroying hand of time, the principal is that of the tutelar saint of the city, beneath the cupola of which, invested with a pall of crimson silk, and enshrined in the odour of sanctity, repose the venerated remains of Sheïkh Hydroos.

An excellent zig-zagged road, imperfectly paved, and raised in parts to the height of twenty feet, extends from the base to the summit of Jebel Shemshán, and, with some few of the disjointed watch-towers, has defied the ravages of centuries. Three enormous pieces of brass ordnance, pierced for a sixty-eight pound shot, and covered with Turkish inscriptions, were the chief symbols of the former strength of this eastern Gibraltar. These were transmitted to England, when their capture, shortly after the present accession, avenged an insult offered to her flag, and wreathed the first laurels around the brow of her youthful Queen.

In general aspect the Cape is not dissimilar from the volcanic islands in the Grecian Archipelago, and viewed from a distance it appears separated altogether from the mainland. The long dead flat of sand by which it is connected with the Arabian continent, rising on either beach scarcely two feet above high water mark, induces the belief that the promontory must on its first production in early ages have been insulated. According to the evidence of the present generation the sea is still receding, and the sand steadily accumulating, but the noble western bay will not be affected for many centuries. Though the glory of Aden may have fled, and her commerce become totally annihilated, her ports will long remain as nature formed them, excellent, capacious, and secure.

Important commercial advantages cannot fail to accrue from the occupation of so secure an entrepôt, which at any season of the year may be entered and quitted with equal facility. The readiest access is afforded to the rich provinces of Hadramaut and Yemen, famous for their coffee, their frankincense, and the variety of their gums, and abounding in honey and wax, of a quality which may vie with the produce of the hives of the Mediterranean. A lucrative market to the manufactures of India and Great Britain is also extended by the facilities attending communication with the African coast, south of Báb el Mandéb, where the high mountain ranges bordering upon the shore are clothed with trees producing myrrh, frankincense, and precious gums, whilst the valleys in the interior pour forth for export, sheep, ghee, drugs, dry hides, gold dust, civet, ivory, rhinoceros horns, peltries, and ostrich feathers, besides coffee of the choicest growth. A wide field is open for mercantile speculation, and it is not a little pleasant to contemplate the approaching improvement of Christian Abyssinia, and the civilisation of portions of Africa even more benighted and remote, through the medium of intercourse with British Arabia.

Under the flag of old England, Aden has enjoyed a degree of happiness and security never previously experienced, even in the days of her greatest glory, when she ranked among the foremost of commercial marts in the East, and when vessels from all the known quarters of the globe thronged her boasted roadstead. Emigrants from the interior as well as from the exterior of Hadramaut and Yemen, and from both shores of the Red Sea, are daily crowding within the walls to seek refuge from grinding oppression, and to free themselves from the galling burthen beneath which they have long groaned at the hand of insatiate native despots. The amazing increase of population and the crowded state of the bazaars form subject for high admiration. In the short space of three years the census has been augmented to twenty thousand souls; substantial dwellings are springing up in every direction, and at all the adjacent ports, hundreds of native merchants do but await the erection of permanent fortifications in earnest of intention to remain, to flock under the guns with their families and wealth. Emerging thus rapidly from ruin and degradation, the tide of lucrative commerce, both from Africa and Arabia, may be confidently expected to revert to its former channel. Blessed by a mild but firm government, the decayed mart, rescued from Arab tyranny and misrule, will doubtless shortly attain a pinnacle far eclipsing even its ancient opulence and renown; and Aden, as a free port, whilst she pours wealth into a now impoverished land, must ere long become the queen of the adjacent seas, and take rank among the most useful dependencies of the British crown.

Chapter Five
Voyage across the Gulf of Arabia

Eight bells were "making it twelve o'clock" on the 15th of May, when the boatswain piped all hands on deck to weigh the anchor, and within a few minutes the Honourable Company's Brig-of-war "Euphrates," having the Embassy on board, and commanded by one of its members (Lieutenant Barker, Indian Navy), set her white sails, and, followed by three large native crafts freighted with horses and baggage, stood across the Arabian Gulf. A favourable breeze pressed her steadily through the yielding bosom of the ocean. The salt spray flew under her gallant bows; and as the hospitable cadjan roofs on Steamer Point, first in order, and then the jagged pinnacles forming the spider skeleton of Aden, sank gradually astern, each individual of the party destined to traverse the unknown wilds of Ethiopia, took the pilgrim's vow that the razor should pass no more over his beard, until his foot had again rested on civilised shores—an event not unreasonably conjectured to be far distant for all, and for some destined never to be realised.

The breeze increasing, the low sandy promontory of Ras Bír on the African coast became visible during the forenoon of the following day; and before evening, notwithstanding a delay of some hours, caused by an accident to the mainyard of one of the tenders, which obliged her to be taken in tow, the brig was passing a group of eight coral islands, elevated about thirty feet above the level of the sea. The remainder of the fleet having parted company during the night, were now perceived standing directly for Mushahh, the nearest of these islets, situated at the mouth of the Gulf of Tajúra, and divided from the Danákil coast by a fathomless channel of seven miles. An iron messenger despatched to bring the convoy to, ricochetted over the blue water, kicking up a column of white spray at every bound, and before the smoke of the gun had cleared the bulwarks, a bald pate protruded between the rigging, was followed by the swarthy person of Aboo Bekr, of the Somauli tribe Aboo Salaam, and commonly styled Durábili, or "the Liar." Nákhuda of a small trading craft which had been employed as a pilot boat during the recent trigonometrical survey of the coast, he was well-known to the officers of the "Euphrates," and was ascertained to be at this moment charged with despatches for Aden, which, whether important or otherwise, had been during three days lying safely at anchor off the island, to admit of enhanced profits by the collection of a cargo of wood.

"Salaam aleikum!" exclaimed the old Palinurus as soon as his foot had touched the deck; "Hamdu-lillah! Praise be unto God! it is you, after all. When I saw those two crazy tubs in your van, I believed that it could not be my old ship, although it loomed so vastly like her; but the moment you took in your studding-sails to let Aboo Bekr come alongside, I knew it must be the Capitan Báshi. Kayf hálut, how fares it with your health?"

The welcome visitor was forthwith accommodated with a chair on the poop; into which having squeezed himself with difficulty, he drew up his knees to his scanty beard, inserted a cigar into his mouth as a quid, and, sipping tea like a finished washerwoman, instituted a train of inquiries relative to the position of affairs in the British possessions across the water.

"Tayyib, tayyib," he ejaculated, when thoroughly satisfied that Cape Aden was not again in the hands of the Arabs. "Marhábba, it is well. All, too, is as it should be at Tajúra. Misunderstandings are adjusted, and the avaricious chieftains have at last, the Lord be praised! got all the dirt out of their bellies. Their palms have been judiciously tickled, and it only now remains to be seen whether the old sultán, who is fully as fond of money as his neighbours—or his ancient rival, Mohammad Ali, is to have the honour of forwarding the English to King Sáloo. My boy has just returned from Hábesh, and shall escort you. Abroo has been twice in Bombay, as you know, Capitan. You have only to tell me if he should misbehave, and I'll trounce the young scamp soundly."

Meanwhile the bold mountain outline of the land of promise, forming a worthy barrier to the unexplored treasures of the vast continent of Africa, had been rapidly emerging from obscurity, and the brown forbidding bluff, styled Ras Dukhán, "the smoking promontory," in height about five or six hundred feet, was now on the starboard quarter; its abrupt summit, as usual, surmounted by a coronet of fleecy clouds, from which, if not from the thermal well at its base, this Cape has probably derived its appellation. The brig was already standing up the bay of Tajúra; but darkness overtaking her, it was resolved to lay to until daybreak; and a gun fired in intimation of approach was presently answered by a display of rockets and blue lights from the Honourable Company's schooner "Constance," riding at anchor in the harbour.

The Arabs lay claim to the invention of the compass; and Aboo Bekr, who believed himself in truth a second Anson, was provided with one, which must certainly have been the first ever constructed. Age having impaired the dilapidated needle, it was forced off its pivot by a quantity of pepper-corns, which are here considered highly efficacious in the restoration of decayed magnetic powers. From the native navigators in the Indian Ocean he had borrowed a primitive nautical instrument for determining the latitude; nor was he a little vain of his practical skill as an observer. Through a perforation in the centre of a plane of wood in size and shape like a playing card, was passed a knotted whipcord, and the distance from each knot was so regulated that the subtended angle should equal the altitude of the polar star at some frequented point on the coast. The knot having been placed between the teeth, and the lower margin of the plane brought in optical contact with the horizon, the position of Polaris must be observed with reference to the upper edge; when, if it be above, the desired haven is known to be to the southward—if below, to the northward, and the course is shaped accordingly.

"I'll take you in this very night, Capitan Báshi, if you so please," resumed the pilot, whose packet had by this time escaped his recollection altogether. "Only give me the order, and, praise be unto Allah! there is nothing that Aboo Bekr cannot do. My head, as you see, is bald, and I may perhaps be a little old-looking now, but wait until we get on shore, and my new wig is bent; Inshállah! I shall look like a child of five years among the youngest of them."

"Now if we had but Long Ali of Zeyla on board," continued the old man, whose merry tongue knew no rest; "if we had only Two-fathom Ali here, you would not make all these difficulties. When they want to lay out an anchor, they have nothing else to do but to hand it over to Ali, and he walks away with it into six or eight feet without any ado. I went once upon a time in the dark to grope for a berth on board of his buggalow, and stumbling over some one's toes, inquired to whose legs they belonged; 'All's,' was the reply. 'And whose knees are these?' said I, after walking half across the deck; 'Ali's.' 'And this head in the scuppers, pray whose is it?' 'Ali's to be sure,' growled a sleepy voice; 'what do you want with it?' 'Subhán Allah, Ali again!' I exclaimed; 'then I must even look for stowage elsewhere.'"

Dawn of the 17th revealed the town of Tajúra, not a mile distant, on the verge of a broad expanse of blue water, over which a gossamer-like fleet of fishing catamarans already plied their busy craft. The tales of the dreary Teháma, of the suffocating Shimál, and of the desolate plains of the bloodthirsty Adaïel, were in that moment forgotten. Pleasure sparkled in every eye, and each heart bounded with exultation at the near prospect of fulfilling the benevolent schemes in design, and of adding one mite to the amelioration of Afric's swart sons.

Those who are conversant with Burchell's admirable illustration of an encampment of Cape farmers, with their gigantic waggons scattered about in picturesque confusion, will best understand the appearance of the group of primitive habitations that now presented itself on the sea-beach. Exceeding two hundred in number, and rudely constructed of frames of unhewn timber, arranged in a parabolic arch, and covered in with date matting, they resembled the white tilts of the Dutch boors, and collectively sheltered some twelve hundred inhabitants. The bold grey mountains, like a drop scene, limited the landscape, and, rising tier above tier, through coral limestone and basaltic trap, to the majestic Jebel Goodah, towering five thousand feet above the ocean, were enveloped in dirty red clouds, which imparted the aspect of a morning in the depth of winter. Verdant clumps of date and palm trees embosomed the only well of fresh water, around which numerous Bedouin females were drawing their daily supply of the precious fluid. These relieved the humble terraced mosque of whitewashed madrepore, whence the voice of the muezzin summoned the true believer to matin prayer; and a belt of green *makanni*, a dwarf species of mimosa with uniform umbrella tops, fringing the sandy shore, completed a pleasant contrast to the frowning blocks of barren black lava which fortify the Gibraltar whereupon the eye had last rested.

As the ship sailed into the harbour, the appearance of a large shark in her wake caused the tongue of the pilot again to "break adrift." "A certain friend of mine," said he, "Nákhuda of a craft almost as fast a sailer as my own, which is acknowledged to be the best in these seas, was once upon a time bound from this port to Mocha, with camels on board. When off Jebel Ján, the high table-land betwixt the Bay of Tajúra and the Red Sea, one of the beasts dying, was hove overboard. Up came a shark, ten times the size of that fellow, and swallowed the carcass, leaving one of the hinder legs protruding from his jaws; and before he had time to think where he was to find stowage for it, up came a second tremendous monster, and bolted his messmate, camel, leg, and all."

In return for this anecdote, the old man was treated to the history of the two Kilkenny cats in the sawpit, which fought until nothing remained of either but the tail and a bit of the flue. "How could that be?" he retorted seriously, after turning the business over in his mind. "Now, Capitan Báshi, you are spinning yarns, but, by Allah, the story I have told you is as true as the holy Korán, and if you don't choose to believe *me*, there are a dozen persons of unblemished veracity now in Tajúra, who are ready to vouch for its correctness."

Chapter Six
Cast Anchor at Tajúra on the African Coast

A scraggy, misshapen lad, claimed by Aboo Bekr as his own most dutiful nephew, now paddled alongside in a frail skiff, the devil dancing in his wicked eye; and having caught the end of a rope thrown by the doting uncle, he was on board in another instant.

During a former cruise of the "Euphrates," this imp had contrived to pass on the purser a basket of half-hatched eggs, which he warranted "new laid," but with which he was subsequently pelted over the gangway. On being greeted as "Sahib el bayzah," "the master of the eggs," and asked if he had not brought a fresh supply for sale, grinning archly, he dragged forward by the topknot a dull, stupid, little wretch—his messmate—whose heavy features formed the exact reverse of his own impudent animation. "Here," he exclaimed, "is the identical young rascal of whom I told you I bought them; he actually stole the whole from under his mother's hen, and then assured me that they were fresh." "Why don't you grow taller as well as sharper?" enquired the party upon whom the precocious child of the sea had imposed; "'tis now twelve months since you cheated me, and you are as diminutive a dwarf as ever."

"How can any one thrive who is starved," was the prompt reply; "were I to eat as immoderately as you do, I doubt not I should soon grow as corpulent."

But the arrival of Ali Shermárki shortly changed this desultory conversation to weightier matters. This worthy old man, sheïkh of the Somauli tribe Aber Gerhájis, possessing great influence and consideration among the entire Danákil population of the coast, had been invited from Zeyla, his usual place of residence, to assist in the extensive preparations making for the journey of the Embassy; and he now represented the requisite number of camels to be on their way down from the mountains, if the assurances of the owners, upon whose word small reliance could be pieced, were to be implicitly believed.

Long faithfully attached to the British government, the sheikh's first introduction arose out of a catastrophe which occurred many years ago—

the loss of the merchant brig "Mary Anne" at Berbera, a sea-port on the Somauli coast, lying immediately opposite to the peninsula of Aden. Deserted from October till March, it becomes, throughout the residue of the year, one uninterrupted fair, frequented by ships from the Arabian shores, by rapacious Banians from India, and by caravans of wandering savages from all parts of the interior—a vast temporary city or encampment, populated by not fewer than fifty thousand souls, springing into existence as if by the magic aid of Aladdin's lamp, and disappearing so suddenly, that within a single week, not one inhabitant is to be seen. Yet another six months, and the purse-proud merchant of Hurrur is again there, with his drove of comely slaves newly exported from the highlands of Abyssinia. There, too, is the wild pagan, displaying coffee, peltries, and precious gums from beyond Gurágue; and, punctual as ever, see the káfilah from the distant gurriahs of Amín and Ogáden, a nomade band, laden with ivory and ostrich plumes, and stained from head to foot, both in person and in garment, by the impalpable red dust traversed during the long march from the southward.

Religious prejudices on the part of the wily Hindoo precluding all traffic in live stock, the Somauli shepherd retains in his own hand the sale of his black-headed flocks; embarked with which in his frail bark of fifty tons, he stands boldly across the gulf, at seasons when the Arab fears even to creep along the coast of the Hejáz. All other trade, however, is engrossed by the subtle Banian, who divides the *adductor pollicis* of the right thumb, in order to increase the span by which his wares are to be measured; and he, during many years, has enjoyed, silently and unobserved, the enormous profits accruing from the riches annually poured out from the hidden regions of Africa. No form of government regulates the commerce; and, in the absence of imposts, barter is conducted solely through the medium of a native broker styled Abán, who, receiving a regulated percentage upon purchases and sales, is bound, at the risk of his own life, to protect his constituent from injury or outrage.

A vessel standing towards the coast proves a signal to all who gain their livelihood by this system, to swim off, and contest first arrival on board; the winner of the aquatic race, in accordance with ancient usage, being invariably received as her Abán. Thus it was that Ali Shermárki became agent to the "Mary Anne," a small English merchantman from Mauritius, whose captain, imprudently landing with the greater portion of his crew, afforded to a party of knavish Somauli an opportunity to cut the cable, when she drifted on shore and was lost. Hoping by his influence to prevail upon the plunderers to desist, the Abán, then a younger man, exerted himself to gain the wreck, but he was repulsed by a shower of spears, and his boat was swamped. A savage rabble next beleaguered his dwelling, and imperiously demanded the persons of the officers and crew, in order to put them to death; but, true to his charge, Ali Shermárki stoutly resisted, and being severely wounded, succeeded with his blood in securing honourable terms, and preserving the lives for which he had made himself responsible. His zealous integrity was duly rewarded by the British Government, and a sword was presented in token of his gallantry, the display of the brilliant setting of which led to the narration of the foregoing history.

The passage from Aden had been made in forty-two hours. As the cable of the "Euphrates" ran through the hawse-holes, and the rest of the squadron feu into their places betwixt herself and the shore, she fired a salute of five guns; and, after considerable delay, a negro was perceived timidly advancing with a lighted brand from among a knot of grey-bearded elders, seated in deep consultation beneath the scanty foliage of an ancient date tree. A superannuated 4 Pr., honey-combed throughout its calibre, and mounted upon a rickety ship carriage, tottered on the beach—the sole piece of ordnance possessed by Sultán Mohammad ibn Mohammad, reputed ruler of all the Danákil tribes. It was, after much coaxing, persuaded to explode in reply to the compliment paid, and for some minutes afterwards, wreaths of white smoke continued to ascend from the chimney-like vent, as though the venerable engine had taken fire, and was being consumed internally.

The commander of the "Euphrates," whose naval functions were now temporarily suspended, having long enjoyed the honour of a personal acquaintance with the potentate bearing the above pompous and high-sounding title, repaired forthwith to the palace, which consists of the stern moiety of the ill-starred "Mary Anne," tastily erected, keel uppermost, in the middle of the town, to serve as an attic story. Letters of introduction from the political authorities at Aden, with many complimentary speeches, duly delivered, permission to land was solicited; and although the formidable array of shipping, whose guns, not two hundred yards distant, sullenly overlooked the royal lodge, had given birth to certain misgivings, the Sultán finally overcame his fears, and acquiesced in the arrangement. A spot of waste land, forming a common near the mosque, was pointed out as the site upon which to encamp, but the favour was granted with this express understanding, that the British Embassy should tarry in so enviable a situation, not one moment longer than the exigencies of the service imperatively demanded; a saving clause in the stipulation to which all parties heartily subscribed.

The bay in which the "Euphrates" now rode, styled, from its wonted smoothness, "Bahr el Bánateen," "the sea of the two nymphs," is a deep narrow estuary, bounded by a bold coast, and extending, in a south-westerly direction, about forty-five miles, when the Eesah and Danákil shores suddenly converge so as to form a straitened channel, which imparts the figure of an hour-glass. Barely three quarters of a mile across, this passage is divided by a barren rocky islet styled "Báb," "the door," as occupying the gateway to the inner bay of Góobut el Kharáb, "the basin of foulness." The vortices formed by the strong tide setting through these confined apertures, assume a most dangerous aspect; and although the water in the bowl, whereof the longer axis measures twelve, and the shorter five miles, is so intensely salt as to create a smarting of the skin during immersion, mud adhering to the lead at one hundred fathoms, is perfectly sweet and fresh. Of four islets, two are rocks; Bood Ali, on the contrary, three hundred feet in height, and perfectly inaccessible, being thickly encrusted with earth and vegetable matter, whilst the sides of its nearest neighbour. Hood Ali, are bare, and present unequivocal traces of more recent volcanic action than are to be found in the surrounding débris.

Immediately outside the bay, on the Danákil coast, there issues from the rock below high water line, a spring which, at the flood tide, is completely effaced; but during the ebb is so intensely hot, that a crab is instantly destroyed and turned red by immersion. At the western extremity of Goobut el Kharáb, a cove three hundred yards in diameter, with sixteen fathoms water, is enclosed by precipitous volcanic cliffs, and the entrance barred by a narrow coral reef, which, at low tide, lies high and dry. In the waters of this recess is presented one of those strange phenomena which are not to be satisfactorily explained. Always ebbing, there is an underflow during even the flood tide; and usually glassy smooth, they become occasionally agitated by sudden ebullition, boiling up in whirlpools, which pour impetuously over the bar; whence the natives, persuaded that there exists a subterranean passage connected with the great Salt Lake, of which the sparkling expanse is visible from an intervening high belt of decomposing lava, term the cove "Mirsa good Ali," "the source of the sea."

Chapter Seven
Reception of the Embassy by the Sultán of the Sea-Port, and Return Visit to his Highness

The first British camp with which the sea-port of Tajúra had been honoured since its foundation, raised its head on the afternoon of the 18th of May; when the Embassy, accompanied by the officers of both ships of war in the harbour, landed under a salute of seventeen guns from the "Euphrates," (commanded by Lieutenant J. Young, I.N.,) and in a spacious crimson pavilion, erected as a hall of audience, received a visit of ceremony from the Sultán and his principal chiefs. A more unprincely object can scarcely be conceived than was presented in the imbecile, attenuated, and ghastly form of this most meagre potentate, who, as he tottered into the marquee, supported by a long witch-like wand, tendered his hideous bony claws to each of the party in succession, with all the repulsive coldness that characterises a Dankáli shake of the hand. An encourager of the staple manufactures of his own country, his decrepit frame was enveloped in a coarse cotton mantle, which, with a blue-checked wrapper about his loins, and an ample turban perched on the very apex of his shaven crown, was admirably in keeping with the harmony of dirt that pervaded the attire of his privy council and attendants. Projecting triangles of leather graced the toes of his rude sandals; a huge quarto Korán, slung over his bent shoulder, rested beneath the left arm, on the hilt of a brass-mounted creese, which was girded to the right side; and his illustrious person was further defended against evil influence by a zone and bandolier thickly studded with mystic amulets and most potent charms, extracted from the sacred book. Enfeebled by years, his deeply-furrowed countenance, bearing an ebony polish, was fringed by a straggling white beard, and it needed not the science of Lavater to detect, in the indifference of his dull leaden eye, and the puckered corners of his toothless mouth, the lines of cruelty, cunning, and sordid avarice.

His Highness's haggard form was supported by the chief ministers of Church and State—Abdool Rahmán Sowáhil, the judge, civil, criminal, and ecclesiastic, and Hámed Bunaïto, the pursy Wazir, whose bodily circumference was in strict unison with the pomposity of his carriage. One Sáleh Shehém, too, occupied a prominent seat in the upper ranks—a wealthy slave-merchant, whose frightful deformities have ennobled him with the title of "Ashrem," which being interpreted signifies, "he of the hare-lip." This trio alone, of all the unwashed retinue, showed turbaned heads, every lesser satellite wearing either a natural or artificial full-bottomed peruke, graced with a yellow wooden skewer, something after the model of a salad fork, stuck erect in hair well stiffened with a goodly accumulation of sheep's-tail fat, the rancid odour whereof was far from enhancing the *agrémens* of the interview. Izhák and Hajji Kásim, two elders of the blood-royal, with whom a much closer acquaintance was in store, were perfectly bald, — their patriarchal bearing and goodly presence affording no bad imitation of the scriptural illustrations by the old masters of the apostles Saint Peter and Saint Paul. True to his word, the wag Aboo Bekr, as full of pleasantries as ever, had donned a preposterous tawny wig, quaintly manufactured of the fleece of a sheep; and in his smirking, facetious physiognomy was found the principal relief to the scowling satanic glances of the ill-favoured rabble, dripping with tallow, and redolent of abominable smells, who crowded the tent to the choking of every doorway.

It having heretofore been the invariable maxim of the Sultán to exact a visit from the stranger before condescending to pay one himself, the departure from established rule in favour of the liege subjects of Her Britannic Majesty could not fail to prove eminently gratifying. Compliments of the most fulsome nature were bandied about with compound interest, as the coffee-cup passed round to the more distinguished of the Danákil guests. Promises of assistance the most specious were lavished by the authorities, in grateful acknowledgment whereof, Cachemire shawls, and Delhi embroidered scarfs of exquisite workmanship, were liberally distributed, and as greedily tucked under the dirty cloth of the avaricious recipients; and although, in accordance with the unpolished custom of the country, no sort of salutation was offered when the conference broke up, the filthy guests departed with a semblance of good humour, that had been observable in none at their first entrance.

Widely different was the mood of the son of Ali Abi, chief of the Rookhba, as he rushed into the pavilion on the exit of his rival, the hereditary Sultán of the Danákil. Lucifer, when gazing forth upon the newly created Paradise, and plotting the downfall of the sinless inmates of the garden of Eden, looked not half so fiend-like as Mohammad Ali, whilst, trembling with jealousy and rage, he demanded the reason of having been so insultingly omitted in the distribution of valuables? "Am I then a dog," he continued, in the highest indignation, "and not worth the trouble of propitiating? whereas that old dotard yonder is to have his empty skull bound with rich shawls from India, and his powerless relatives decorated from head to foot.

Inshállah, we shall see anon whether the Sultán of the sea-beach, or the son of Ali Abi, keeps the key of the road to Hábesh."

Unlike the succession of every other government in the universe, the nominal sovereignty of the united tribes composing the Adaïel of Danákil nation, whereof Tajúra is the seat, is alternately vested in the Adáli and the Abli, a Sultán drawn from the one, being succeeded by his Wazir, who is invariably a member of the other, whilst the individual to fill the post vacated by the latter, is elected by suffrage from the family of the Sultán deceased. The town is besides the rendezvous of the petty chiefs of all the surrounding clans, who, to the number of eight or ten, claim an equal voice in the senate, and with about an hundred litigious followers each, make it their head-quarters during the greater portion of the year. Mohammad Ali is the principal of these, and his powerful tribe occupying a central position on the road to Abyssinia, he asserts the right to escort all parties proceeding thither—a right which the Sultán denies. The necessity of propitiating at one time, and in the same place, two rival savages, possessing equally the means of annoyance, whilst neither is sufficiently strong to afford protection against the interference of the other, rendered the negotiation one of considerable difficulty and delicacy; nor was it without a vast expenditure of honied words, that the ruffled temper of the malcontent was finally soothed, and he was persuaded to waive the assertion of his recognised claim, until a more suitable opportunity.

All the tents having been erected, the steeds landed and picketed in the rear, and the heterogeneous mass of property which strewed the sea-beach reduced to a something less chaotic state, a return visit to His Highness was paid in full uniform; and the cortège being swelled by the naval officers, an exceedingly gay procession of cocked hats, plumes, and gold lace, passed along the strand to the palace, under a befitting salute from the Brig of war. The lounging population were altogether lost in amazement at the sight of such magnificence—old and young, of both sexes, thronging the wayside, with features indicative of unequivocal admiration at the brilliancy of so unwonted a display.

The thunder of artillery, to which the nervous old Sultán does not conceal his insuperable aversion, still shook the unpretending couch whereon he quailed, as the procession entered the fragile tenement of stakes and matting which constituted the Divan; and which, without possessing any pretensions to exclude either sun or rain, proved just sufficiently large to include the entire party. A renewal of hand-shaking in its coldest form, and a repetition of yesterday's compliments, and of yesterday's promises mode only to be broken, was followed by a general sipping of coffee, prepared, not in the royal kitchen, but in the cuisine of the Embassy; and after being scrutinised during ten minutes of suffocating heat by numerous female eyes glistening through an infinity of chinks and perforations in the envious matting, the party returned, bearing as a costly token of His Highness's regard, a cloth similar to that composing the royal mantle.

It did indeed, in this instance, form matter of heartfelt congratulation, that the regal custom was dispensed with, of investing the honoured guest with a garment from the imperial wardrobe! As the cavalcade, duly impressed with this sentiment, remounted at the gate of the thorn inclosure which fortifies the palace, the Sultana vouchsafed a glimpse of her bedizened person from the stern cabin window of the "Mary Anne"—the withered frame of the ancient beldame, embedded in spells, beads, amulets, and grease, forcibly reminding the spectator of the witch of Endor, and rendering her in very truth, a right seemly partner for her wrinkled lord.

Chapter Eight
Tajúra, "The City of the Slave-Merchant"

In the heart of the peninsula of Arabia, environed on every side by rocky mountains, there stood, in the middle of the sixth century, a celebrated pagan shrine, that had been held in the most exalted veneration during fourteen hundred years. The edifice was believed to cover the hallowed remains of Ishmaël, the father of the wandering Bedouin, and it contained a certain sacred black stone, whereon the Patriarch Jacob saw the vision of angels ascending into heaven. On its site, according to the Arab tradition, Adam pitched his tent when expelled from the garden of Eden, and there died Eve, the partner of his fall, whose grave of green sods is shown to the present day, upon the barren shores of the Red Sea.

This shrine, of course, was none other than the famous temple of the Sun at Mecca, since so consecrated by the lawgiver of the Mohammadans, as to form the focus of attraction to every true believer. The extraordinary veneration it received in those early days, concentrating the tide of commerce, rendered it the absorbing mart of Eastern trade. Abyssinia at that period held in occupation the adjacent provinces of Arabia Felix, and Abrahah, the vicegerent of Yemen, conceiving the idea of diverting the channel to his own advantage, erected in the country of the Homerites a splendid Christian church, which, under the title of Keleïsa, he endowed with the same privileges, immunities, and emoluments, that had pertained, from all antiquity, to the shrine of Sabaean idolatry.

"If," says Gibbon, "a Christian power had been maintained in Arabia, Mahomet must have been crushed in his cradle, and Abyssinia would have prevented a revolt which has changed the civil and religious aspect of the world." But alarmed at the prospect of the desertion of their temple both by votaries and merchants, the Beni Koreish, who held the keys of the black stone in hereditary right, polluted the rival fane at Saana, which had no equal, saving the palace of the Hamyar kings, and was calculated to ensure the veneration of every pilgrim. Out of this sacrilege and affront arose the event celebrated in the Korán as "the war of the Elephant." Mounted on a huge white elephant, Abrahah, surnamed El Ashrem, placing himself at the head of a vast army, proceeded to take revenge on the idolaters; but, misled by intelligence artfully given by Aboo Táleb, grandfather to the Apostle of God, he destroyed, instead of the Kaaba, a temple of Osiris at Taïef, and the first recorded appearance of the small-pox, shortly afterwards annihilated the Christian forces.

The wars that distracted all Arabia, between the Greeks and Persians in the first instance, and subsequently between Mahomet and the population in support of his divine mission, had greatly impaired the traffic carried on by general consent at the temple of Mecca. A caravan scarcely ever ventured forth by any road, that it was not plundered by the opposing partisans, and merchants as well as trade gradually departed south of the Arabian Gulf, to sea-ports which in earlier times had been the emporia of commerce with the East. Raheïta, Zeyla, Tajúra, and a number of other towns in the Indian Ocean, thus recovered their importance and their lost prosperity. The conquest of the Abyssinian territories in Arabia, drove every Ethiopian to the African shores. Little districts now grew into great consideration. Mara, Hadea, Aussa, and Adel, amongst other petty states, assumed unto themselves the title of kingdoms, and shortly acquired power and wealth eclipsing many of the more ancient monarchies.

The miserable town of Tajúra, "the city of the slave-merchant," as it exists at the present day, demands no further description. It was for two years in the hands of the Turks, who occupied it after the taking of Massowah, and converted into a fort a venerable mosque, now in ruins, on the sea-beach near the palace. But no consistent chronicle, either of the capture or evacuation, is to be expected where every man is notorious equally as a boaster and a liar, and making himself the individual hero in every passage of arms, never foils to extol his own clan as immeasurably superior in valour to every other. The melancholy aspect of the place is but too well calculated to convey to the traveller a foretaste of the sufferings inseparable from a pilgrimage through any portion of the country denominated Adel; and each barbarian of the entire population of Tajúra will be found, on sad experience, a type of the Dankáli nation!

Bigoted Mohammadans, punctual to the call of the Muezzin, praying three times in excess of the exactions of the Prophet, often passing the entire night in the mosque, or sitting in council at its threshold; sedulously attentive to the outward forms of their creed, though few have sufficient energy to undertake a pilgrimage to the Kaaba, and content, like other hypocrites, with a rigid observance of externals—the Danákil rise from their devotions well primed with Moslem intolerance, and are perfectly ready to lie and cheat as occasion may offer. Unoccupied, and at a loss for honest employment, idlers without number sauntered about the pavilion at all times and seasons, entering at pleasure, and monopolising chairs and tables with the insolent independence which forms one of their most prominent features. Supported by a long staff, the ruffians gazed for hours together at the novel splendour of the equipage; and invariably disfigured by a large quid of tobacco adulterated with ashes, squirted the redundant saliva over the carpet, although squatted on the outside of the door, with ample space at command. But although thieves by profession on a grand scale, they fortunately contrived to keep their hands from picking and stealing; and notwithstanding that the tents were thus thronged from morning till night, and the sea-beach for many weary days was strewed with boxes and bales of truly tempting exterior, nothing whatever was abstracted.

The classic costume of the people of this sea-port consists of a white cotton robe, thrown carelessly over the shoulder, in the manner of the old Roman toga; a blue-checked kilt reaching to the knees, simply buckled about the waist by a leathern belt, which supports a most formidable creese, and a pair of rude undressed sandals to protect the feet of such as can afford the luxury. The plain round buckler and the broad-headed spear, without which few ever cross their threshold, renders the naturally graceful and manly figure of almost every individual a subject for the artist's pencil; but the population are to a man filthy in the extreme, and the accumulated dirt upon their persons and apparel leaves a taint behind, that might readily be traced without the intervention of a bloodhound. Rancid mutton fat, an inch thick, frosts a bushy wig of cauliflower growth, which harbours myriads of vermin. Under the melting rays of a tropical sun, the grease pours copiously over the skin; and the use of water, except as a beverage, being a thing absolutely unheard-of, a Dankáli pollutes the atmosphere with an effluvium, such as is only to be encountered elsewhere in the purlieus of a tallow-chandler's shop.

All are vain of scars, and desirous of displaying them; but little favour is shown for other outward ornament; and the miserly disposition which pervades the breast both of young and old, inducing an effort towards the concealment of property possessed, a paltry silver ring in the ear, a band of copper wire round the junction of the spear-blade with the shaft, or pewter mountings to the creese, form the sum total of decoration on the arms and persons even of the most extravagant. Fops in numbers are to be seen at Tajúra, who have called in the aid of moist quick-lime towards the conversion of the naturally jet black peruke to a most atrocious foxy red—when judicious frizzing, and the insertion of the wooden skewer, used for scratching, completes the resemblance to a carriage mop. But this novel process of dyeing, so contrary to that employed by civilised beaux, is only in fashion among the Somauli, who, in common with the Danákil dandies, employ, in lieu of a down pillow, a small wooden bolster, shaped like a crutch, which receives the neck, and during the hours of presumed uncomfortable repose, preserves the periwig from derangement.

Massy amulets in leathern envelopes, or entire Koráns in quarto or octavo, are borne on the unpurified person of almost every individual; and the ancient Arab remedy of swallowing the water in which passages from the holy book have been washed from the board or paper whereon they were inscribed, is in universal repute, as a sovereign medicine for every ailment to which frail flesh is heir—the firm of Sultán, Wazir and Kázi, who alone possess the privilege of wearing turbans, holding the monopoly, and driving a most profitable trade by the preparation of this simple, but potent specific. Large doses of melted sheep's-tail fat are moreover swallowed on certain occasions; and a native Esculapius gave proof of the perfection to which the dentist's art has attained at Tajúra, by dexterously detaching a carious tooth from the stubborn jaws of a submissive old woman, with the patent machinery of a rusty nail as a punch, struck with a heavy stone picked up on the sea-beach, where the operation was performed for the edification of the encampment. Applications were nevertheless frequent for European aid—a venerable priest numbering threescore years and ten, peremptorily demanding, in addition to a philter, the instantaneous removal of two obstinate cataracts, which had long dimmed his sight, and upon which he had vainly expended the teeth of half the mules in Tajúra, roasted, and reduced to an impalpable powder.

Education, to the extent of spelling the Korán, is general, and all speak Arabic as well as Dankáli; the lore of the most learned being however restricted to a smattering of the holy book, with a very confused idea of numerals, and ability to endite a scraggy Arabic letter, which, when completed with infinite labour, the writer is often puzzled to decipher. To the immortal honour of the Sultán be it here recorded, that although the oldest male inhabitant of Tajúra, he is a solitary instance of non-acquaintance with the alphabet. The swarthy cheek of every urchin who distinguishes himself by diligence or quickness, receives in token thereof, a dash of white chalk, a black streak in like manner disgracing the idle and stupid; but the pedagogue would appear to omit the residue of this oriental custom—the stuffing the mouths of the well-behaved with sugar-candy, which would doubtless prove a source of much greater enjoyment.

In the evening the ingenuous youth of the town, each armed with a creese in case of quarrel, convene in numbers on the common, to play a game which combines hockey and football; the residue of their time being spent in angling, when the juvenile Walton stands up to the chin in the salt sea, and employing his head as a substitute for the reel, spins out a dozen yards of line in a truly fisherman-like manner. Numbers spent the period of their relaxation from study in gaping with the adults at the door of the pavilion, whilst the magic effect of the magnet was exhibited, or fire produced from the human mouth by means of a promethean, here emphatically denominated "the devil."

The softer sex of Tajúra, whilst young, possess a tolerable share of comeliness, and a pleasing expression withal; but they are speedily past the meridian of beauty. A close blue chemise, a plain leathern petticoat, or a cloth reaching to the ankles, and a liberal coat of lard over extravagantly braided ringlets, which are knotted with white beads, form the toilet of maid, wife, and widow. An occasional necklace of coloured beads falling over the sable bosom, a pendant of brass or silver wire of no ordinary dimensions in the ear, and large ivory bracelets or anklets, proclaim the besetting foible of the sex: but ornaments are by no means general. Mohammadan jealousy tends to the seclusion of the better order of females to a certain extent; but a marriage in high life, when the procession passed close to the encampment, afforded an opportunity not always enjoyed, of beholding the beauty and fashion of the place. The matrimonial shackles are here easily loosed; and the greater portion of the population being deeply engaged in the slave trade with the interior, have their rude houses filled with temporary wives, who are from time to time unceremoniously shipped for the Arabian market, in order that the funds accruing from the sale of their persons may be invested in new purchases.

Agriculture there is none. Every man is a merchant, and waxes sufficiently rich on his extensive slave exportations, to import from other climes the produce he requires. An extensive traffic is carried on with Aussa and Abyssinia, in which nearly all are engaged at some period of the year. Indian and Arabian manufactures, pewter, zinc, copper and brass wire, beads, and salt in large quantities, are at these inland marts exchanged for slaves, grain, ivory, and other produce of the interior,—salt and human beings forming, however, the chief articles of barter. Virgin Mary German crowns of Maria Theresa, 1780, as integrals, and strips of raw hide for sandal soles, as fractionals, form the currency of the sea-port; beads, buttons, mirrors, trinkets, empty bottles, snuff, and tobacco, for which latter there is an universal craving, being also received in exchange for the necessaries of life.

Avarice is the ruling passion—the salient point in the character of the Dankáli. His whole soul is engrossed in amassing wealth, whilst he is by nature indolent and lazy, and would fain acquire riches without treading the laborious uphill path towards their attainment. Miserly in disposition, there is not an individual of the whole community, from the Sultán downwards, who would not infinitely prefer the present receipt of two pieces of silver, to a promissory note for twenty at the expiration of a week, upon the very best security. "Trees attain not to their growth in a single day," remarked Ali Shermárki, after remonstrating with the grasping ruler on his inordinate love of lucre—"take the tree as your text, and learn that property is only to be accumulated by slow degrees."

"True," retorted the old miser—"but, Sheikh, you must have lost sight of the fact, that my leaves are already withered, and that if I would be rich I have not a moment to lose."

Chapter Nine
Foretaste of Danákil Knavery

A share of thirty thousand German crowns, the annual profits accruing from the sale of three thousand human beings kidnapped in the interior, renders every native of Tajúra a man of competent independence. It is not, therefore, surprising that the usual rates of transport hire, added to a knowledge of the exigencies of the Embassy, should have produced in this avaricious, but indolence-loving race, no particular desire to bestir themselves. All are camel-owners to a greater or less extent; but the presence of so many interested parties tended not a little to increase the difficulties inseparable from dealings with so listless and dilatory a set of savages—it being of course requisite to consult the advantage of all, to which, as might be conjectured, all are most feelingly alive. The ashes of ancient feuds were still smoking on the arrival of the British; and notwithstanding that it was matter of notoriety that the amount disbursed at the time of departure for Shoa, would be diminished in the exact ratio of the delay experienced— and although, to judge from the surface, affairs looked prosperous enough towards the speedy completion of carriage, there was ever an adverse under-current setting; and the apathy of the savage feeding upon listless delays, the party were doomed for a weary fortnight to endure the merciless heat of the Tajúra sun, whose tardy departure was followed by a close muggy atmosphere, only occasionally alleviated by the bursting of a thunder-storm over the peak of Jebel Goodah, and to be perpetually deceived by the falsest promises, without being able to discover where to lay the blame. Bribes were lavished, increased hire acceded to, and camels repeatedly brought into the town; but day after day found the dupes to Danákil knavery still seated like shipwrecked mariners upon the shore, gazing in helpless melancholy at endless bales which strewed the strand, as if washed up by the waves of the fickle ocean.

During this tedious detention, which, as the sun shone fiercer and the close nights grew hotter with the rapidly advancing season, waxed daily more irksome and insupportable, and even threatened to arrest the journey altogether, the most conflicting accounts were received from various interested parties, of the actual extent of the Sultán's jurisdiction, averred by himself to have no limits nearer than the frontier of Efát. His revenues were ascertained to be restricted to two hundred head of oxen, camels, sheep, and goats, paid annually by the adjacent Danákil tribes, and it was certain that he enjoyed circumscribed prerogatives, based upon ancient usage; but although nothing is done or undertaken, without his concurrence duly obtained, he possesses no discretion to punish disobedience of his will, and is precluded from acting in the most trivial matter without the consent in full conclave, of the majority of the chiefs. Possessing little or no power over his nominal subjects, he is merely a puppet, looked up to by the wild tribes as the head of the principal family—infirmity and utter imbecility of character rendering His Highness at the same time, little better than a laughing-stock.

Faithless and rapacious, his insatiable avarice induced him to take every extortionate advantage of the helpless party at his mercy, whilst his tottering sway debarred him the power of reserving to himself the exclusive right of pillage. Private as well as public *kaláms* were daily held for hours at the sacred threshold of the mosque, during which new schemes of villainy and plunder were devised; and date leaves were indolently plaited by a host of apathetic legislators, as the propriety of permitting the departure inland of the Christian Kafirs was fully discussed and deliberated over with all the vicious bigotry of the Moslem zealot.

In order to ascertain how far fraud and impertinence might be carried with impunity, a deputation of the artful elders beleaguered the pavilion during the dead of night, to complain, in no measured terms, that certain of the followers, regardless of orders, had been seen endeavouring, with beads and trinkets, to betray the virtue of females who drew water at the well—a tale which proved, on due inquiry instituted, to be, like other Danákil asseverations, devoid of the slightest truth or foundation. Not even a paltry water skin was to be purchased from a schoolboy under the disbursement of a silver *fuloos*, value four sterling shillings; and a courier, who had, at three times the established charge, been furnished on the security of the high and mighty Sultán, to convey to Ankóber a letter advising the King of Shoa of the advent of the Embassy, was, after being three entire days and nights in possession of his ill-gotten wealth, discovered to be still snug within his mat-house, in the bosom of his family.

The letter in question had fixed the day of departure, and had been written in the most public manner before the assembled chiefs, in order, if possible, to counteract in some measure the tissue of underplots hourly developing, and to demonstrate to the Danákil capacity, that, whether camels were forthcoming or not, the journey would positively be undertaken; and the nefarious detention of the document, after the receipt of such exorbitant hire, being perfectly in keeping with the outrageously unprincipled and underhand treatment experienced from the first moment of arrival, the Sultán was at last plainly informed that further shuffling and falsehood would avail him nothing; since, if carriage were not immediately furnished in accordance with the plausible agreement concluded, the heavy baggage would be reshipped for Cape Aden, and the party would advance in defiance of opposition, with ten camels that had been brought by sea from Zeyla, by the nephews of Sheïkh Shermárki. Mohammad Ali, too, was now heart and hand in the cause, and his jealous rival, on receipt of this unpleasant intimation, began plainly enough to perceive that his guests were in right earnest, and that the golden opportunity of filling his coffers was passing rapidly away.

The royal salute, fired alternately from the decks of the brig and the schooner, each tricked out in all her colours, with gay signal flags in honour of the natal day of her Most Gracious Majesty the Queen, enveloped the town during forty minutes in a dense white smoke, accompanied by a most unpleasant smell of gunpowder; and during the entire day the beach in front of the British encampment wore the semblance of a disturbed ant-hill. European and native—master and servant—the latter from every nation under the sun, Arab, Persian, Nubian, Armenian, Egyptian, Syrian, Greek, and Portuguese,—all in a state of most active bustle, were selecting light baggage for the approaching departure; whilst crowds of oily savages, squatted on their hams, looked on in smiling apathy at the heaps of valuable commodities that were tossing about the sands. Twenty-one British officers subsequently sate down to dinner in the crimson pavilion, and the health of Queen Victoria having been given with nine times nine, another salute bursting from the sides of the vessels of war, shook the frail town to its foundations, and re-echoed long and loud among the mountain-glens— flights of rockets ascending at short intervals to illumine the dark sky.

The deafening din of the 32 pound stern chaser of the "Constance," which pointed directly towards the royal abode, proved too much for the nerves of the timid Sultán; and no sooner had the lights been extinguished, than his spectral figure, which ever shunned the day, glided into the tent unannounced, and ghostlike, muttered the agreeable intelligence that His Highness, after consulting the horoscope, and ascertaining beyond all doubt that the journey would prove propitious—a fact not previously determined—had come to the resolution, wise though late, of supplying the desired carriage without further delay, and deputing his own son as a safeguard through the tribes—services for which the apparition felt confident of receiving a suitable reward. The voice of the chieftains had become unanimous. At the last of a long succession of meetings convened for the purpose of taking the affair into full consideration, Abdool Rahmán, the Kázi, in his capacity of lawgiver, had risen from his seat in the assembly, and ably demonstrated to his mat-weaving audience, why all animosities and heart-burnings must be sunk in the general object of making money, and getting rid as expeditiously as possible of a party of Kafirs, whose guns, unshotted, threatened the destruction of the mosque of the true believer, and the total demolition of Tajúra. The Fátheh, being the first chapter of the holy Korán, was duly read, and the Danákil conclave with one voice vociferated a loud Ameen, even so let it be!

Chapter Ten
Long Adieu to the Unprincipled Sultán

From this eventful epoch each sultry day did indeed bring a numerical accession to the beasts of burthen collected in the town; but they were owned of many and self-willed proprietors; were, generally speaking, of the most feeble description, melancholy contrasts to the gigantic and herculean dromedary of Egypt and Arabia; and no trifling delay was still in store through their arrival from distant pastures bare-backed, which involved the necessity of making up new furniture for the march. The Dankáli saddle is fortunately a simple contrivance; a mat composed of plaited date leaves thrown over the hump, supporting four sticks lashed together in couples, and kept clear of the spinal process by means of two rollers as pads, having been proved by centuries of experience to be not more light than efficient. Accoutrements completed, and camels ready for the march, other provoking excuses for delay were not wanting, to fill, even to overflowing, the measure of annoyance. The demise of a nephew of the Sultán—the protracted funeral obsequies of the deceased—and the almost nightly abstraction of one or more hired camels by the lurking Bedouin, all contributed their mite. At length however no further pretext could be devised, and nine loads being actually in motion towards Ambábo, the first halting ground on the road to the kingdom of Shoa, the schooner "Constance," getting under weigh, stood up the bay of Tajúra, and cast anchor off the incipient camp, of which the position was denoted by a tall cluster of palms.

Endless objections being now provokingly raised to the shape, size, and weight of the boxes to be transported, it next became requisite to reduce the dimensions of the greater number, in the progress of which operation it was discovered that the hurry of transhipment at Aden had resulted in the substitution of several dozens of choice marasquino, for a similar number of cases, of equal size, freighted with round shot for the galloper-guns. The work in hand was one of no ordinary labour and difficulty; and, after all, its completion proved insufficient to satisfy the parties. One blockhead complained that his load was heavier than his neighbour's, who had wisely risen earlier in the morning to make his selection; another, that his case, although confessedly light, was not of convenient size; one was too long, another not long enough, a third too deep, and a fourth too loosely packed. From earliest dawn, until final close of day, on a sandy beach, under a broiling sun, was this torment continued without intermission, until the 30th of May, when, by dint of coaxing, menacing, and bribing, every article had been removed saving an unwieldy hand-organ, at which every camel-owner had shaken his wig in turn, and a few stand of arms which had been removed from wooden cases, and repacked in mats and tarpaulins. A great hulking savage finally proposed to carry these latter, upon condition of their being transversely divided with a saw to suit the backs of his wretched hip-galled camels. "You are a tall man," quoth Aboo Bekr drolly, "suppose we shorten you by the legs?"

"No, no," cried the barbarian, "I'm flesh and blood, and shall be spoiled."

"So will the contents of these cases, you offspring of an ass," retorted the old pilot, "if you divide them."

The almost insurmountable difficulties thus experienced in obtaining carriage, but now happily overcome, had so far delayed the advance of the Embassy, as to oblige it to cross the Teháma during the height of the fiery and unwholesome blast which, during the months of June and July, sweeps over that waterless tract from the south-west; and had moreover rendered it impossible to reach Abyssinia before the setting-in of the annual heavy rains, when the river Hawásh becomes impassable for weeks together. Independently of the natural apathy of the camel-owning population, the fact of the season of all intercourse with the interior, by Káfilah, having already passed away, rendered every one averse, under any consideration of gain, to so hazardous a journey. Grain was to be carried for the consumption of horses and mules during the passage of arid regions, where, during the hot season, neither vegetation nor water exists; and the wells and pools having notoriously failed in every part of the road, during three consecutive seasons of unusual drought, it was necessary to entertain a large proportion of transport for a supply of water sufficient to last both man and beast for two and three days at a time; whilst, neither grass nor green food remaining near the sea-shore, the hundred and seventy camels now forming the caravan, had been individually assembled from various grazing grounds, many miles distant in the interior.

A sufficient number of water-skins had fortunately been purchased at exorbitant prices to complete the equipment, together with mules for the conveyance of the European escort and artillery; and the greedy Sultán, besides receiving the lion's share of the profits on all, had sold his own riding beast for three times its worth in solid silver. But the forage brought over from Aden being long since consumed, the whole were fed upon dates, and to the latest moment the greatest difficulty continued to exist in regard to followers. The services of neither Dankáli, Bedouin, nor Somauli, were obtainable at whatever wages; and the whole of the long train of live stock was consequently to be attended by a few worthless horse-keepers, enlisted at Aden, aided by a very limited number of volunteers from the shipping, whose indifferent characters gave ample promise of their subsequent misdeeds.

On the departure of the last load, a general begging commenced on a grand scale, on the part of all who flattered themselves that they had in the most remote manner been so fortunate as to render assistance during the protracted sojourn of the Kafirs. Many, whose claims were far from being apparent, after confessing themselves satisfied *in propriis personis*, modestly urged demands on behalf of their still more worthless neighbours; and in order to have any chance of passing in safety to the mountains with so long a line of camels, it was only prudent to propitiate each and all of this predatory hosts of locusts, before entering upon their lawless country.

With a feeling of pleasure akin to that experienced by Gil Blas, when he escaped from the robbers' cave, the party at length bade adieu to Tajúra. Of all the various classes and denominations of men who inhabit the terrestrial globe, the half-civilised savages peopling this sea-port, are perhaps the most thoroughly odious and detestable. They have ingeniously contrived to lose every virtue wherewith the rude tribes to which they pertain, may once have been adorned; and having acquired nothing in exchange, save the vices of their more refined neighbours, the scale of abject degradation to which they are now reduced, can hardly descend lower. Under this sweeping and very just condemnation, the impotent Sultán, Mohammad ibn Mohammad, stands pre-eminently in relief; and the old miser's rapacity continuing unsated up to the very latest moment, he clutched his long staff betwixt his skinny fingers, and hobbled forth from his den, resolved to squeeze yet another hundred dollars as a parting memento from his British victims. The European escort were in the act of mounting the mules already harnessed to the galloper-gun, which he had vainly persuaded himself could never be transported from the coast, since no camel-owner consented to take it, and repeated attempts that he had witnessed to yoke a pair of oxen to the limbers had proved unsuccessful, even after their stubborn noses were pierced. But mule harness had been ably manufactured to meet the exigency, and when his lustreless eyes beheld the party in horse artillery order, firmly seated in their saddles, and moving along the strand towards Ambábo—forgetting the vile errand upon which he had come, he involuntarily exclaimed, "In the name of Allah and the holy Prophet, whither are those fellows going?" "*Raheen el Hábesh,*" "to Abyssinia," was the laconic reply that fell upon his astounded ears as the whips cracked merrily in succession; and His Highness was long after seen, still leaning on his slender crutch, and staring in idiotic vacancy after the departing cavalcade, as it disappeared under a cloud of dust from before his leaden gaze.

Chapter Eleven
Iniquitous Proceedings at Ambábo, and Understanding with the Ras El Káfilah

The tall masts of the schooner of war, raking above the belt of dwarf jungle that skirts the tortuous coast, served as a beacon to the new camp, the distance of which from the town of Tajúra was less than four miles. A narrow footpath wound along the burning sands, across numerous water-courses from the impending mountain range of trachyte and porphyry, whose wooded base, thickly clothed with mimosa and *euphorbia antiquorum*, harboured swine, pigmy antelope, and guinea-fowl in abundance. Many large trees, uprooted by the wintry torrent, had been swept far out to sea, where in derision of the waves that buffet their dilapidated, stag-horn looking arms, they will long ride safely at anchor. The pelican of the wilderness soiled through the tossing surf, and files of Bedouin damsels, in greasy leathern petticoats, bending beneath a load of fuel from the adjacent hamlets, traversed the sultry strand; whilst a long train of wretched children, with streaming elf-like locks, who had been kidnapped in the unexplored interior, wended their weary way with a slave caravan, towards the sea-port, whence they were to be sold into foreign bondage.

An avenue through the trees presently revealed the white tent, occupying a sequestered nook on the course of a mountain stream near its junction with the shore. Here horses and mules were doing their utmost, by diligently cropping the scanty tufts of sun-burnt grass, to repair their recent long abstinence from forage, whilst the abbreviated tails of those which had been improved by mutilation, formed the jest of a group of grinning savages. Clumps of lofty fan palms, and date trees loaded with ripe orange-coloured fruit, still screened from view the village of Ambábo, the straggling Gothic roofed wigwams composing which have the same waggon-like appearance as the huts of Tajúra,—a similar style of architecture extending even to the unostentatious mosque, alone distinguishable from the surrounding edifices, by uncarved minarets of wood.

Greasy ragamuffins still intruding, here continued their teasing persecutions, and Mohammad Mohammad, the son, though not the heir to the throne of the Sultán, having been specially appointed by his disreputable sire to the important post of reporter and spy, unceremoniously occupied one of the chairs, to the exclusion of the lawful proprietor during the entire day. He however proved useful in so far that he was versed in the chronicle of Ambábo. The Nákhuda of one of his uncle's buggalows having contrived a quarrel with a member of the tribe Hassóba, one of the manifold subdivisions of the Danákil, the man threw the gauntlet of defiance by cutting off the prow of the boat. Meeting shortly afterwards in deadly conflict, the insulted mariner slew his antagonist on the spot, and took refuge in the hills, until, tired of long concealment, and believing the affair to be consigned to oblivion, he ventured to settle with his family at Ambábo, and thus founded the present village; but after some years of repose, he was discovered by the relatives of the slain, and, as usual in all blood feuds, ultimately assassinated. Occupying a site proverbially unhealthy, and scourged during the rains by insupportable clouds of musquitoes, the miserable hamlet is but thinly peopled, and the Sheikh being on far from amicable terms with the authorities of Tajúra, it is likely soon to be abandoned in favour of some more eligible location.

A red savage, falsely representing himself to be one of the household of his Christian Majesty of Shoa, arrived during the afternoon from Ankóber, with letters for Aden, and having safely deposited his packet on board the "Constance," was readily induced to return whence he came, with the Embassy. Déeni ibn Hámed, a liar of the first magnitude, but the only Dankáli who had voluntarily attached himself to the fortunes of the party, conceiving the arrival of this courier to afford an opening for the exercise of his talents which ought on no account to be neglected, immediately proceeded to tax his lively ingenuity in disclosing the contents of a document which he pretended had been received from Sáhela Selássie by the old ruffian from whose clutches his audience had just thankfully escaped; and the mass of gratuitous falsehoods that he contrived to string together with an unblushing front, must be admitted to reflect ample credit upon his fertile invention.

Lying appeared in fact to be the chosen occupation of this youthful warrior, who, however, unlike the mass of his compatriots, did possess some redeeming qualities, though they were by no means so conspicuous as his scars. The insuperable aversion to veracity which he evinced on every occasion, renders it difficult to determine what degree of credit may be attached to the tragic tale that he was pleased to connect with a deep gash over the temple, which distorted his vision; and if not received in a less honourable *rencontre* than he pretended, affords another to the ten thousand instances on record of the savage rancour with which blood feuds are prosecuted. "My maternal uncle, and a native of Zeyla," said Déeni, "becoming embroiled, mutually unsheathed their creeses in mortal strife, fought desperately, and died. The brother of the latter sought my life in revenge, as being the nearest of kin; but after receiving this slash upon my forehead, and another on my arm, which I shall also carry to the grave, I closed, stabbed the Somauli villain to the heart with this good creese, and, glory be to God I divided his windpipe with his own sword."

Profiting by the amiable example of the illustrious ruler of Tajúra, the Sheïkh of Ambábo, a most notable extortioner, resolved to put his chum to a sum of ready money beyond a shadow of doubt, placed a strong Bedouin guard over the only well; and although he had every reason to be satisfied with the success of his nefarious schemes, he did not possess sufficient gratitude to prevent the commission of a robbery during the night, which might have proved more serious than it did. Solace under all misfortunes and annoyances was, however, found in the arrival of Mohammad Ali on the 31st, with a welcome accession of camels for the carriage of water, which rendered certain the prospect of departure on the morrow, it having been distinctly promised by the Sultán, in return for a handsome pecuniary consideration, that his brother Izhák, who had been unanimously appointed Ras el Káfilah, his son, his nephew, and seven other persons of undoubted influence on the road, should be in readiness without fail, to escort the Embassy on the 1st of June, and that the reward of their services should be paid, *ad valorem*, upon safe arrival within the kingdom of Shoa.

Three hours after midnight, the galloper-gun, fired within the limits of the British camp as a summons to the drowsy camel-drivers to be up and doing, was echoed, according to previous agreement, by the long stern chaser of the "Constance,"—a signal to the "Euphrates," still anchored off Tajúra, to thunder a farewell salute as the day dawned. The work of loading was merrily commenced—the tent went down—and camel after camel moved off towards Dullool; when, on the departure of the last string, it was observed with dismay that the ground was still strewed with baggage, for which carriage had unquestionably been paid and entertained, but for which none was forthcoming. The greasy proprietors were, after some search, discovered below the bushes, engaged in the operation of jerking mutton,—a process sufficiently nauseous in itself to repel any close advance; but persuasion and threats proved alike unavailing. Some had already sent their camels to graze at a distance; others insolently expressed their intention of doing so after the completion of their interesting work, and by far the greater number would vouchsafe no explanation whatever. At length the provoking riddle was solved by the arrival of a peremptory message from the Sultán, naming the price of the attendance of his brother with the promised escort, and modestly requesting that the amount might forthwith be disbursed, or the bargain must be considered null and void!

In this awkward dilemma, one of the party was immediately despatched to create a diversion among the Philistines, and to remonstrate against so gross a breach of good faith; whilst the residue, awaiting his tardy return, passed the sultry day beneath the mock shelter afforded by a low date bush, shifting position with the deceitful shadow, which, before any further tidings were received of the delinquent old Sultán and his ungovernable myrmidons, was cast full on the eastern side. At length the anxiously straining eye was relieved by the appearance of the messenger on his way back. After a world of trouble, he had succeeded in hunting out some of the elders, who, however, would only consent to accompany him on the payment of every stuiver of the demand made in the morning, and, quietly possessed of the dollars, they had thought proper to detain the escort.

Izhák, backed by Ibrahim Shehém, the most renowned warrior in the next ten tribes, sat as orator on the occasion. The demeanour of the Ras bordered closely on the insolent. A heavy load of impudence could be detected under his broad pudding face; and his desire to be impertinent was favoured in no small degree by the presence of heaps of valuable baggage lying at his mercy upon the ground. The deputation was received quite as coldly as their dishonest and most provoking behaviour demanded; a silence of several minutes affording to each, leisure to pick out his curly locks, and cool himself a little, the whole having walked out in the broiling sun, and become considerably excited withal. Distant inquiries were at length instituted relative to the august health of the Sultán and the royal family, which were stiffly responded to after the current Dankáli fashion, "Hamdu-lillah," "thanks be unto God!"

The conference then opened with a bluster concerning the movement of the Káfilah from Ambábo without the presence, order, or consent of the Ras, who, after sneering at the attempt as a most unprecedented proceeding, and indulging in a very gratuitous *tirade* against Mohammad Ali, whom he styled in derision "the supplier of water," and was anxious to make appear the only culprit on the occasion, added, in conclusion, that his own being "a house of mourning," he had given up his intention of proceeding to Abyssinia, and had finally resolved to wash his hands of the business.

He was gravely answered that the caravan had started upon express orders given in consequence of a distinct understanding and pledge, purchased the preceding day of the Sultán and himself. He was reminded that every hire and remuneration for camels, guides, and escort, exorbitant though they were, had been paid in full at Tajúra; and was distinctly informed that if the terms of the agreement were not fully complied with, ere the night fell, the property of the British Government would be left on the ground, where it then lay, whilst the Embassy proceeded to Dullool, off which place the "Constance" had already anchored, reshipped all the baggage that had been sent to the advance camp, and set sail for Aden.

It was further added, that as the consequences of this step would rest upon the head of those who had entered into an express engagement, upon receipt of whatever terms they had demanded as the price of their services, it should be borne in mind that further offensive and unprincipled demonstrations might terminate in unpleasant results.

As the interpreter proceeded to unfold this high-toned remonstrance, Izhák was seen to fidget uneasily upon his hams, whilst he sought to conceal his agitation by tracing figures on the sand; and, as the last intimation fell upon his ear, seizing his sandal, he relieved his excited feelings by shovelling a pointed stick through the very centre of the leather. But the swaggering air which he had assumed had now entirely disappeared, and, after a hurried whispering consultation with his confederates, he declared that he had been toiling day and night in the service of the English; that he was perfectly ready to perform every thing required of him, and that, notwithstanding the recent calamity with which his family had been visited, and the dangerous illness of his mother, he would escort the Embassy in person, with trustworthy colleagues; that he would be responsible for all the property left at Ambábo, and only petition for two days' grace to put his house in order before repairing to Dullool. This point being tardily accorded, he rose with Ali Shermárki, who had ridden in as mediator during the heat of the conference, and each offering his hand, in earnest of the matter being finally and amicably concluded in full accordance with the original stipulations of the covenant, set out on his return to Tajúra.

Chapter Twelve
Dullool—The Ras Unpleasantly Reminded of his Pledge—Sagállo and Warelissán

Izhák's absent camels, which had been kept close at hand pending the issue of this stormy debate, being now brought in, the ground was speedily cleared of the remaining baggage; and satisfied with the specious assurance of the Ras el Káfilah, that he would on no account tarry beyond nightfall of the following day, the party, relieved from their anxiety, mounted after five o'clock, and galloped seven miles along the sea-beach to the camp at Dullool,—the loose sand being so perforated and undermined in every part by the hermit crab, as to render the sieve-like road truly treacherous and unpleasant.

The grassy nook occupied by the tent was situated at the abutment of a spur from the wooded Jebel Goodah, evidently of volcanic origin, which gradually diminishes in height, until it terminates, one hundred yards from the shore, in a thick jungle of tamarisk and acacia, the former covered with salt crystals. Hornblende, in blocks, was scattered along the beach, and, wherever decomposed, it yielded fine glittering black sand, so heated under the noontide sun as to burn the naked foot. The movable camp of a horde of roving Bedouin shepherds, who, with very slender habitations, possess no fixed abode, was erected near the wells; and a quarrel with the followers, respecting the precious element, having already led to the drawing of creeses, silver was again in requisition to allay the impending storm.

The heat on the 2nd of June was almost insupportable; but the sultry day proved one of greater quiet than had fallen to the lot of the Embassy since its first landing. Late in the evening, when a cool sea-breeze had set in, Ali Shermárki rode into camp, and delivered a letter which had been slipped into his hand by the Sultán, appealing against the hardship of being left without remuneration for his diligent services, praying that his old heart might be made glad, and hoping that all might meet again ere death should call them—a wish responded to by no single individual of the British party.

Neither Izhák nor any of his followers made their appearance, notwithstanding that the redemption of the solemn promise passed was anxiously watched until midnight. At gun-fire the next morning, however, the arrival of the whole being reported, orders were issued to strike the tent, a measure which was doggedly opposed by the Ras el Káfilah, whose brow again darkened as he declared his resolution not to stir from Dullool until three of his camels, which were said to have strayed, should be recovered; and deaf alike to remonstrance or entreaty, he finally withdrew to a distance, taking his seat in sullen mood beneath a tree.

The schooner had meanwhile fished her anchor, and was now getting under weigh for the purpose of standing up within range of the next halting ground. The mules were harnessed to the gun, and the tent and baggage packed. Ali Shermárki was deputed to acquaint Izhák with these facts, and to intimate firmly, that unless the order to load were given without another moment's delay, minute guns would be fired as a signal to bring up the brig from Tajúra, when the promise made yesterday by the English would be found more binding than those of the Danákil had hitherto proved. This menace had the desired effect, and after three hours of needless detention, the party commenced its third hot march along the sea-beach, whence the hills gradually recede. Bedouin goat-herds occupied many wells of fresh water, which were denoted by clumps of date trees entwined by flowering convolvuli, whose matted tendrils fix the movable sands of the shore; and late in the forenoon the camp was formed at the pool of Sagállo, only three miles from the former ground, but affording the last supply of water to be obtained for thirty more.

An extensive and beautiful prospect of the western portion of the Bay of Tajúra had now opened, bound in on all sides by a zone of precipitous mountains, in which the gate leading into Goobut el Kharáb was distinctly marked by a low black point, extending from the northern shore. The schooner's services were volunteered to admit of a nearer inspection of the "basin of foulness;" but no sooner had she stood out to sea than signal guns fired from the camp announced the arrival of another packet from Shoa. The courier had been forty-four days on the journey, and the tidings he brought respecting the road, although highly satisfactory, added yet another instance to the many, of the small reliance that can be placed on information derived from the Danákil, who, even when disinterested, can rarely indeed be induced to utter a word of truth.

The strong party feeling entertained towards Mohammad Ali by the magnates of Tajúra, now vented itself in divers evil-minded and malicious hints, insinuating the defection of the absentee, who had been unavoidably detained by business, some hours after the last of the sea-port heroes had joined. "Where now is your friend Ali Mohammad?" "Where is the man who was to supply water on the road?" were the taunting interrogatories from the mouths of many; but come the son of Ali Abi did, to the confusion of his slanderers, long ere the sun had set, bringing secret intelligence that he had sent to engage an escort from his own tribe; and the whole party being now at last assembled, it was resolved in full conclave, that as not a drop of water could be procured for three stages in advance, the entire of the next day should be devoted to filling up the skins, which done, the caravan should resume its march by night—a manoeuvre that savoured strongly of a design to favour the clandestine return to Tajúra of certain of the escort, who had still domestic affairs to settle.

Thus far the conduct of the son of the Rookhba chief had formed a notable contrast to the proceedings of his backbiters. Whilst Izhák and his stubborn partisans had positively declined to move according to their agreement, unless a further most extravagant and unconscionable sum were paid in advance for their anticipated services, and had altogether assumed a bullying tone, coupled with a most impertinent and overbearing demeanour, this scion of a savage house that holds in its hands the avenues betwixt Shoa and Tajúra, and could at pleasure cut off communication with the coast, had never applied for aught save a trifling sum for the present maintenance of his family, and since the first éclaircissement, had, to the best of his ability, striven to render himself useful and agreeable to the party about to pass through his country.

A most unprofitable discussion, which was prolonged until eleven the following night, had for its object to persuade the transmission of baggage in advance to the Salt Lake, in consequence of the carried supply of water being, after all, considered insufficient for three days' consumption. But the proposal was negatived upon prudent grounds, the honesty of the intentions by which it had been dictated, seeming at best, extremely questionable, and no one feeling disposed to trust the faithless guides further than they could be seen, with property of value.

Scarcely were the weary eyes of the party closed in sleep, than the long 32-pounder of the "Constance," proclaiming the midnight hour, sounded to boot and saddle. The Babel-like clamour of loading was at length succeeded by a lull of voices, and the rumbling of the galloper wheels over the loose shingle, was alone heard in the still calm of the night, above the almost noiseless tread of the cushion-footed camels, which formed an interminable line. The road, lit by the full moon, shining brightly overhead, lay for the first two or three miles along the beach, and then, crossing numerous water-courses, struck over the southern shoulder of Jebel Goodah, the distance from whose lofty peak each march had reduced.

Blocks and boulders varying in size from an 18 pound shot, to that of Ossa piled upon Pelion, aided by deep chasms, gullies, and waterways, rendering the ascent one of equal toil and peril, cost the life of a camel, which fell over a precipice and dislocated the spine; whereupon the conscientious proprietor, disdaining to take further heed of the load, abandoned it unscrupulously by the wayside. Gáleylaféo, a singular and fearful chasm which was navigated in the first twilight, did not exceed sixty feet in width; its gloomy, perpendicular walls of columnar lava, towering one hundred and fifty feet overhead, and casting a deep deceitful shadow over the broken channel, half a mile in extent. Déeni, in his customary strain of amplification, had represented this frightful pass to be entered through a trap-door, in order to clear which it was necessary for a loaded camel to forget its staid demeanour, and bound from rock to rock like a mountain kid. The devil and all his angels were represented to hold midnight orgies in one of the most dismal of the many dark recesses; and the belief was fully confirmed by the whooping of a colony of baboons, disturbed by the wheels of the first piece of ordnance that had ever attempted the bumping passage.

Dawn disclosed the artillery mules in such wretched plight from their fatiguing night's labour, that it was found necessary to unlimber the gun, and place it with its carriage on the back of an Eesah camel of Herculean strength, provided for the contingency by the foresight of Mohammad Ali; and although little pleased during the imposition of its novel burthen, the animal, rising without difficulty, moved freely along at a stately gait. The same uninteresting volcanic appearance characterised the entire country to the table-land of Warelissán, a distance of twelve miles. Dreary and desolate, without a trace of vegetation saving a few leafless acacias, there was no object to relieve the gaze over the whole forbidding expanse. In this barren unsightly spot the radiation was early felt from the masses of black cindery rock, which could not be touched with impunity. The sand soil of the desert reflecting the powerful beams of the sun, lent a fearful intensity to the heat, whilst on every side the dust rose in clouds that at one moment veiled the caravan from sight, and at the next left heads of camels tossing in the inflamed atmosphere among the bright spear-blades of the escort. But on gaining the highest point, a redeeming prospect was afforded in an unexpected and most extensive bird's eye view of the estuary of Tajúra, now visible in all its shining glory, from this, its western boundary. Stretching away for miles in placid beauty, its figure was that of a gigantic hour-glass; and far below on its glassy bosom were displayed the white sails of the friendly little schooner, as, after safely navigating the dangerous and much-dreaded portals of Scylla and Charybdis, never previously braved by any craft larger than a jolly boat—bellying to the breeze, she beat gallantly up to the head of Goobut el Kharáb.

Chapter Thirteen
Gloomy Passage of Rah Eesah,
the Descensus ad Inferos

Although Warelissán proved nearly seventeen hundred feet above the level of the blue water, a suffocating south-westerly wind, which blew throughout the tedious day, rendered the heat more awfully oppressive than at any preceding station. The camp, unsheltered, occupied a naked tract of table-land, some six miles in circumference, on the shoulder of Jebel Goodah—its barren surface strewed with shining lava, and bleached animal bones; sickly acacias of most puny growth, sparingly invested with sun-burnt leaves, here and there struggling through the fissures, as if to prove the utter sterility of the soil; whilst total absence of water, and towering whirlwinds of dust, sand, and pebbles, raised by the furnace-like puffs that came stealing over the desert landscape, completed the discomfiture both of man and beast.

During the dead of night, when restless unrefreshing slumbers on the heated ground had hushed the camp in all its quarters, the elders, in great consternation, brought a report that the Bedouin war-hawks, who nestle in the lap of the adjacent wild mountains, were collecting in the neighbourhood with the design of making a sudden swoop upon the káfilah, for which reason the European escort must be prepared for battle, and muskets be discharged forthwith, to intimidate the lurking foe. They were informed, in reply, that all slept upon their arms, and were in readiness; but Mohammad Ali came shortly afterwards to announce that matters had been amicably adjusted with the aid of a few ells of blue cloth; and under the care of a double sentry, the party slept on without further disturbance until two in the morning, prior to which hour, the moon, now on her wane, had not attained sufficient altitude to render advance practicable.

The aid of her pale beams was indispensable, in consequence of the existence of the yawning pass of Rah Eesah, not one hundred yards distant from the encampment just abandoned, but till now unperceived. It derives its appellation, as "the road of the Eesahs," from the fact of this being the path usually chosen by that hostile portion of the Somauli nation, on the occasions of their frequent forays into the country of the Danákil, with whom, singularly enough, an outward understanding subsists. Its depths have proved the arena of many a sanguinary contest, and are said, after each downpouring of the heavens, to become totally impassable, until again cleared of the huge blocks of stone, the detritus from the scarped cliffs, which so choke the bed of the chasm, as to impede all progress. The labour of removing these, secures certain immunities to the wild pioneers, who levy a toll upon every passing caravan, and who in this instance were propitiated, on application, by the division of a bale of blue cotton calico, a manufacture here esteemed beyond all price.

A deep zig-zagged rent in the plateaux, produced originally by some grand convulsion of nature, and for ages the channel of escape to the sea of the gathered waters from Jebel Goodah, winds like a mythological dragon through the bowels of the earth, upwards of three miles to the southward. Masses of basalt of a dark burnt brown colour, are piled perpendicularly on either side, like the solid walls of the impregnable fortresses reared by the Cyclops of old; and rising from a very narrow channel, strewed with blocks of stone, and huge fallen fragments of rock, tower overhead to the height of five or six hundred feet. One perilous path affords barely sufficient width for a camel's tread, and with a descensus of one foot and a half in every three, leads twisting away into the gloomy depths below, dedicated to the son of Chaos and Darkness, and now plunged in total obscurity.

It was a bright and cloudless night, and the scenery, as viewed by the uncertain moonlight, cast at intervals in the windings of the road upon the glittering spear-blades of the warriors, was wild and terrific. The frowning basaltic cliffs, not three hundred yards from summit to summit, flung an impenetrable gloom over the greater portion of the frightful chasm, until, as the moon rose higher in the clear vault of heaven, she shone full upon huge shadowy masses, and gradually revealed the now dry bed, which in the rainy season must often-times become a brief but impetuous torrent.

No sound was heard save the voice of the camel-driver, coaxing his stumbling beasts to proceed by the most endearing expressions. In parts where the passage seemed completely choked, the stepping from stone to stone, accomplished with infinite difficulty, was followed by a drop leap, which must have shaken every bone. The gun was twice shifted to the back of a spare camel, provided for the purpose; and how the heavily-laden, the fall of one of which would have obstructed the way to those that followed, kept their feet, is indeed subject of profound astonishment. All did come safely through, however, notwithstanding the appearance of sundry wild Bedouins, whose weapons and matted locks gleamed in the moonbeam, as their stealthy figures flitted in thin tracery from crag to crag. A dozen resolute spirits might have successfully opposed the united party; but these hornets of the mountains, offering no molestation, contented themselves with reconnoitring the van and rear-guards from heights inaccessible through their natural asperity, until the twilight warned them to retire to their dens and hiding places; and ere the sun shone against the summits of the broken cliffs, the straggling caravan had emerged in safety from this dark descent to Eblis.

Goobut el Kharáb, with the singular sugar-loaf islet of Good Ali, shortly opened to view for the last time, across black sheets of lava, hardened in their course to the sea, and already rotten near the water's edge. Many years have not elapsed since the Eesah made their latest foray to the north of the pass, which has since borne their name; and sweeping off immense booty in cattle, halted on their return at Eyroladába, above the head of the bay. Under cover of the pitchy darkness, five hundred Danákil warriors, passing silently through the gloomy defile, fell suddenly in the dead of night upon the marauders, when, in addition to the multitude slain by the spear and creese, numbers in the panic created by the surprise, leapt in their flight over the steep lava cliffs, and perished in the deep waters of the briny basin.

The schooner, although riding safely at anchor near the western extremity, was altogether concealed by precipitous walls that towered above her raking masts, and kept the party in uncertainty of her arrival. Crossing the lone valley of Marmoríso, a remnant of volcanic action, rent and seamed with gaping fissures, the road turned over a large basaltic cone, which had brought fearful devastation upon the whole surrounding country, and here one solitary gazelle browsed on stubble-like vegetation scorched to a uniform brown. Skirting the base of a barren range, covered with heaps of lava blocks, and its foot ornamented with many artificial piles, marking deeds of blood, the lofty conical peak of Jebel Seeáro rose presently to sight, and not long afterwards the far-famed Lake Assál, surrounded by dancing mirage, was seen sparkling at its base.

The first glimpse of the strange phenomenon, although curious, was far from pleasing. An elliptical basin, seven miles in its transverse axis, half filled with smooth water of the deepest caerulean blue, and half with a solid sheet of glittering snow-white salt, the offspring of evaporation— girded on three sides by huge hot-looking mountains, which dip their bases into the very bowl, and on the fourth by crude half-formed rocks of lava, broken and divided by the most unintelligible chasms,—it presented the appearance of a spoiled, or at least of a very unfinished piece of work. Bereft alike of vegetation and of animal life, the appearance of the wilderness of land and stagnant water, over which a gloomy silence prevailed, and which seemed a temple for ages consecrated to drought, desolation, and sterility, is calculated to depress the spirit of every beholder. No sound broke on the ear; not a ripple played upon the water; the molten surface of the lake, like burnished steel, lay unruffled by a breeze; the fierce sky was without a cloud, and the angry sun, like a ball of metal at a white heat, rode triumphant in a full blaze of noontide refulgence, which in sickening glare was darted back on the straining vision of the fainting wayfarer, by the hot sulphury mountains that encircled the still, hollow, basin. A white foam on the shelving shore of the dense water, did contrive for a brief moment to deceive the eye with an appearance of motion and fluidity; but the spot, on more attentive observation, ever remained unchanged—a crystallised efflorescence.

As the tedious road wound on over basalt, basaltic lava, and amygdaloid, the sun, waxing momentarily more intensely powerful, was reflected with destructive and stifling fervour from slates of snow-white sea-limestone borne on their tops. Still elevated far above the level of the ocean, a number of fossil shells, of species now extinct, were discovered; a deep cleft by the wayside, presenting the unequivocal appearance of the lower crater of a volcano, situated on the high basaltic range above, whence the lava stream had been disgorged through apertures burst in the rocks, but which had re-closed after the violence of the eruption had subsided.

Dafári, a wild broken chasm at some distance from the road, usually contains abundance of rain-water in its rocky pool, but having already been long drained to the dregs, it offered no temptation to halt. Another most severe and trying declivity had therefore to be overcome, ere the long and sultry march was at an end. It descended by craggy precipices many hundred feet below the level of the sea, to the small close sandy plain of Mooya, on the borders of the Lake—a positive *Jehannam*, where the gallant captain of the "Constance" (Lieutenant Wilmot Christopher, I N) had already been some hours ensconced under the leafless branches of one poor scrubby thorn, which afforded the only screen against the stifling blast of the sirocco, and the merciless rays of the refulgent orb overhead.

Adyli, a deep mysterious cavern at the further extremity of the plain, is believed by the credulous to be the shaft leading to a subterranean gallery which extends to the head of Goobut el Kharáb. Déeni, most expert and systematic of liars, even went so far as to assert that he had seen through it the waters of the bay, although he admitted it to be the abode of "gins and efreets," whose voices are heard throughout the night, and who carry off the unwary traveller to devour him without remorse. The latest instance on record was of one Shehém, who was compelled by the weariness of his camel to fall behind the caravan, and, when sought by his comrades, was nowhere to be found, notwithstanding that his spear and shield had remained untouched. No tidings of the missing man having been obtained to the present hour, he is believed by his disconsolate friends to have furnished a meal to the gins in Adyli; but it seems not improbable that some better clue to his fate might be afforded by the Adrúsi, an outcast clan of the Débeni, acknowledging no chief, though recognising in some respects the authority of the Sultán of Tajúra, and who wander over the country for evil, from Sagállo to the Great Salt Lake.

Foul-mouthed vampires and ghouls were alone wanting to complete the horrors of this accursed spot, which, from its desolate position, might have been believed the last stage in the habitable world. A close mephitic stench, impeding respiration, arose from the saline exhalations of the stagnant lake. A frightful glare from the white salt and limestone hillocks threatened destruction to the vision; and a sickening heaviness in the loaded atmosphere, was enhanced rather than alleviated by the fiery breath of the parching north-westerly wind, which blew without any intermission during the entire day. The air was inflamed, the sky sparkled, and columns of burning sand, which at quick intervals towered high into the dazzling atmosphere, became so illumined as to appear like tall pillars of fire. Crowds of horses, mules, and fetid camels, tormented to madness by the dire persecutions of the poisonous gad-fly, flocked recklessly with an instinctive dread of the climate, to share the only bush; and obstinately disputing with their heels the slender shelter it afforded, compelled several of the party to seek refuge in noisome caves formed along the foot of the range by fallen masses of volcanic rock, which had become heated to a temperature seven times in excess of a potter's kiln, and fairly baked up the marrow in the bones. Verily! it was "an evil place," that lake of salt: it was "no place of seed, nor of figs, nor yet of vines; no, nor even of pomegranates; neither was there any water to drink."

Chapter Fourteen
Fearful Sufferings in the
Pandemonium of Bahr Assál

In this unventilated and diabolical hollow, dreadful indeed were the sufferings in store both for man and beast. Not a drop of fresh water existed within many miles; and, notwithstanding that every human precaution had been taken to secure a supply, by means of skins carried upon camels, the very great extent of most impracticable country to be traversed, which had unavoidably led to the detention of nearly all, added to the difficulty of restraining a multitude maddened by the tortures of burning thirst, rendered the provision quite insufficient; and during the whole of this appalling day, with the mercury in the thermometer standing at 126 degrees under the shade of cloaks and umbrellas—in a suffocating Pandemonium, depressed five hundred and seventy feet below the ocean, where no zephyr fanned the fevered skin, and where the glare arising from the sea of white salt was most painful to the eyes; where the furnace-like vapour exhaled, almost choking respiration, created an indomitable thirst, and not the smallest shade or shelter existed, save such as was afforded, in cruel mockery, by the stunted boughs of the solitary leafless acacia, or, worse still, by black blocks of heated lava, it was only practicable, during twelve tedious hours, to supply to each of the party two quarts of the most mephitic brick-dust-coloured fluid, which the direst necessity could alone have forced down the parched throat, and which, after all, far from alleviating thirst, served materially to augment its insupportable horrors.

It is true that since leaving the shores of India, the party had gradually been in training towards a disregard of dirty water—a circumstance of rather fortunate occurrence. On board a ship of any description the fluid is seldom very clean, or very plentiful. At Cape Aden there was little perceptible difference betwixt the sea-water and the land water. At Tajúra the beverage obtainable was far from being improved in quality by the taint of the new skins in which it was transferred from the only well; and now, in the very heart of the scorching Teháma, when a copious draught of *aqua pura* seemed absolutely indispensable every five minutes, to secure further existence upon earth, the detestable mixture that was at long intervals most parsimoniously produced, was the very acmé of abomination. Fresh hides stripped from the rank he-goat, besmeared inside as well as out with old tallow and strong bark tan, filled from an impure well at Sagállo, tossed, tumbled, and shaken during two entire nights on a camel's back, and brewed during the same number of intervening days under a strong distilling heat—poured out an amalgamation of pottage of which the individual ingredients of goat's hair, rancid mutton fat, astringent bark, and putrid water, were not to be distinguished. It might be smelt at the distance of twenty yards, yet all, native and European, were struggling and quarrelling for a taste of the recipe. The crest-fallen mules, who had not moistened their cracked lips during two entire days, crowding around the bush, thrust their hot noses into the faces of their masters, in reproachful intimation of their desire to participate in the filthy but tantalising decoction; and deterred with difficulty from draining the last dregs, they ran frantically with open mouths to seek mitigation of their sufferings at the deceptive waters of the briny lake, which, like those of Goobut el Kharáb, were so intensely salt, as to create smarting of the lips if tasted.

Slowly flapped the leaden wings of Time on that dismal day. Each weary hour brought a grievous accession, but no alleviation, to the fearful torments endured. The stagnation of the atmosphere continued undiminished; the pangs of thirst increased, but no water arrived; and the sun's despotic dominion on the meridian, appeared to know no termination. At four o'clock, when the heat was nothing abated, distressing intelligence was received that one of the seamen, who during the preceding night had accompanied the captain of the schooner-of-war from Goobut el Kharáb, and had unfortunately lost his way, could nowhere be found—the gunner, with six men, having long painfully searched the country side for their lost messmate, but to no purpose; Abroo, the son of whom old Aboo Bekr was justly proud, and who was indeed the flower of his tribe, immediately volunteered to go in quest of the missing sailor, and he subsequently returned with the cheering intelligence that his efforts had been crowned with success. Overwhelmed by heat and thirst, the poor fellow, unable to drag his exhausted limbs further, had crept for shelter into a fissure of the heated lava, where he had soon sunk into a state of insensibility. Water, and the use of a lancet, with which the young midshipman who heroically accompanied the exploring party had been provided, restored suspended animation sufficiently to admit of his patient being conveyed on board the "Constance" alive; but, alas! he never reached Tajúra; neither did one of the brave tars who sought their lost comrade under the fierce rays of the sun, nor indeed did any of the adventurous expedition, escape without feeling, in after severe illness, the unwholesome influence upon the human constitution of that waste and howling wilderness.

But the longest day must close at last, and the great luminary had at length run his fiery and tyrannical course. String after string of loaded camels, wearied with the passage of the rugged defile of Rah Eesah, were with infinite difficulty urged down the last steep declivity, and at long intervals, as the shadows lengthened, made their tardy appearance upon the desert plain; those carrying water, tents, and the greater portion of the provisions most required, being nevertheless still in the rear when the implacable orb went down, shorn of his last fierce ray. The drooping spirits of all now rose with the prospect of speedy departure from so fearful a spot. The commander of the friendly schooner, which had proved of such inestimable service, but whose protecting guns were at length to be withdrawn, shortly set out on his return to the vessel with the last despatches from the Embassy, after bidding its members a final farewell; and in order to obtain water, any further deprivation of which must have involved the dissolution of the whole party, no less than to escape from the pestilential exhalations of the desolate lake, which, as well during the night as during the day, yielded up a blast like that curling from a smith's forge—withering to the human frame—it was resolved as an unavoidable alternative, to leave the baggage to its fate, and to the tender mercies of guides and camel-drivers, pushing forward as expeditiously as possible to Goongoonteh, a cleft in the mountains that bound the opposite shore, wherein water was known to be abundant. Pursuant to this determination, the European escort, with the servants, followers, horses, and mules, were held in readiness to march so soon as the moon should rise above the gloomy lava hills, sufficiently to admit of the path being traced which leads beyond the accursed precincts of a spot, fitly likened by the Danákil to the infernal regions.

Dismal, deadly, and forbidding, but deeply interesting in a geological point of view, its overwhelming and paralysing heat precluded all possibility of minute examination, and thus researches were of necessity confined to the general character of the place. Latitude, longitude, and level were however accurately determined (These will be found in the Appendix, Number One), and many were the theories ventured, to account for so unusual a phenomenon. Obviously the result of earthquake and volcanic eruption—a chaos vomited into existence by

"Th' infuriate hill that shoots the pillar'd flame,"

Dame Nature must indeed have been in a most afflicting throe to have given birth to a progeny so monstrous; and there being no locality to which the most vivid fancy could assign aught that ever bore the name of wealth or human population, little doubt can exist that the sea must have been repelled far from its former boundaries. The oviform figure of the bowl, hemmed in on three sides by volcanic mountains, and on the fourth by sheets of lava, would at the first glance indicate the site of an extensive crater, whose cone having fallen into a subterranean abyss, had given rise to the singular appearance witnessed. But it is a far more probable hypothesis that the Bahr Assál, now a dead sea, formed at some very remote period a continuation of the Gulf of Tajúra, and was separated from Goobut el Kharáb by a stream of lava six miles in breadth, subsequently upheaved by subterranean action, and now forming a barrier, which, from its point of greatest elevation, where the traces of many craters still exist, gradually slopes eastward towards the deep waters of the bay, and westward into the basin of the Salt Lake. Whilst no soundings are found in the estuary of Tajúra, Goobut el Kharáb gives one hundred and fifteen fathoms, or six hundred and ninety feet; and premising the depression of the lake to have been formerly correspondent therewith, one hundred and twenty feet may be assumed as its present depth. To this it has been reduced by the great annual evaporation that must take place— an evaporation decreasing every year as the salt solution becomes more intensely concentrated, and evinced by the saline incrustation on the surface no less than by a horizontal efflorescence, in strata, at a considerable height on the face of the circumjacent rocks.

In the lapse of years, should the present order of things continue undisturbed from below, the water win probably disappear altogether, leaving a field of rock salt, which, when covered in by the débris washed down from the adjacent mountains, will form an extensive depôt for the supply of Danákil generations yet unborn; and the shocks of earthquakes being still occasionally felt in the neighbourhood, it seems not improbable— to carry the speculation still further—that Goobut el Kharáb, divided only by a narrow channel from the Bay of Tajúra, will, under subterranean influence, be, in due process of time, converted into a salt lake, in no material respect dissimilar from the Bahr Assál—another worthy type of the Valley of the Shadow of Death.

Chapter Fifteen
Dismal Night-March along the Inhospitable Shores of the Great Salt Lake

Scarcely had the moon dipped her first flickering beam into the unruffled surface of the oval lake, and lighted the bluff cliffs for some hours previously shrouded in gloomy obscurity, than a loud war-cry from the adjacent heights echoed the assembly to arms, and the shrill blast of the Adaïel conch summoned all to the rescue. Abandoning his occupation, each stalwart warrior seized spear and buckler, which had been laid aside whilst he aided in the task of reloading the camels for the approaching night-march, and with respondent yells rushed towards the spot whence the alarm proceeded. The Europeans, springing from their broken slumbers on the parched sands, stood to their arms. A long interval of silence and suspense succeeded, which was at last relieved by the return of Mohammad Ali, one of whose beasts had unfortunately slidden with its burden over a steep precipice, when the water-skins bursting incontinently, had scattered the filthy but precious contents over the thirsty soil—an irreparable catastrophe which had occasioned the call for assistance, believed by all to indicate a hostile gathering of the wild Bedouin clans.

Of two roads which lead to Goongoonteh from the shores of the dreary Bahr Assál, one skirts the margin of the lake by a route utterly destitute of fresh water; whilst the other, although somewhat more circuitous, conducts over high lava banks stretching some distance inland to Haliksitan, and past the small well of Hanlefánta, where the drained pitcher of the fainting wayfarer may be refilled. On finally quitting the bivouac under the scraggy boughs of the dwarf acacia, where the tedious and most trying day had been endured—which each of the half-stifled party did with an inward prayer that it might never fall to his lot to seek their treacherous shelter more—a fierce dispute arose amongst the leaders of the caravan as to which path should be adopted. "What matters it," urged the intolerant Mohammadan from Shoa, who had accidentally been found starving at Ambábo, and been since duly fed by the embassy—"what matters it if all these Christian dogs should happen to expire of thirst? Lead the Kafirs by the lower road, or,

Allahu akbar, God is most powerful, if the waters of the well prove low, what is to become of the mules of the Faithful?"

But the breast of the son of Ali Abi fortunately warmed to a more humane and charitable feeling than the stony heart of the "red man." With his hand upon the hilt of his creese, he swore aloud upon the sacred Korán to take the upper path, and stoutly led the way, in defiance of all, after Izhák and the ruthless bigots in his train had actually entered upon a route, which the event proved must have involved the destruction of all less inured than the savage to the hardships of the waste wilderness.

'Twas midnight when the thirsty party commenced the steep ascent of the ridge of volcanic hills which frown above the south-eastern boundary of the fiery lake. The searching north-east wind had scarcely diminished in its parching fierceness, and in hot suffocating gusts swept fitfully over the broad glittering expanse of water and salt whereon the moon shone brightly—each deadly puff succeeded by the stillness that foretells a tropical hurricane—an absolute absence even of the smallest ruffling of the close atmosphere. Around, the prospect was wild, gloomy, and unearthly, beetling basaltic cones and jagged slabs of shattered larva—the children of some mighty trouble—forming scenery the most shadowy and extravagant. A chaos of ruined churches and cathedrals, *eedgahs*, towers, monuments, and minarets, like the ruins of a demolished world, appeared to have been confusedly tossed together by the same volcanic throes, that when the earth was in labour, had produced the phenomenon below; and they shot their dilapidated spires into the molten vault of heaven, in a fantastic medley, which, under so uncertain a light, bewildered and perplexed the heated brain. The path, winding along the crest of the ridge, over sheets of broken lava, was rarely of more than sufficient width to admit of progress in single file; and the livelong hours, each seeming in itself a century, were spent in scrambling up the face of steep rugged precipices, where the moon gleamed upon the bleaching skeleton of some camel that had proved unequal to the task—thence again to descend at the imminent peril of life and limb, into yawning chasms and dark abysses, the forbidding vestiges of bygone volcanic agency.

The horrors of that dismal night set the efforts of description at defiance. An unlimited supply of water in prospect, at the distance of only sixteen miles, had for the brief moment buoyed up the drooping spirit which tenanted each way-worn frame; and when an exhausted mule was unable to totter further, his rider contrived manfully to breast the steep hill on foot. But owing to the long fasting and privation endured by all, the limbs of the weaker soon refused the task, and after the first two miles, they dropped fast in the rear.

Fanned by the fiery blast of the midnight sirocco, the cry for water, uttered feebly and with difficulty by numbers of parched throats, now became incessant; and the supply of that precious element brought for the whole party falling short of one gallon and a half, it was not long to be answered. A tiny sip of diluted vinegar for a moment assuaging the burning thirst which raged in the vitals, and consumed some of the more down-hearted, again raised their drooping souls; but its effects were transient, and after struggling a few steps, overwhelmed, they sunk again, with husky voice declaring their days to be numbered, and their resolution to rise up no more. Dogs incontinently expired upon the road; horses and mules that once lay down, being unable from exhaustion to rally, were reluctantly abandoned to their fate; whilst the lion-hearted soldier, who had braved death at the cannon's mouth, subdued and unmanned by thirst, finally abandoning his resolution, lay gasping by the wayside, and heedless of the exhortation of his officers, hailed approaching dissolution with delight, as bringing the termination of tortures which were not to be endured.

Whilst many of the escort and followers were thus unavoidably left stretched with open mouths along the road, in a state of utter insensibility, and apparently yielding up the ghost, others, pressing on to arrive at water, became bewildered in the intricate mazes of the wide wilderness, and recovered it with the utmost difficulty. As another day dawned, and the round red sun again rose in wrath over the Lake of Salt, towards the hateful shores of which the tortuous path was fast tending, the courage of all who had hitherto home up against fatigue and anxiety began to flag. A dimness came before the drowsy eyes, giddiness seized the brain, and the prospect ever held out by the guides, of quenching thirst immediately in advance, seeming like the tantalising delusions of a dream, had well nigh lost its magical effect; when, as the spirits of the most sanguine fainted within them, a wild Bedouin was perceived, like a delivering angel from above, hurrying forward with a large skin filled with muddy water. This most well-timed supply, obtained by Mohammad Ali from the small pool at Hanlefánta, of which, with the promised guard of his own tribe, by whom he had been met, he had taken forcible possession in defiance of the impotent threats of the ruthless "red man," was sent to the rear. It admitted of a sufficient quantity being poured over the face and down the parched throat, to revive every prostrate and perishing sufferer; and at a late hour, ghastly, haggard, and exhausted, like men who had escaped from the jaws of death, the whole had contrived to straggle into a camp, which, but for the foresight and firmness of the son of Ali Abi, few individuals indeed of the whole party would have reached alive.

A low range of limestone hillocks, interspersed with strange masses of coral, and marked by a pillar like that of Lot, encloses the well of Hanlefánta, where each mule obtained a shield full of water. From the glittering shores of the broad lake, the road crosses the saline incrustation, which extends about two miles to the opposite brink. Soiled and mossy near the margin, the dull crystallised salt appears to rest upon an earthy bottom; but it soon becomes lustrous and of a purer colour, and floating on the surface of the dense water, like a rough coarse sheet of ice, irregularly cracked, is crusted with a white yielding efflorescence, resembling snow which has been thawed and refrozen, but which still, as here, with a crisp sound, receives the impress of the foot. A well trodden path extends through the prismatic colours of the rainbow, by the longitudinal axis of the ellipse, to the northeastern extremity of the gigantic bowl, whence the purest salt is obtainable in the vicinity of several cold springs, said to cast up large pebbles on their jet, through the ethereal blue water.

At some distance from the beach was a caravan of Bedouin salt-diggers, busily loading their camels for the markets of Aussa and Abyssinia, where it forms on article of extensive traffic and barter. Two other basins of a similar stamp, but inferior extent, which exist at no great distance to the northward, are styled "Ullool" and "Dus." The first of these producing salt of most exquisite lustre, is preferred by the Mudaïto tribes, from whose capital Aussa, it is not more remote than Doba, as they term the Bahr Assál, the right to frequent which is asserted as an exclusive privilege by the Danákil, who for centuries have actually held the monopoly undisputed. Transferred in bulk in long narrow mat bags, wrought of the date-leaf, it is exchanged for slaves and grain, and not only forms, as in other climes, one of the chief necessaries of life, but possesses a specific value for the rock salt of the north, which, cut into rectangular blocks, passes as a circulating medium.

A second low belt of hills, gypsum and anhydrite, succeeded by limestone overstrewed with basaltic boulders, forms the western bank of the molten sea, and opens into a mountain ravine. Taking its source at Allooli, the highest point of the Gollo range, this torrent strives to disembogue into the extremity of the lake, although its waters seldom arrive so far, save during the rainy season. The high basaltic cliffs that hem in the pebbly channel, approximating in the upper course as they increase rapidly in altitude, form a narrow waist, where the first running stream that had greeted the eye of the pilgrims since leaving the shores of Asia, trickled onwards, leaving bright limpid pools, surrounded by brilliant sward.

Bowers, for ever green, enlivened by the melodious warbling of the feathered creation, and the serene and temperate air of the verdant meadows of Elysium, were absent from this blessed spot, but it was entered with feelings allied for the moment to escape from the horrors of purgatory to the gates of Paradise; and under the shade cast by the overhanging cliffs, which still warded off the ardent rays of the ascending sun, it was with thankful hearts that the exhausted party, after the terrors of such a night, turned their backs upon the deadly waters of the stagnant lake, to quaff at the delicious rivulet of Goongoonteh an unlimited quantity of cool though brackish fluid.

Here terminated the dreary passage of the dire Teháma—an iron-bound waste, which, at this inauspicious season of the year, opposes difficulties almost overwhelming in the path of the traveller. Setting aside the total absence of water and forage throughout a burning tract of fifty miles— its manifold intricate mountain passes, barely wide enough to admit the transit of a loaded camel, the bitter animosity of the wild bloodthirsty tribes by which they are infested, and the uniform badness of the road, if road it may be termed, everywhere beset with the huge jagged blocks of lava, and intersected by perilous acclivities and descents—it is no exaggeration to state, that the stifling sirocco which sweeps across the unwholesome salt flat during the hotter months of the year, could not fail, within eight and forty hours, to destroy the hardiest European adventurer. Some idea of the temperature of this terrible region may be derived from the fact of fifty pounds of well packed spermaceti candles, having, during the short journey from Tajúra, been so completely melted out of the box as to be reduced to a mere bundle of wicks. Even the Danákil, who from early boyhood have been accustomed to traverse the burning lava of the Teháma, never speak of it but in conjunction with the devouring element, of whose properties it partakes so liberally, and when alluding to the Lake of Salt, invariably designate it "Fire."

Chapter Sixteen
Afflicting Catastrophe at Goongoonteh

Goongoonteh, a deep gloomy zig-zagged fissure, of very straitened dimensions, is hemmed in by craggy lava and basaltic walls, intersected by dykes of porphyry, augitic greenstone and pistacite, with decomposed sulphate of iron, all combining to impart a strangely variegated appearance. Scattered and inclined in various directions, although towering almost perpendicularly, they terminate abruptly in a rude pile of rocks and lulls, through a narrow aperture in which the path to the next halting ground at Allooli, where the torrent takes its source, strikes off at an angle of 90 degrees.

Huge prostrate blocks of porphyry and basalt, which have been launched from the impending scarps, and now reduce the channel to this narrow passage, are in places so heaped and jammed together by some mighty agency, as to form spacious and commodious caverns. In the rainy season especially, these doubtless prove of wonderful convenience to the wayfarer; and no tent arriving until late the following day, the re-assembled party were fain to have recourse to them for shelter against the fierce hot blast from the Salt Lake, which, unremitting in its dire persecutions, now blew directly up the ravine. But the rocks soon became too hot to be touched with impunity, and the oblique rays of the sun, after he had passed the meridian, darting through every aperture, the caves were shortly converted into positive ovens, in which the heat, if possible, was even more intolerable than ever. Unlike former stations, however, there was, in this close unventilated chasm, a luxurious supply of water to be obtained from the living rill which murmured past the entrance, and although raised to the temperature of a thermal spring by the direct influence of the solar rays, and withal somewhat brackish to the taste, it was far from being pronounced unpalatable.

Notwithstanding that the neighbourhood afforded neither the smallest particle of forage nor of fuel, it became necessary, in consequence of the non-arrival of one half of the camels, no less than from the exhaustion of many of the party, to halt a day in the hot unhealthy gully; and this delay afforded to the treacherous creese of the lurking Bedouin an opportunity of accomplishing that which had only been threatened by drought and famine. The guides objecting strongly to the occupation of the caves after nightfall, on account of the many marauding parties of Eesah and Mudaïto, by whom the wady is infested, every one, as a measure of precaution, slept in the open air among the baggage, half a mile lower down the ravine, where the caravan had halted. The dry sandy bed of the stream was here narrow, and the cliffs—broken for a short distance on either side into hillocks of large distinct boulders—again resumed their consistency after an interval of one hundred yards, and enclosed the camp in a deep gloom.

The straitened figure of the bivouac rendered it impossible to make arrangements with much regularity in view to defence. The horses were picketted in the centre of the ravine. The European escort occupied a position betwixt them and the northern side, and the scanty beds of the officers of the party were spread close to the southern bank. A strong picket of the Danákil was placed a little distance in advance; and, in addition to the numerous other native guards in various quarters, the usual precaution was observed of mounting a European sentry, whose beat extended the length of the front of the encampment. Old Izhák slept close to the beds of the embassy, and, evidently in a state of considerable trepidation, solaced himself until a late hour by recounting bloody tales of murder and assassination, perpetrated, within his knowledge, by the mountain *Buddoos* haunting the ravine of Goongoonteh, which, being the high road to the Salt Lake, forms the resort of numerous evil disposed ruffians, who are ever on the prowl to cut throats, and to do mischief.

The first night, although awfully oppressive from the heat exhaled from the baked ground, and the absence of even the smallest zephyr, passed quietly enough; and after another grilling day, which seemed to have no termination, spent within the caverns, the same nocturnal arrangement as before was observed with undiminished precaution. An hour before midnight a sudden and violent sirocco scoured the wady, the shower of dust and pebbles raised by its hot blast, being followed by a few heavy drops of rain, with a calm, still as the sleep of death. The moon rose shortly afterwards, and about two o'clock a wild Irish yell, which startled the whole party from their fitful slumbers, was followed by a rush of men, and a clatter of hoofs, towards the beds of the Embassy. Every man sprang instinctively on his feet, seized a gun, of which two or three lay loaded beside each, and standing on his pillow with weapon cocked, prepared for the reception of the unseen assailants. Fortunate was it that no luckless savage, whether friend or foe, followed in the disorderly retreat, or consequences the most appalling must inevitably have ensued; but the white legs of half-naked and unarmed artillerymen having passed at speed, were followed only by a crush of horses and mules that had burst from their pickets. So complete was the panic caused by a sudden start from deep sleep to witness the realisation of the murderous tales of midnight assassination which had been poured into their ears, that the flying soldiery, who in the battle field had seen comrades fell thick around them, and witnessed death in a thousand terrific forms, were rallied with difficulty. But a panic is of short duration if officers perform their duty, and the word "Halt!" acted like magic upon the bewildered senses of the survivors, who, falling in, formed line behind the rifles.

Hurrying to the spot which they had occupied, a melancholy and distressing sight presented itself. A sergeant and a corporal lay weltering in the blood with which their scanty beds were deeply stained, and both were in the last agonies of death. One had been struck with a creese in the carotid artery immediately below the ear, and the other stabbed through the heart; whilst speechless beside their mangled bodies was stretched a Portuguese follower, with a frightful gash across the abdomen, whence the intestines were protruding. Aroused in all probability during this act of cold-blooded murder, and attempting to give the alarm, he had received a fatal slash as the dastards retreated; but almost instantaneous death had followed each previous blow of the creese, which, whilst the back of the sentinel was turned, had been dealt with mortal and unerring precision.

Two human figures being perceived at the moment the alarm was first raised, crossing the lower gorge of the ravine, and absconding towards the hills which bounded the further extremity of the camp, were promptly pursued by Mohammad Ali and his band of followers, who had seized spear and shield with the utmost alacrity; but although the moon shone bright, and the stars twinkled in the clear firmament, the broken and stony nature of the ground facilitated the escape of the miscreants under the deep shadow cast by the overhanging mountains, where objects could not be distinguished.

This afflicting catastrophe gave birth in the breast of all to a by no means unnatural feeling of distrust towards the escort engaged on the sea-coast, not only as to their ability, but also as to their intention to afford protection. The European party had lain down in full and entire confidence, only to be aroused by the perpetration of this most diabolical and fiendish deed; and although those who had been so fortunate as to escape might, now that they had become aware of the existing peril, defend their own lives, yet such an alternative, involving the abandonment of all the government property in charge, was far from being enviable. Upon after investigation, however, it appeared probable, as well from the evil character borne by the gloomy ravine, as from the numberless murders known to be annually committed under similar circumstances of wanton atrocity amongst the native káfilahs *en route*, that a party of the Eesah Somauli, inhabitants of the opposite coast of Goobut el Kharáb, but who, to gratify an insatiate thirst for human blood, are in the habit of making frequent incursions into the country of the Danákil, had seized the opportunity afforded by the absence of the sentry at the further extremity of his beat, to steal unperceived down the inumbrated bank of the hollow, and perpetrate the dastardly and cold-blooded outrage.

No attempt to plunder appeared as an excuse for the Satanic crime, and the only object doubtless was the acquisition of that barbarous estimation and distinction which is only to be arrived at through deeds of assassination and blood. For every victim, sleeping or waking, that falls under the murderous knife of one of these fiends in human form, he is entitled to display a white ostrich plume in the woolly hair, to wear on the arm an additional bracelet of copper, and to adorn the hilt of his reeking creese with yet another stud of silver or pewter—his reputation for prowess and for bravery rising amongst his clansmen in proportion to the atrocity of the attendant circumstances. At perpetual strife with the Danákil, although the chiefs of the tribes are on outward terms of friendship, and even of alliance, no opportunity is lost of retaliating upon the mountain Bedouin—every fresh hostility creating a new blood feud, and each life taken on either side, being revenged two-fold, *ad infinitum*.

Ere the day dawned the mangled bodies of the dead, now stiff and stark, were consigned by their sorrowing comrades to rude but compact receptacles of boulder stones—untimely tombs constructed by the native escort, who had voluntarily addressed themselves to the task. And a short prayer, suited to the melancholy occasion, having been repeated as the mortal remains of each gallant fellow, enveloped in a blood-stained winding sheet, were lowered to their wild resting-place, three volleys of musketry, paying the soldier's last tribute, rang among the dark recesses of the ravine, when the hurried obsequies were concluded by scaling the entrance to the cemeteries, in which, however, it is not probable that the dastardly sons of Satan—still doubtless watching with savage satisfaction from some inaccessible cranny—long suffered their victims to sleep.

In the grave-like calm of the night, under the pale light of the wan moon, which only partially illumined the funereal crags that hemmed in the dreary chasm, and rose in gloomy sadness over the vaults of the departed, the scene was mournful and impressive. Mohammad Ali, Izhák, and Hajji Kásim, with all their retainers, appeared deeply touched by the fatal occurrences that had so thinned the ranks of a party for whose lives they had made themselves responsible; but they referred the event to fate and to the Almighty fiat, adding that, although they were unable to restore the dead to life, or undo that which by the will of Heaven had been done, their own eyes should never close in sleep so long as danger was to be apprehended from the dreaded Eesah, whose only honour and wealth consists in the number of foul butcheries with which their consciences are stained, and whom even savages concur in representing as sanguinary and ferocious monsters, "fearing neither God nor Devil."

Chapter Seventeen
The Stricken Follower Dies—Cairns of the Murdered—Allooli and Bedi Kurroof

It had been intended to march at break of day to Allooli, the source of Wady Goongoonteh; but the absence of several of the camels, which had gone astray during the nocturnal confusion, caused delay in this den of iniquity until ten o'clock. The altered deportment of the chiefs meanwhile tended materially to banish from the mind suspicion of treachery. Heretofore, with the single exception of Mohammad Ali, all had been cold, unfriendly, or insulting; but from the moment of the late catastrophe their manner was visibly changed, and the anxiety evinced for the safety of the survivors under their charge was unremitting. They formed a circle round the party whensoever seated, and not a single white face was for a moment suffered to wander beyond their sight unattended by a clump of spears.

The wound of the unfortunate Portuguese had been pronounced mortal, and his dissolution was hourly expected; but life still glimmering in the socket, he lingered on with fearful groans, although speechless, and too nearly insensible to be aware of what had passed. Placed upon a litter, arranged as comfortably as circumstances would permit, the attempt was made to convey him to the next ground, but the rough motion of the camel doubtless hastened the termination of his sufferings; and the wretched man breathing his last ere he had journeyed many miles from the scene of his misfortunes, was interred under a date tree by the road-side, in a grave ready prepared for his reception.

The last rains having washed away an artificial bank of stones which had formerly facilitated the ascent of the difficult and dangerous passage leading from Goongoonteh into the Wady Kélloo—as the upper course is denominated—a delay of two hours was at first starting experienced in the bed of the torrent, during which all were on the alert. Two huge pointed rocks abutting on opposite angles of the acute zig-zag, reduced it to a traversed waist, so narrow, that room for the load to pass was only afforded when the long-legged dromedary swung its unwieldy carcass alternately from side to side—the steepness of the acclivity rendering it very frequently necessary to perform this inconvenient evolution upon the knees. Many became jammed, and were unladen before they could regain an erect position; whilst others were, with infinite difficulty, by the united efforts of a dozen drivers, who manned the legs and tail, saved from being launched with their burthens over the steep side of the descent, which consisted of a treacherous pile of loose rubbish.

To the surprise of every spectator the train passed through the defile without any material accident, and thence proceeded to pick their steps among the rocks, pools, and fissures, which abound in every mountain torrent whose course is short and precipitous. Flanked by perpendicular sheets of basalt and porphyry, of unwholesome sulphury appearance, beneath which many deep pools of cool water had collected, the tortuous road was at intervals enlivened by clumps of the *doom* palm, environed by patches of refreshing green turf—sights from which the eye had long been estranged. Nine miles of gradual ascent brought the caravan safely to the encamping ground at the head of the stream—a swamp surrounded by waving palms and verdant rushes, occupying high table-land, and affording abundance of green forage to the famished cattle. Most fortunately the sky had proved cloudy, or the march, performed during the hottest hours of the day, would indeed have been terrific.

Hence to Sagállo, the dismal country is in the exclusive occupation of a wandering race of the Danákil, who, notwithstanding that the Sultán of Tajúra claims the sovereignty of the entire waste, only acknowledge his impotent authority during their occasional temporary sojourn among the huts of that sea-port. The guides asserted, with many imprecations, that from time immemorial few káfilahs had ever halted at Allooli without losing one or more of its members by the Adrúsi creeses, or by those of the Eesah; and on the bank opposite to the shady clump of *doom* palms, under whose canopy the residue of the day was passed, numerous cairns, consisting of circular piles of stone, similar to those left at Goongoonteh to commemorate the outrage of the preceding night, stood memorials of the dark deeds that had been perpetrated.

During about three years the road from Abyssinia to the sea-coast was completely closed by hordes of these ruffian outcasts, who continued their murderous depredations on every passer-by, until Loheïta, the present Akil of the Débeni, a young, daring, and warlike chieftain, succeeding to the rule on the demise of his father, routed the banditti after a severe struggle, and re-opened the route. The Wady Kélloo is, however, still permanently infested by parties of wild Bedouins, who skulk about the rocky passes: lie in wait for stragglers from the caravan: assassinate all who fall into their ruthless clutches: and, when time permits, further gratify their savage propensities, by mangling and mutilating the corpse.

"See how the cowardly scoundrels marked me," exclaimed the fiery old warrior Ibrahim Shehém Abli, drawing aside his checked kilt, and displaying sundry frightful seams, which had doubtless been the work of a sharp knife. "Behold these tokens of Eesah steel upon my thigh; I received them in this wild wady; but, by Allah, I had a life for every one of them. We have a blood feud now, and it behoves all who are not weary of the world, to look well to their own throats."

Lurking bandits excepted, who prowl about like the midnight wolf, the Adaïel tribes, although sufficiently barbarous and quarrelsome by nature, are fortunately in a great measure restrained from deeds of ferocity by the certain consequences of spilling blood. None are anxious to involve their family or tribe in a mortal feud, nor would any warrior, incurring the almost inevitable consequences of a two-fold retribution, find support from his clansmen, unless sufficient cause could be shown; and thus, even in the most lawless states of society, are checks imposed by absolute necessity, which prove almost as powerful as the more civilised legal restraint upon the human passions.

Although Allooli was represented to be even more perilous than Goongoonteh, it possessed, in point of locality, immense superiority; and every advantage that could be devised, was taken of its capabilities for defence. The baggage, formed in a compact circle on an open naked plain, was surrounded by a line of camels, and the mules and horses were placed in the centre next to the beds of the party. Guards and sentinels patrolled under an officer of the watch; and at the solicitation of the Ras el Káfilah, who was exceedingly anxious to avoid the inconvenient consequences of a blood feud, a musket was discharged every hour at the relief of sentries, in order to intimate to the evil-minded that all within the breastwork were not asleep.

Notwithstanding the presence, in the immediate neighbourhood, for several days previously, of a large band of Eesah, the hot night passed without any alarm. The non-arrival, until long after daybreak, of the camels lost at Goongoonteh, added to the length of the next march, obliging the abandonment of the intention entertained, to speed beyond the pale of this site of assassination, the party halted on the 10th. Allooli stands two hundred and twenty-eight feet above the sea, and although intensely hot, and its waters saline, it proved a paradise when compared with every preceding station. Here animal life was once more abundant. A horde of pastoral savages, who from time to time appeared on the adjacent heights, were made acquainted with the effect of rifle bullets, by the slaughter from the tent door of sundry gazelles that visited the swamp; and the venison afforded a most seasonable accession to the empty larder, which was further replenished from the trees overhead, whose fan-like leaves gave shelter to a beautiful variety of the wood pigeon.

Shortly after midnight the march was resumed by the moon's light over a succession of small barren terraces, confined by conical and rounded hills. In the lone valley of Henráddee Dowár, which opens into the wide level plain of Gurgúddee, there stood by the wayside a vast pile of loose stones, half concealed among the tall jaundice-looking flowers of the senna plant. Towards this spot ensued a general race on the part of escort and camel-drivers, who each added a pebble whilst repeating the Arabic auguration, *"Nauzu billahi mina Shaytani r rajím."*—"Let us flee for refuge to God from Satan the stoned." A tragic legend was attached to the cairn, which, from the dimensions attained, must have dated from a remote epoch. A hoary old man, accused in days long gone of incestuous intercourse with his own daughter, was arraigned before a tribunal of his assembled tribe, and, being fully convicted, was on this spot stoned to death, together with his fair partner in guilt. Throughout Syria and Palestine it is to this day the practice of all who pass the mounds raised over those who die in crime, and whose memory it is intended to dishonour, thus to contribute a stone, as well with a view to perpetuate the monument, as to shield themselves from evil by manifesting the detestation entertained of the infamy commemorated.

Gurgúddee, eight miles in length, and stretching on either hand to the far horizon, is bounded by steep mountain ranges, whence an alluvial deposit washed down by the rains, presented over the whole of the level plain a surface of cracked and hardened mud, like that of a recently-dried morass. From the southern side, where the clayey tract is thickly clothed with stunted tamarisk and *spartium*, a road strikes up the valley in a north-westerly direction to the Mudaïto town of Aussa, distant some three days' journey for a caravan. As the day dawned, the steeple necks of a troop of ostriches were perceived nodding in the landscape, as the gigantic birds kicked the dust behind their heavy heels; and a herd of graceful gazelles were seen scouring towards a belt of stony hillocks which skirted the dry pebbly bed of a river, that expends its waters on the sun-dried plain. Ascending this stream, in which were a few stagnant pools of bitter unpalatable water, a human figure was detected skulking behind some thick green tamarisks by which they were overshadowed. But on being perseveringly hunted down by Mohammad Ali and his wild myrmidons, the prisoner proved to be a Débeni in quest of truant camels—his attempt at concealment having, according to his own account, arisen from the appearance of so many mounted cavaliers, whom he had mistaken for a foraging party of the Eesah, and was naturally desirous of eluding.

The caravan halted early at Bedi Kurroof, after a march of sixteen miles, and the camp was formed on a stony eminence of basalt and lava, affording neither tree nor shade. A day of fierce heat succeeded. There was no forage for the cattle; the water was of the most brackish description; and the spot being of old infested by Bedouins, the party passed a restless and watchful night.

A legend of blood too was attached to this wild bivouac, as to most others on the road, and thus it was related. One of the young men of a Danákil caravan returning from Abyssinia, fatigued by the hot journey, lay down to rest his weary limbs beneath the shadow of a rock, near which the tent of the Embassy now stood. It was yet broad daylight, but a band of lurking Eesah presently pounced upon the wayfarer, like the eagle on its prey, and, ere he could resume his weapons, had stabbed him to the heart. The dying groans of the murdered man being heard by his comrades, a number of warriors started in hot pursuit of the flying assassins, and after a severe chase, succeeded in capturing the whole gang. Two were immediately speared to death upon the principle of two drops of blood for one; and the remaining miscreants, four in number, having been stripped of their clothes and arms, were kicked forth out of the place.

"The Eesah of these lulls," continued the narrator of this tale, as, by the light of the blazing watch-fire, he fashioned a rude wooden bolster for the preservation of his greasy peruke during approaching slumbers, "are perfect *Shaytans*. Outcasts from their tribe, bands of ten or more here wander up and down like wild beasts, cutting the throats of all they meet, whether infidels or true believers—not for the sake of gain or plunder, but purely to gratify an innate propensity to murder. The monsters train for these blood forays upon raw flesh and marrow, and, well anointed with sheep's-tail fat, can travel day and night, during the hottest season, without suffering from fatigue. *Allahu akbar*! but they are devils incarnate!"

"Who has seen the Eesah, who has heard the Eesah?" wildly challenged Mohammad ibn Izhák, starting upon his feet, and clashing his now finished bolster against his buckler, as he concluded this harangue. "Who has seen the Eesah, who has heard the Eesah?" shouted a dozen voices in various quarters of the extended camp. "Uncover your shields, uncover your shields! Count well their spears, that not a man of them escape!"

"We have not seen them, we have not heard them," responded the patroles on duty. "No Eesah are here. Sleep on in peace!"

Chapter Eighteen
Territories of the Danákil Débeni—
Suggadéra, Murrah, Dúddee, and Gobaad

Some hours before dawn on the 12th, the káfilah was again loaded and in motion across a low belt of stony eminences which gradually descend to the Kóri Wady, a long water-course, varying in width from two to four hundred yards. Threading the moist channel of this stream, where the foot often absolutely left an impression on the sand, and passing the watering pool of Leilé, the road ascended a deep valley to the halting ground at Suggadéra, in the country of the Danákil Débeni. The entire borders were flanked by dwarf palms and drooping tamarisk, bounded by low hills with cliffs of conglomerate and sandstone, which disclosed dykes of porphyry at an acute angle. Flocks of goats, diligently browsing on the fat pods which fall at this season from the acacia, were tended by ancient Bedouin crones in greasy leathern petticoats, who plaited mats of the split date-leaf; whilst groups of men, women, and children, lining the eminences at every turn, watched the progress of the stranger party.

A pastoral race, and subsisting chiefly upon the fermented juice of the palm, and upon the milk derived from numerous flocks of sheep and goats, or from a few breeding camels, the Débeni, a division of the Danákil, are during certain months of the year engaged in the transportation of salt from the deadly Bahr Assál to the Mudaïto town of Aussa, where it is bartered for grain. Architecture affords no term applicable to a structure of any kind inferior to a hut or hovel, or it might with propriety be applied to the base jumble of rough stone and shavings of the date stalk, tenanted by these nomade savages, who are divided into clans, and have no fixed habitations. Nevertheless there was something cheering in the aspect even of these frail edifices, the first human tenement which had greeted the eye since leaving the sea-coast, now ninety miles distant. Bare, desolate, and fiery, the entire intervening tract, although infested by the lurking robber and the midnight assassin, may be pronounced in all its sultry parts, utterly unfitted for the location of man.

Water of rather an improved description was obtained at Suggadéra, under basaltic rock, stained green by carbonate of copper. But not a particle of forage was to be had; and the heat, reflected from a pebbly hill beneath which the tent was erected, brought the mercury in the thermometer to 118 degrees, during the greater portion of the day; and the evil appearance of the place, surrounded by gloomy hills cast into the deepest shadow, led to the maintenance of a vigilant watch during the dark night.

Although disturbed at the early hour of 2 a.m., and denied further repose save on the bare ground, the loss of a camel, which was not recovered until late, so far retarded advance, that only four miles were achieved on the 13th. The road continued to wind with a gentle ascent along the bed of the Wady Kóri, the hills gradually diminishing in apparent height until they merged into the elevated plain of Murrah, which exhibited pebbles of pink quartz, with a few scanty tufts of sweet-scented grass, yellow and withered. Here, at the distance of two miles from a puddle of dirty rain-water, in defiance of the impotent Ras el Káfilah, the camel-drivers, who studiously avoid trees and the vicinity of a pool, resolved to halt, as being a place after their own hearts.

In the dry water-course just left, the chirruping of some solitary hermit bird, and the bursting bud of a certain dwarf shrub which clothed the borders, agreeably reminded the traveller of more favoured climes. But most completely was the illusion dispelled by the forbidding aspect of the sultry plain of Murrah. Monotonous fields strewn with black boulders, glaring in the sun, distressed the gaze wheresoever it was turned—each cindery mass seeming as though it had been showered down during a violent eruption of some neighbouring volcano; although, on nearer inspection, it proved to be the time-worn fragment of an extensive lava sheet. The bare stony plain was decorated with numerous cairns, marking deeds of treachery and blood; and at the distance of twenty miles rose a lofty range of hot table-land, behind which the Abyssinian river Háwash is lost in the great lake at Aussa.

The presence at the watering-place of a host of wild Bedouins, whose appearance was far from prepossessing, again induced the cautious elders to anticipate an attack; and the camp occupying a very unfavourable position for warlike operations, no little difficulty was experienced in making defensive dispositions. A gloomy black hill threw its impenetrable shadow immediately in front; and on the flank, a pile of half-ruined sheepfolds, constructed of blocks of lava, afforded extensive concealment. The night however passed away without any alarm, and the intense heat of the day giving place to a somewhat cooler atmosphere, admitted of sleep by turns in some comfort—parties of the Danákil escort contriving by chanting their wild war-chorus, to keep their heavy eyes longer open than usual.

An hour after midnight the loading commenced, and the steep rocky hill having been surmounted by a path strewed with loose stones, a terrace of slow ascent, presenting the same dreary appearance of rocks and lava boulders, continued during the residue of the moon's reign. At break of day, however, the aspect of the country began rapidly to improve. Gaining the higher and more salubrious level of Gulámo, the bare sterile land, strewed with black blocks of lava which tore the feet with their jagged edges, was fast giving place to sandy plains covered with dry yellow grass—a most welcome prospect for the exhausted cattle. Heretofore, saving in the wadys, no tree had been seen except small stunted leafless acacias, few and far between, and scarcely deserving of the name. Several small ravines were now choked with continuous groves, and a mountain stream termed Chekaïto, which rises in the country of the Eesah, and in the rainy season disembogues into the lake at Aussa, was thickly clothed on both sides with green belts of tamarisk, wild caper, and other wood, overhung with creeping parasites, and affording food and shelter to birds. The pensile nests of the long-tailed loxia depended from the boughs; and whilst the stems, covered with drift to the height of fifteen feet, gave evidence of a headlong course during the rains, water, even at this season, was here and there to be obtained.

Heaps of loose stones thrown carelessly together, mark in almost every direction the spot where the victim lies who has been cut off by some cold-blooded miscreant—melancholy monuments connected each with a tale of assassination. But on the banks of the Chekaïto many acres of ground are covered with stones of memorial, such as were raised over Absalom, and over Achan the king of Ai, each surrounded by a circular cordon which bears the stamp of high antiquity, and has evidently witnessed the passage of ages. These sepulchres are said to cover the bones of the heroes who fell in a battle fought on the spot at the period that the country was first wrested from the shepherds. "Hai," the designation of the spot itself, is applied also to the entire surrounding district, which is stated to have been formerly peopled by the Gitteréza, a gigantic pastoral race, who, under the chief Sango, were at enmity with all the surrounding tribes, but are now extinct.

After five times crossing the serpentine bed to the point of junction with the Sagulli, where ostriches cropped the grass around numerous deserted sheep-pens, the caravan finally halted at Dúddee, no great distance from Ramudéle. For days together the pilgrimage had led across dreary and desolate wastes, and through sterile ravines where no verdure relieved the eye, no melody broke upon the ear, and so few living creatures were to be seen, that the unwonted appearance of a solitary butterfly which had become bewildered in the desert, was duly hailed as an event. The general character is that of a stern wilderness, parched by the intolerable heat of a vertical sun blazing in fierce refulgence over the naked landscape, of which the chief varieties consist in immense plains of dry cracked mud, or in barren rocks towering towards an unclouded and burning sky. The utter sterility of the soil is rather marked than alleviated by occasional sickly plants of most puny growth, and by the scanty verdure of the few valleys wherein water is to be found, generally in a state of stagnation. But at Dúddee, forage and fuel were abundant. The water obtained by digging in the channel of the stream was no longer brackish. The heat, although the thermometer rose to 110 degrees, was infinitely more endurable than it had hitherto proved; and the insatiable thirst by which all had been incessantly tormented on the lower ground, had well nigh disappeared.

A march of twelve miles over a succession of grassy plains, untenanted by man or beast, but presenting the first cone of the termites that had been seen, brought the party on the 15th to the enclosed valley of Gobaad, a thousand and fifty-seven feet above the ocean. Volcanic ashes, jasper, chalcedony, and quartz, strewed the sandy route, low volcanic ridges, of comparatively recent formation, intersecting the landscape from west to east. The encamping ground, among heaps of hard gravel, near which water was good and plentiful, had only two years previously formed the scene of the discomfiture of the Ras el Káfilah and his party, who had been plundered of all they possessed by two hundred and fifty mounted Eesah. The recollection of the disaster being green in his memory, he had, before leaving Dúddee, donned his folio Korán, in the place of a duodecimo edition which previously graced his shoulder. This was a not-to-be-mistaken sign of *"khouf fee"* (i.e. There is danger to be apprehended) and with a terror-stricken face he now came to intimate, that the presence of a band of these lawless ruffians in the opposite hills, together with a gathering of the Mudaïto at the neighbouring pools of Sábala and Dagatéli, leaving no sort of doubt upon his mind of a meditated attack during the night, it behoved every man to be more than usually on the alert.

The equanimity of the brother of the Sultán of Tajúra was somewhat disturbed at the assurance in reply to this exhortation, that the Danákil camel-owners were the thieves most to be dreaded, their dirty and dishonest fingers being unhesitatingly thrust into the bags of rice and dates, whensoever opportunity proved favourable; and that the hired escort, whose business it was to prevent this malappropriation of the property of the Embassy, far from assisting to keep watch, left the duty to be performed by the Europeans, and invariably went to sleep on their posts.

"Not one of them shall close his eyes to-night, at all events," grumbled the Ras. "I shall myself superintend the business, and see to the safety of the camp; for, by the life of the Prophet, this is an evil spot!"

As the red sun went down there was certainly a considerable display of erect spears; but their number gradually diminished as the night closed in; and when the ten o'clock sentry was relieved, Izhák was snoring aloud, according to his wont, whilst each doughty warrior lay fast asleep, with his greasy head upon his shield, and his broad lance in the precise position that it assumed, when it fell from the relaxed grasp of the slumberer.

Chapter Nineteen
Interview with the Ogre

Loheïta ibn Ibrahim, Makobúnto, Akil, or chief of the Débeni and a section of the Eesah, asserting supremacy over Gobaad, as a portion of his princely dominions, which extend from the Great Salt Lake to Ramudéle, a messenger had, immediately upon the arrival of the caravan, been despatched to his encampment in the neighbourhood, to invite the hero to the tent; and the peaceful night passed, having inspired the leader of the alarmist party with new confidence, the non-arrival of the expected visitor was made an excuse for halting the following day.

Attended by a numerous and disreputable retinue, dragging as a gift an obstinate old he-goat, the potent savage, whose exploit of clearing the high road of the restless marauders, who long obstructed the passage of káfilahs, has already been noticed in terms of commendation, sauntered carelessly in during the early hours of the forenoon. Not one whit better clad than the ragged and greasy ruffians in his train, he was yet distinguished by weapons of a superior order—the shaft of his spear, which resembled a weaver's beam, being mounted below the broad glittering blade with rings of brass and copper, whilst the hilt and scabbard of a truly formidable creese were embellished in like ostentatious fashion. The wearer's aristocratic air, and look of wild determination, were well in unison with the reputation he had acquired as a warrior chief. Long raven locks floated like eagle's feathers over a bony and stalwart frame. A pair of large sinewy arms, terminated in fingers tipped with nails akin to bird's claws, and the general form and figure of the puissant Makobúnto, brought forcibly to mind the Ogre in the nursery tale, who breakfasted on nought save the flesh of tender innocents, and was cut short in his career of cannibalism by Jack the Giant-killer. A mighty man of valour, and presiding over a numerous clan of fierce and savage warriors, he is feared and respected by all the country round, and seemed to be right well aware of his consequence upon the road.

For some reason of his own, which he did not think proper to divulge, the audience was deferred until dusk, when the warrior stalked consequentially into the tent, and deposited himself between the arms of a chair placed for his reception, with as much dignity and self-possession as if he had never in his life been seated upon the ground. Although his covering was restricted to a very dirty cotton cloth, he wrapped himself in the impenetrable mantle of silence, and, comprehending no Arabic, gave ear to all the compliments that were translated for his edification into the Dankáli tongue, with the most perfect indifference and mental abstraction; until, having swallowed a sufficiency of hot coffee, and stuffed his nostrils with a becoming modicum of Regent's mixture, he deigned to lay aside a portion of his reserve, and in slow, measured language, vouchsafed a brief detail of the energetic measures that had been adopted at his behest, towards the recovery of certain horses sent by his ally, the King of Shoa, to Her Britannic Majesty, and which had, by some unfortunate chance, been stolen in their transit through Gobaad: adding, that he would impart to the Embassy the boon of his protection, and in earnest thereof might probably condescend the favour of his countenance a few stages in advance.

Izhák with his compeers sate in gloomy silence during the entire conference, evidently annoyed at the good understanding that subsisted betwixt his rival Mohammad Ali, and the illustrious guest. The presents designed for the propitiation of the Ogre having been duly transferred, were eagerly clutched and hastily conveyed beneath his buckler, or below the ample folds of his greasy garb, as being far too choice for the prying eyes of attendants; and after sitting another half hour in taciturn dignity, the prince of savages rose deliberately from his chair, and, loaded with broad-cloth and trinkets, walked away as he had come, without condescending to pay attention to, or say a parting syllable to any one.

The extraordinary hour chosen for this curious audience, had obviously been dictated by a desire to conceal from the covetous gaze of the wild spirits around him, the tribute which he had reasonably calculated upon receiving from the British pilgrims, on the occasion of their transit through his territories; for, in truth, it must be confessed that the social state of these savages does not by any means betray that primitive simplicity so lauded and extolled by Rousseau. Rude barbarians they are, saturated with Moslem intolerance as with mutton fat; and although they tend their flocks in the parched valley after the most approved Arcadian fashion, yet the persons of even the boldest chiefs are not always secure: and however poets may have embroidered the subject with the flowers of their fancy, there is not to be found one individual of the whole community, who would hesitate to cut a throat for the sake of the last remaining button on a waistcoat.

Betwixt savage and civilised existence there yawns a wide gulf. The savage man and the civilised man, although descended from a common parent, can scarcely be said to belong to the same stock of humanity, and he who has been pronounced the only true man, the lordly lord of the wilderness, might here more appropriately be designated a devil incarnate. An interesting trait in the children of nature was witnessed on the occasion of the slaughter of the rank buck goat presented to the Embassy by Loheïta ibn Ibrahim. No sooner had the razor-like creese been drawn across the throat, with the concomitant ejaculation, "Bismilláhi rahmáni rahím," —"in the name of God, the compassionate, the merciful," —than a savage threw himself upon the expiring animal; and having, vampire-like, quaffed as much of the hot flowing blood as he could obtain, besmeared his greasy features with the residue, and wiped them on the still quivering carcass. No tiger could have acted in more ferocious guise, or displayed a greater relish for the tide of life.

This had been a day of feasting and carousal; for both Izhák and the son of the Rookhba chief had likewise received sheep, and the slaughter of each had been followed by a general tussle for the possession of the caul. For the purpose of larding the head this is a prize infinitely preferred even to the tail, which appendage in the Adel sheep is so copiously furnished, that the animal is said to be capable of subsisting an entire year upon the absorption of its own fat, without tasting water. It was truly delightful to witness the process of greasing the poll at the hands of the Danákil barber. The fat having been melted down in a wooden bowl, the operator, removing his quid, and placing it in a secure position behind the left ear, proceeded to suck up copious mouthfuls of the liquid, which were then sputtered over the frizzled wig of a comrade, who, with mantle drawn before his eyes to exclude stray portions of tallow, remained squatted on his haunches, the very picture of patience. The bowl exhausted, the operator carefully collects the suet that has so creamed around his chaps as to render him inarticulate; and having duly smeared the same over the filthy garment of him to whom it in equity belongs, proceeds, with a skewer, to put the last finishing touch to his work, which, as the lard congealed, has gradually assumed the desired aspect of a fine full-blown cauliflower.

The Dankáli who has prevailed over his foe, adorns his cranium with a perfect frost of tallow, dons a leopard-skin decorated with monkey tails three times in excess of the highest bashaw in the Ottoman empire, and tricks himself out with feathers in all the variety of savage fancy, the lobe of his ear being pierced for the reception of pewter rings, which denote the number of his victories achieved. Many warriors thus distinguished had strolled in during the day; for there had been an onslaught upon the Eesah, who, among other recent atrocities, had only the preceding week ripped up six pregnant Débeni females. The same wearisome string of enquiries on the part of each member of the káfilah, were responded to in the same cold monotonous drawl, and then bandied back by the new arrival—apathy and indifference pervading the features of both parties throughout the endless mechanical repetitions of "*Wogérri?*" and "*Wogérri maani?*"

To Gobaad, from the shores of Lake Abhibbab, which is formed by the waters drained from Abyssinia, it is said to be one easy day's journey for the pedestrian. Amongst other Mudaïto visitors from its borders, there came one of the Galeyla, an outcast from his clan, who bore amongst his fellows the reputation of being a *veritable* cannibal. This villain became at once the cynosure of every eye, and stood confessed the vilest of the vile. A coil of putrid entrails which encircled his neck had been distended with mutton fat into the figure of monstrous sausages; and the shaggy mane of a filthy hyena, that he had destroyed and devoured the preceding day, being twined in a becoming wreath around his dark brow, mingled wildly with his dishevelled locks. Under the gaze of so great a crowd, his calm repose was calculated to elicit the highest admiration; and fully sensible of his own merit, the man-eater endured the scrutiny of the curious populace with an air of conscious dignity, which was scarcely disturbed when the temerity of the more juvenile spectators called imperatively for the interference of his heavy mace.

It is difficult to comprehend the motives which may have induced this worthy to venture thus rashly among his bitterest foes; but the nature of the terms occasionally subsisting between the Mudaïto and the Danákil are not more singularly anomalous than those that bind the Danákil and the Eesah, over a portion of which latter Loheïta ibn Ibrahim exercises nominal supremacy. Making common cause, and assisting each other against the Mudaïto, international hostilities are nevertheless almost unceasing; and mutual interest, added to the aversion entertained to the perpetuation of blood feuds, affords perhaps the only substantial argument for their temporary cessation.

Of three chieftains who take the title of Ougass, and whose authority is in some sort acknowledged by the Eesah, the principal is Ougass Robiley, who resides with the Gidderboosi, south of Zeyla. Hoossain ibn Fara, the next in order, is related by marriage to the Makobúnto of the Débeni, and asserts influence from the Reahmoosa tribe of Somauli, bordering on Goobut el Kharáb, to Kore Korágureet, within thirty miles of Zeyla, where commences the country of the Hebrowal—thence south to the limits of the Galla territory, and north-west to Killulloo. Here it is bounded by Errur, the residence of the old sheikh of the Wóema, and by the independent Mohammadan principality of Hurrur, whose Ameer annually confers upon each Eesah chief a conical skull cap and turban, in recognition of his alliance.

Not a cloud blotted the sparkling vault overhead, which now blazed out in a perfect galaxy of light, engirdled by the luminous zone of the milky way. Attention was early directed to its beauties by the shower of meteors that in rapid succession shot through the innumerable host of heaven, and temporarily eclipsed their brilliancy. The night was already somewhat advanced when Loheïta sent to demand a private audience upon two points of vital importance; and Mohammad Ali being the agent employed, no time was lost in arranging the desired interview. "My beard is troublesome," whispered the Ogre in a most mysterious tone, after he had been some minutes seated in silence; "my tough beard is not readily trimmed with a creese, and a razor would therefore have been desirable." A first-rate Savigny was immediately placed within his grasp. "And, secondly," he continued, trying the keen edge upon the largest of his formidable talons, "my sister, who is far advanced in her pregnancy, has lately rejected food— mutton, beef, every thing in fact has been offered, and equally loathed. Now I am desirous of trying whether she might not fancy a bag of dates."

Chapter Twenty
Showing how the Ogre Acquitted Himself at Gootabélla

Many and tragic were the tales narrated of the prowess of the Ogre when the hot blood of youth boiled in his warrior veins. The first feat of his early days, ascribed to the year of the great comet, is still green in every recollection; and as it was recounted by Ibrahim Shehém, so was it vouched for by those of the Danákil braves, who during the recital crowded around the watch-fire at Gobaad.

The grey-bearded elders had sate for many nights in deep consultation, and the chicken-hearted of the Débeni had exhausted all the usual epithets upon the countless number of the foe, and the consequences of rash and fool-hardy adventure, when the youthful chief raised his manly form in the circle, and his brawny proportions seemed to dilate into colossal stature in the dimness of the evening mist.

"Listen to my words," he exclaimed, "for they are the sentiments of my heart. Children of Loheïta, hearken to the voice of your leader! Has the spirit of the foul hare entered into the breast of the warrior? Is the shield no longer to clash, nor the broad spear to glitter in the valley of Gobaad? Are the Débeni tamely to suffer their wives and their daughters to be carried into captivity, their flocks and their herds to be swept off, their wells to be taken possession of, and their very name made the scorn and the laughing-stock of the dastardly Mudaïto, without one struggle to prevent it? Dust be upon my head if the brave sons of the desert should thus root themselves in a quiet spot, like the withered and dying acacia, without a single thorn to avenge an insult! Rouse ye, my children, for in the name of the most holy Prophet I will even dare the danger of the war; and ignominy sully the fame of him who shall suffer his chief to mingle singly in the strife."

Reseating his sinewy form upon the rock, Loheïta covered his face in the folds of his garment, and in anxious silence awaited the result of this appeal. But the chord of feeling had been struck by a master hand. A low murmur of voices was quickly followed by the deep hum of approbation accompanying the confused clatter of the bucklers, and the elders, rising simultaneously, proclaimed, "It is the voice and the will of the Most High. Even so let it be!" The erect spears sank with one accord to the ground, and the stern "Ameen" of the assembled tribe, rolled ominously amongst the surrounding cliffs.

For some days after this harangue, the Débeni maintained a peaceable demeanour: but it was now the still, treacherous calm which precedes the hurricane. The Galeyla Mudaïto, who had already possessed themselves of all the choicest grazing grounds in the neighbourhood, and completely closed the caravan route from Abyssinia to the sea-coast, meanwhile continued their depredations with impunity; one subdivision of the tribe settling in the small valley of Gootabélla, where they erected permanent habitations, and boasted of their unmolested vicinity to the graves of the ancestors of Loheïta.

The Galeyla subdivision of the great nation of Mudaïto had rendered itself more particularly obnoxious by its aggressions. Many were the young men of Gobaad who had fallen under their sharp knives. Scornful taunts were ever rife upon the tips of their insulting tongues; and few indeed of the huts in the valley had not at some period sent forth the voice of wailing and lamentation for captive maids or for harried flocks. But the day of dire retribution was fast speeding on. The wane of the moon was the appointed signal of rendezvous to the heretofore slothful tribe; and as the darkness of the unlit night shrouded the valley and the hill, all those members of the clan whose spirit had not been utterly quelled by the frequent disasters experienced at the hand of the sanguinary invader, mustered around their youthful chief.

Silently, like the descending wreath of snow, the files of warriors poured in from every quarter of his extensive though distracted domain. The nation had responded to the call of its leader; and the wrinkled brow, and the full oily cheek: the thin sinewy shank of the veteran, and the graceful form of the untried but aspiring stripling, were soon mingled together. The sun set upon a busy scene in the lone valley of Gobaad. Two thousand savages, enjoying the rude feast that had been amply provided for their wants, were engaged in close whispering consultation on the coming strife; and wrought to a pitch of frenzy by the spirit-stirring words of their warlike chief, no less than by the exhortations of his wily emissaries, who ever and anon mixed with the carousing groups, to feed their panting passions against the hereditary foe, each warrior firmly clenched his teeth in dread determination, whilst he whetted his sharp weapon to the keenest edge upon the nearest stone.

As the fire blazed brightly upon shield, and spear, and stalwart frame, Loheïta moved forth in front of his enclosure, buckled for the fray. His active form was fully revealed by the fitful flame; and a dark smile played for the moment over his stern visage, as his followers, rising with one accord, unsheathed their murderous creeses, and, bursting into a loud murmur of applause, swore by the Sacred volume that the steel should that night reek in the hot blood of the accursed Mudaïto.

Placing himself at the head of his animated retainers, the chief now led the advancing van, and the tramp of the eager savage fell light over the steep mountain and the boundless plain. Deep darkness was esteemed of small account by these children of the desert, who, like the course of the falling thunderbolt, held on their progress in the true direction. Starting as the dense phalanx advanced, the timid gazelle scoured in terror over the valley, and the prowling lion yielded the path to men who were now in a mood not less desperate than his own.

The last rocky defile gained, a deep impenetrable gloom pervaded the scene. The very stars were hid under a partial mist, and naught gave token of the habitation or the presence of man, save at intervals the disturbed bleat of captive Débeni flocks. "They were ours once," scornfully muttered the chief betwixt his closed teeth, "and Wullah! if there be faith in the sharp steel of a true believer, they shall this night return to their pastures."

"All know the valley of Gootabélla," observed the narrator, "closely hemmed in on three sides by towering cliffs, over one perpendicular rock at the neck of which, the river Chekaïto, leaping, extends its sandy bed throughout the entire centre, so that ten resolute spirits might defend the only outlet against countless legions. None save the sons of asses would have pitched their tents in that spot; but the Galeyla were overweeningly conceited and vain of their exploits, and held in utter contempt the dispossessed proprietors of the soil, whom they had hitherto so easily despoiled."

No timely note of alarm announced the approach of danger; and the noiseless step of the foe gliding unheard round the devoted hamlet, it was encompassed on every side. Infuriate warriors in appalling silence beleaguered the narrow aperture of each matted wigwam. The recollection of captive and murdered relatives, of burning huts and harried flocks, entered deep into the stern soul of each grim assailant; and as the edge of the naked creese was passed cautiously along the finger, a prayer was breathed on high to the throne of the Eternal Avenger.

The unsuspecting inmates of every abode were hushed in deep repose. The spear lay entangled in the folds of the scattered garments, the shield had been cast idly in the corner, and the warrior, surrounded by his wives and little ones, was wrapped in peaceful rest, such as he was wont to enjoy when lulled by the gentle murmur of the breaking waves of the Bahr el Shub, in his own far distant land.

The suffocating fumes of smoke soon stole upon the sense of the drowsy slumberers; the crackling of flames aroused all abruptly from their dreams of security, and the lurid glare that enveloped the blazing hamlet caused each affrighted inmate to rush to the door, where the crooked steel, driven by the hand of desperate revenge, was sheathed in many a bare bosom.

Sudden, electric, and complete was the surprise, and vain were the efforts of the unarmed warrior. Loheïta raged through the scene like the demon of the angry element, and each follower ruthlessly strove to emulate his example. A dozen spear-blades transfixed the body of every fugitive. Two thousand of the foe fell during the murderous onslaught; and in that fearful night all ancient injuries were well washed out in the warm blood of the Mudaïto.

The pent-up wrath of the savage, like the checked waters of an impetuous mountain torrent, bursting all bounds, careered along without restraint. Mockery and insult were bandied back to the frantic screams of the women, as their tender babes were barbarously pitched into the hissing flame; and the red sun rose above the beetling crags to witness a frightful scene of carnage and desolation.

Flocks and herds had burst from their folds, and betaken themselves to the wilderness. Scorched and mangled bodies thickly strewed the ground, or lay half consumed among the smouldering embers of the pile. The groans of the dying mingled with the bitter wailing of captive females bereft of husband and offspring; and the chief surrounded by his exulting host sat in grim triumph beside the dense column of smoke, which with an eddying flame ascended high into the vault of heaven from the black and burning monument to Débeni vengeance.

A deep fissure in the bowels of the hill had given refuge to a determined few who had sought safety within its rocky sides: but the keen eye was not long in discovering the track of the fugitives; and the insatiate chieftain, speeding upon the trail, tore from the aperture the thorns and overhanging shrubs, and dashed into the cave with spear and buckler. The only resistance made during the foray was in this last stronghold; and Loheïta received a deep wound on the breast, the scar of which will be borne to his grave. Desperation nerved the limbs of the surviving Galeyla, who, well knowing that no quarter would be granted, sullenly fought on with the few weapons they had snatched up in their hurried flight; but all died in the unequal strife upon the spot where they had taken their last stand.

Crowned with brilliant success, the return of the dauntless young chief from his first expedition was swelled by troops of captive maids and by the pillaged herds of years. But the triumph had been achieved with no trifling loss to his clan. The bodies of thirteen braves, borne by their comrades upon green branches of the palm, closed the order of march, and the war-chorus pealed wildly among the rocks as the victorious host poured back through the valley of Gobaad.

A burst of savage acclamation, which rose shrill and high in the noontide heat from the assembled population, was succeeded by a solemn pause as the dread tidings were imparted to the relatives of the fallen. A path was cleared through the now hushed and silent phalanx, whilst muffled females, beating their bare breasts, passed towards the biers between the open ranks. The boldest and the bravest had been untimely cut off; and their widows, throwing themselves upon the lifeless bodies, indulged for a season in the most piercing shrieks and extravagant grief. But the deep loud chaunt of the elders, "It is the decree of the Most High," drowned the hysterical sobs of the bereaved; and the host again moved on in boisterous mirth to indulge, after the successful foray, according to the bent of their inclinations, and prepare for a series of achievements, which have since cleared the surrounding plains.

To this day none but the boldest dare, after nightfall, to enter the valley of skulls. The moans of the Galeyla warriors who fell in the affray are heard amidst the funereal sighing of the wind; the plaintive song of the Bedouin maid still chronicles the event; and long will be remembered in the red house of Mudaïto the night of the massacre of Gootabélla.

Chapter Twenty One
Sankul, and Suggagédan. Dawáylaka and Amádoo in the Limits of the Galeyla Mudaïto

Ascending by an extremely bad road the broken range to the southward, which commands a fine prospect over the valley of Gobaad, the káfilah reached Sankul on the 17th. It forms the focus of several small dales converging from the table-land, and shut in from all breeze by the surrounding steep black cliffs of basalt, passing into hornblende. A small cave near the encamping ground was occupied by a colony of industrious bees, and at the only well, flocks of the diminutive black-faced Berbera sheep were drinking from a trough formed of an ox-hide stretched between four stakes, to which the water was transferred in gourds by greasy Bedouin shepherdesses. The evening was passed in perpetual wrangling with these matrons during the operation of filling up the water-skins; and sad presage was afforded of a coming day of drought, which the exhausted and sinking cattle of the caravan were hourly waxing less able to endure.

The next march led over the high table-land of Hood Ali, a stony level thickly studded with dry grass, and extending in one monotonous plateau far as the eye could reach. The fetid carrion-flower here presented its globular purple blossoms among the crevices, and a singular medicinal plant, termed Lab-lubba, was detected by the keen eye of a savage who had before evinced a latent taste for botanical studies. The usual encamping ground at Arabdéra was found to be pre-occupied by a nomade tribe of Bedouin goat-herds, who monopolised the scanty water. Descending the range, therefore, the bluff brow of which commanded an extensive prospect over the wide level valley of Dullool, the káfilah halted at Suggagédan. This arid spot in the strand-like waste was covered with masses of lava and with blocks of basalt from the adjacent hills. It was parched by a burning atmosphere, and afforded no water whatever—calamities which resulted in the abandonment of a horse and two of the mules that were no longer able to bear up against thirst and fatigue; whilst many others now dragged their weary limbs with difficulty, and seemed but too well disposed to follow the example.

Dullool is one thousand two hundred and twenty-eight feet above the level of the sea—a perfect flat, covered with alluvial deposit, and studded with extensive tracts of coarse dry grass in tufts, among which, as the almost interminable string of camels crossed the following morning, both ostriches and gazelles were descried. It is bounded by a bold mountain range, and the further extremity of the plain, towards the foot of Jebel Márie, is perfectly bare, stretching away to the westward, in one uninterrupted sheet of hard compact mud, which imparts the aspect of the Runn of Cutch. A herd of wild asses, precisely similar to those found on the Indian salt desert, materially enhanced the resemblance; and the sun, which had now attained considerable altitude, casting his rays in a full blaze over the naked plain, called up the dancing mirage that was alone wanting to complete the picture.

On this level expanse, which terminates in a *cul-de-sac*, shut in by high basaltic walls, inaccessible either to man or beast, the Adaïel affect to ride down the wild ass, upon lean mules forsooth, and to rip up the quarry with their creeses. There had been much vain-glorious talking upon this head, but it ended, like every Danákil boast, in nothing. The hawk-eye of the Ogre detected an out-lying mare among the ravines at the foot of the range, and he dashed off the road with such lightning speed, that the animal narrowly escaped being hemmed into a corner; but once on the broad desert, and she tossed her arched neck, kicked up her wanton heels, and laughed at the absurd efforts of her impotent pursuers.

Loose stones again strewed the approach to the Márie range, which is of trap formation, of a slaty texture, stained with red iron oxide, and intersected by veins of iron clay. A breach in the hills, here about a thousand or twelve hundred feet high, formed a steep sloping ridge of lava rocks, containing quantities of carbonate of lime, disposed in rhomboids and hexagonal sheets. In this nook, surrounded by a thick jungle of acacia, were sundry basins filled with clear water, to which the solar rays had not penetrated. They afforded most refreshing draughts; and the skins having been replenished, the encampment was formed at Dawáylaka, a full mile beyond. Márie is not a word of either Arabic or Dankáli derivation; whence it seems not improbable that this bold range of hills may in days of yore have been named by some wanderer from the West.

A fine fresh morning succeeded to a very sultry night, passed upon the hard hot stones; and at break of day, the cattle having been taken to the pools, where, at so early an hour, they would drink but little, the skins were again replenished, and the caravan pursued its march to Oomergooloof, which can boast of no water at any season. Of two roads, the lower, but more level, was adopted, in consequence of the exhaustion of the beasts of burthen. It led across a dry desert plain of six miles, over which the delusion of mirage was complete. Covering the valley far as the eye could reach, to the foot of the hills which rise abruptly on all sides, it imparted the appearance of an extensive bay, shut in by projecting headlands—a still calm lake, so unmoved by the wind that every cliff was most distinctly reflected on the mirror of its glassy bosom.

Approaching from a higher level, a ripple played upon the surface of the visionary water; and the vapour being too subtle to screen irregularities of the ground, the aqueous expanse soon became gradually disunited, until it ultimately vanished altogether. The scene, cool and pleasant whilst it endured, formed a striking contrast to the baked alluvial desert under foot, destitute of even a vestige of vegetation, but over which was wafted a zephyr as unlooked-for as refreshing. Thrown in a particular way, and on certain atoms, rays of light produce illusions to the vision which are often embodied after the likeness of objects most deeply dwelling in the imagination. Thus it was that the character of the headlands of Dullool, square and perpendicular, together with an islet riding like a ship at her cable in the centre of the molten basin, aided the striking similarity of names in the respective neighbourhoods, to bring vividly before the eyes of all, the apparition of the bay of Goobut el Kharáb.

Immediately opposite to Oomergooloof is a projecting spur from Jebel Oobnoo, a lofty range visible to the westward; and this divides the plain into two valleys, whereof the southern-most is denominated Wady Arfa. The Márie range here towers overhead, steep and precipitous, to the height of about nine hundred feet; stupendous masses of rock which have been detached from the summit, and strew the entire base, corroborating the assertion of the Danákil that earthquakes are frequently felt in the vicinity. Nomade tribes with their families and flocks, having settled at the wells which exist at a distance, had compelled the gentler portion of the Libyan creation to resort to regions more blest with water; and not even a desert-loving gazelle was espied during the march of twelve miles.

Ibrahim Shehém Ablí had long viewed with the eye of bigoted disapproval, the attentions paid by one of the Mohammadan followers to two canine companions of the party, pets that had survived the passage of the fiery Tehámá, but whose feet had become so lacerated by the hot lava boulders as to incapacitate them from walking. Quilp—for so the offending Moslem was styled from his striking resemblance to that notable character—was in the act of extricating his wire-haired charge from the panniers wherein they travelled, when the irascible little warrior approached, and, drawing his trenchant blade, swore with a dreadful anathema to exterminate him on the spot. "Dog, and father of dogs," he exclaimed, seizing the dismayed mortal by the throat, "beware how thou again defilest thy fingers with those accursed curs, or by the beard of the Prophet I will sever thy gullet as one who has brought foul discredit upon the faith." Then relaxing his grasp, and sheathing his creese with a horizontal flourish, he threw himself into the attitude of a slaughtered victim, and closed the significant lecture by mimicry of the gurgle heard in a divided windpipe, whence the tide of life is welling.

Several herds of cattle pertaining to the Issehirába Mudaïto, grazed in the neighbourhood; and these were said to derive their supply of water from pools formed by a cluster of hot sulphureous springs at the further extremity of the plain, which, with a loud noise, rise bubbling from the earth at a boiling temperature. Possessing marvellous medicinal properties, they are believed to be a panacea for every malady: but the tribe not being on terms with the Danákil, these thermal wells could not be visited, neither could water be obtained either for man or beast. A few Mudaïto females, with their children, strolled into the camp to sell sheep, and stare at the Feringees; but the Ras el Káfilah would scarcely permit them to be spoken to, and was in a nervous fidget until they departed. Avowing that these greasy dames had come for no other purpose than to spy out the nakedness of the land, and that the creeses of their liege lords would prove troublesome during the night, he strictly interdicted all wandering beyond camp limits, and insisted upon the discharge of several volleys of musketry in addition to the cartridge expended at guard-mounting, and at every relief of sentries.

The sky having become gradually overcast towards evening, a deluge, equally to be desired and dreaded, was deemed close at hand, but the threatening appearance passed off with the hot blast of the Shimál, accompanied by a cloud of dust, and followed by a close oppressive night. Skirting the Márie range to a tract thickly strewed with rounded masses of lava and basalt, the detritus from the adjacent hills, the road now wound over a volcanic ridge which divides the valley of Dullool from that of Amádoo, running exactly parallel to it. In this latter the caravan halted on the 21st, about a mile from a large pool of rain-water, occupying a rocky nook formed by huge blocks of basalt. The stagnant green fluid was far more palatable than it looked, although troubled by a legion of horned cattle, asses, goats, and sheep, the property of the Galeyla Mudaïto, who were encamped in great force in the neighbourhood, and looked what they are said to be—most desperate villains.

Altogether it was a bustling scene. Herdsmen shouted in every direction to their kine, whose sinister glances and lowered heads proclaimed their dislike of the white intruders; flocks of Somauli sheep, with incommodiously overgrown tails, swam about like otters to cool their heated skins; numbers of Bedouin damsels, after laving their own greasy persons, replenished their dirty water-skins; and one wrinkled old hag, in direct breach of the Moslem prejudice against "man's friend," was absolutely detected in the act of cleansing the rough coat of her own pet-dog.

This pastoral scene of savage life, where the peaceful occupation of the shepherd contrasted strangely with the presence of spear and buckler, was about mid-day exchanged for the tent. A crowd of listless, tattooed savages, bearing very indifferent characters for honesty, soon swaggered in to see what they could pick up, and presently waxed so passing insolent that it was deemed prudent to intimidate them by a display of rifle-practice. Emboldened by numbers, they had begun to question old Izhák regarding his right to conduct strangers through the country without the permission, first duly obtained, of the "lords of the soil;" but seeing the stones fly about in splinters at two hundred and fifty yards they were not long in decamping, and gave no further annoyance. The Galeyla tribe of Mudaïto, which still boasts of the most expert and notorious thieves in the country, is, as might be conjectured, on no very amicable terms with the Danákil; and the very severe chastisement it received at the hands of Loheïta ibn Ibrahim sufficiently accounted for the sudden desertion of the unattended Ogre, who donned his seven-league boots, and strode back to his castle from Dawáylaka, after he had pledged himself to accompany the party to the borders of the territory occupied by Mohammad Ali's clan.

From Amádoo, Aussa was represented to be only one day's journey for a swift mule, and two for a caravan of laden camels, the road branching off across Wady Arfa, and over the Jebel Oobnoo range, by which the extensive valley is bounded. At this point, moreover, had ceased the pretended influence of Mohammad ibn Mohammad, Sultán of Tajúra, the utter futility of propitiating whom had long been sufficiently apparent. Although in the eyes of the uninitiated it was no difficult matter to invest this avaricious imbecile with supreme authority over a fiery desolate tract, in most parts obviously unfitted for human location, his own immediate retainers did not now conceal that Mirsa Dukhán, and the Gollo mountains near the Salt Lake, bound even his nominal jurisdiction. He is in fact Sultán of the sultry strand whereon his frail tenement is erected; for the few lawless wanderers beyond, over whom he would assert supremacy, are universally thieves and murderers, who disdain all fixed abode, disclaim all mortal control, and acknowledge their own unbridled inclinations as their only master.

Chapter Twenty Two
Red House of Mudaïto—Chronicle
of the Conquest of Aussa

Distinguished like the houses of York and Lancaster by their respective colours, "the white house" of Débenik-Wóema, composed of various Adaïel clans, who in time of need rally under one standard, is banded against the Assa-himéra, "the red house" of the Mudaïto, with the same bitter feud and animosity which spread desolation through the fair domains of England, and poured out the best blood of her heroic sons. Well would it be for the cause of humanity were these savage combatants animated also with the same noble and chivalrous feelings which in days of yore reigned paramount in the breast of the British knight, and met together only in the open field of honourable contest. But the case is widely different indeed; and under whatever circumstances the hated and hereditary foe may here be discovered, the unarmed bosom of the lone, sleeping, or unsuspecting wanderer, rarely fails to prove a sheath for the murderous knife of the assassin.

Aussa, formerly an important town, was, less than a century ago, the capital and principal seat of the united tribes of Mudaïto, who extend thence to Ras Billool, and are represented to be countless as the hairs of a Danákil head. Regarded as the seat of wisdom and learning, and governed in the latter days of its strength by Yoosuf Ali ibn Ajdáhis, a brave and martial sultán, whose armoury boasted of many matchlocks, and of several small pieces of cannon, it long flourished in powerful independence—a bright spot of beauty in a waste of barrenness. But the sun of its prosperity at length set; and the predatory hostilities long exercised towards the various united tribes of Adaïel, leading to a general invasion on the part of the Ado-himéra, the prince was slain, the stronghold of the "red house" sacked, and its garrison put to the sword: nor in these degenerate days is this once important place more than an extensive encampment, whereat is held a perpetual fair, frequented by all the tribes of Danákil, Eesah, Somauli, and Mudaïto.

The site of Aussa, a wide-stretching valley, described to be from eight to ten days' journey across for a caravan, is hemmed in by lofty mountains, and fertilised in all its extended quarters by the Lakes Guraaïd, Abhibbab, Hilloo, and Dugód—the first situated a little to the eastward of the town, and the last by far the largest of the four. These vast stagnant basins in the plain receive the Abyssinian waters of the Háwash and its tributaries, in addition to the contributions of all the streams from Jebel Oobnoo and other collateral ranges—the abundance of fluid thus lost upon volcanic formation, so enriching the soil as to enable this district to produce wheat, juwarree, barley, Indian com, pepper, and tobacco, in quantities sufficient for the supply of the entire coast.

The Háwash may be conjectured to have experienced interruption in its course to the Bahr Assál and Bay of Tajúra, at the same period that volcanic agency divided the waters of the great Salt Lake from Goobut el Kharáb. Miles around the wonted boundaries of each lagoon now become annually inundated during the spreading of the great freshes; and, as the floods, carried off by absorption and evaporation, again recede, the soil is covered with a fertilising sediment—a fat alluvial deposit, which with little labour yields an ample return. Even the lazy and listless Danákil, who neither sows nor reaps elsewhere, is here induced to turn agriculturist; but not a single acre of ground in any direction is to be found under the plough from the sea even to the mountains of Abyssinia—a distance exceeding three hundred and fifty miles.

Pastoral as well as agricultural pursuits engage the population of Aussa; but whilst the cultivating portion of the inhabitants are permanent residents on the soil, the shepherds are annually driven away by the gad-fly, which attacks the flocks from the setting-in of the rainy season until the termination of the fast of Ramzan, when the waters have again subsided, and the herdsman, descending from the mountains, returns to his occupation in the valley. An extensive commercial intercourse is moreover carried on with Tajúra. Salt from the Bahr Assál, blue calico, which is in high demand for the caps universally worn by the married Bedouin females, zinc, pewter, and brass or copper wire, used both for personal ornament, and for the decoration of weapons, are bartered for the produce of the luxuriant soil—some few caravans crossing the Háwash, and pursuing their journey along the western bank to Dowwé, on the frontier of the Wollo Galla, in order to purchase slaves; or striking into the main road at Amádoo, and so prosecuting their way to Shoa for a similar purpose.

Mudaïto tribes occupy the entire plain of Aussa, but they are now divided into five distinct nations. The Assa-himéra are under the rule of Humferi, a descendant of the ancient house of Ajdáhis, who preserves the empty title of Sultán, and resides at the decayed capital. Eastward are the Issé-hirába, governed by Das Ali, an independent chief, and the Galeyla, under Daamer Ibrahim; south are the Dár, who own allegiance to Akil Digger Myárgi; and west are the ferocious Koorhá, under the sway of Yoosuf Aboo Bekr, who, also with the title of Akil, resides at Alta, and wages war indiscriminately on both Assa-himéra and Débenik-Wóema.

South-westward of the valley of Aussa are the independent Adaïel tribes Hurruk Bodaïto, over whom presides Gobuz Elincha, a powerful chieftain, who has espoused Léni, daughter of Birru Lubo, the Prince of Argóbba, and through whose territories lies the high caravan route to Dowwé, with which the traffic is considerable. On the north, the Mudaïto are bounded by the distinct nation styled Hírto, under the rule of Yingool Ali—Mohammadans, deriving their origin from the Arab invaders of the seventh century, and speaking a language not very dissimilar from the Adaïel, who claim the same descent.

Aussa is still the abode of all the Uleemas, Aukál, and learned doctors, for whom the Mudaïto have ever been renowned, but the present government is singularly constituted. The aged Sultán Humferi, son of Yoosuf Ali ibn Ajdáhis, has retained with his high-sounding title the mere shadow of authority, which is in truth vested in Mohammad Ali, the vicegerent of the Débenik-Wóema, appointed by general suffrage from Tajúra. Residing at Kulloo, and ruling with an iron hand, he admits of little interference; and, in all cases where disputes between the "red" and "white" houses of the proprietors of the soil and their invaders, terminate fatally to the latter, takes two lives for one, according to the immemorial observance in blood feuds.

Ameer Sulaam, the Wuzír of the Mudaïto, is head of all the sages, and he is aided in the administration of justice by Hurrur Hássan, Téeoh, and Bérbera or "Pepper" Ali, the latter so styled from the volubility of his sarcastic tongue. This triumvirate of venerable sheikhs, whose wisdom and learning is reputed to be *kum el báhr*, "profound as the sea," is referred to on all occasions where knotty points are at issue, whether amongst the Ado-himéra or Mudaïto; and even the Sultán of Tajúra was on a late occasion held bound to abide by their arbitration, relative to the projected marriage of his son to a bride from another clan of the "white house," a measure which was resisted, and which he was desirous of enforcing. Yet a transit duty of fifty per cent, is levied by Mohammad ibn Mohammad upon all exports made by the Mudaïto, whereas ten per cent, only is exacted from the numerous Danákil tribes.

"A large Arab force from Zeylá," observed Ibrahim Shehém Abli, who was well versed in the chronicles of Aussa, "was induced to join the

Débenik-Wóema in their invasion of the predatory Mudaïto hordes; and overtures of capitulation having been made by Yoosuf Ali ibn Ajdáhis, they were thrown off their guard. During the night the Wóema, who knew with what villains they had to deal, bivouacked upon the heights of Dugódlee and Hy Tunkóma, where they rested safely enough. But the blockheads of Arabs choosing to sleep in the plain, the garrison took advantage of their folly to make a *goom*: and so cleverly was it managed, that by Allah! they succeeded in drawing their creeses across the throats of all save one."

Nothing intimidated by this reverse, and joined by fresh allies from the coast, the Wóema were not long in renewing the attack; and the whole of the Adaïel tribes who rally under the standard of "the white house," making common cause, the Mudaïto sustained a murderous defeat, when their stronghold, which had maintained its integrity unimpaired for so many centuries, fell at last into the hands of their hereditary foe.

A long term of years elapsed, but the hearts of the scions of the "red house" still rankled under this disaster; and, bent upon retaliation, the assembled clans, designing to plunder the now decayed sea-port whence their Arab invaders had been furnished, made a rapid inroad into the country of the Eesah Somauli. Unprepared, the tribe fled before the host in dismay, but presently recovering from the panic created by the sudden burst of war, rallied in great numbers, fell furiously upon the foe, and left not one marauding Mudaïto alive to tell the issue of the disastrous day. The "great battle," as this signal rout is still termed, was about three years ago fought within sight of Zeyla, on the plains of Takoosha, now white with the skeletons of a tribe.

"Brave men are these Mudaïto," continued the old warrior, playing carelessly with the hilt of his creese, which was seldom suffered to repose quietly in his girdle; "but they are not to be compared with us. *Hamdu-lillah,* 'Praise be unto the Lord,' I slew their sheikh with my own hand; and here is the identical scratch that I received in the scuffle. As for the Eesah," he concluded, "with their childish bows and arrows, they are sad cowards. One Dankáli spear is an over-match for fifty of their best marksmen in a fair fight; and I have myself dealt single-handed with six, although the villains came like thieves in the dark."

Ibrahim Shehém was requested to reconcile this character with the issue of the great battle just recounted, wherein the despised tribe had so signalised itself. "That," quoth he of Tajúra, "was a dastardly surprise; and *Wullah,* had I been the invader with a handful of Danákil spearmen, there would have been another tale to tell."

Bas Ali, late sheikh of the cultivating portion of the Aussa population, some years since made an attempt to restore the exclusive rule to the Mudaïto, and to this end headed a conspiracy sworn upon the Korán to plough the field no more until the head of the Wóema vicegerent should be exalted upon a pole at the city gate, and his body have been cast out to the hyaenas. He was however waylaid and assassinated by Ibrahim Shehém Abli, who received a wound in the cheek. The numerous scars which adorned the diminutive person of this hero proclaimed him to have made one in many an affray; and, if his own account might be believed, all were honourably gained. Nevertheless the singular aversion that he displayed to passing certain watering-places in brood daylight, and his skulking port at Amádoo more especially, had tended not a little to confirm the disparaging anecdotes maliciously narrated by his compatriots, relative to the mode in which some of these much-prized distinctions had been acquired.

The veteran Ali Arab had sat in gloomy silence during the early part of the conversation, but his light wicker cap started to the apex of his bald crown as he rose in wrath at the last vaunting words of the son of the Débeni. "Heed not the empty boast of that braggart," he exclaimed, with boiling indignation, forgetting his wonted taciturnity—"Brave as the lion's whelp are the hardy children of Yemen, and but for the cowardly desertion of their false allies there would have been a different issue to the fell night at Aussa. Do the Wóema to this hour not pay tribute to Zeyla in acknowledgment of the assistance rendered? The event was written in the sealed volume of Fate. The decree of the Almighty was fulfilled. But lest you should have believed the disparaging statements of this vain-glorious scorner, I will even recount the misfortunes of a campaign fraught with sad disaster to my kindred."

Uttering these words, he led the way to his enclosure, reared of bales of the most costly wares which had been committed to his tried integrity; and there, seated upon the rich shawls of Cachemire, or upon the choicest manufactures of the British loom, the party, provided each with a tiny cup of most potent coffee, gave ear in silence to the old man's tale, which in the two ensuing chapters shall be presented in the form that would appear best calculated to afford a picture of warfare in the Desert.

Chapter Twenty Three
Arab March over the Téhama

All was bustle and confusion in the small sea-port town of Zeyla. Camels were screaming as the well-filled sacks were tied tightly upon the saddles. The idle portion of the population had assembled to admire the pride and pomp of war. Women were running to and fro with more than usual briskness, to deliver some forgotten package to a body of men who stood under arms in the market-place; and crowds streamed to join the group through the narrow bazaar, which had been lit up for the occasion, whence arose a confused hum of higgling and barter, as each last want was supplied by the merciless Hindoo trader, on the credit of a successful return from the foray.

A motley diversity prevailed in the age, dress, arms, accoutrements, and bearing of the assembled party; but the turban and the checked kilt, the frequency of the long, ornamented matchlock, and the thousand strange-fashioned leathern pouches and pockets, dangling from every part of the person, proclaimed the presence of a body of warriors of the Faithful. And more than sufficient for the sultry climate was the cumbrous attire of the foreign mercenaries. Every colour of the rainbow had been appropriated to their full varied vestments. Red, and yellow, and green, surmounted the dark elf-like locks of the soldiers of Yemen; knives and long heavy swords glittered in their rich shawl waist-cloths; and the national cloak of Arabia, clasped across the tawny breast, floated gaily over each stalwart frame.

Numerous mules stood ready saddled in the busy square, and many were the long provident bags and water-skins strapped behind each high wooden cantle. The band had not been engaged to act as cavalry, but Arab troops are somewhat self-willed as to their tactics and style of movement, and at no time relish interference in any of those little private arrangements which they can afford for their personal comfort.

The grey eye and the grisly beard of the veteran from Hejáz, and the fierce glance and the long raven hair of the inhabitant of Medina, were exhibited together under the light of a blazing fire; and it might have been observed that the strongest current of female attention set towards the spot where the youth were collected, hammering the hard bullets down their rusty matchlocks.

"God is great!"—ejaculated a gaily-bedecked stripling, as he added an extra pinch of powder, for good luck, to the handful already poured into his long culverin. "Bring me alien, that he may feel the hands of the mighty, and *Inshallah!* if the leader of the expedition be of my mind, we shall not return empty-handed to have our beards laughed at by these fat kafirs from Hinde. Better were it to quaff at once the waters of immortality. But alas! Amru! the star was little on the ascendant when, forsaking the pleasant terraces and the cypress-waisted damsels of Mocha, thy stupid head dreamt of receiving two piastres a day from the treasury of the Sheriffe, or of being cooped up with infidels in a perfect *Jehánnam* upon earth."

This speech was received with considerable applause, for the Reis Amru was well liked by his comrades in arms. Jokes passed freely among the youth, who were all in high good humour at being released from the dull stupidity of a hot garrison; and each talked gaily of his future deeds of prowess, although as yet nothing had transpired as to the nature or object of the enterprise.

But the veterans were crowded together in a mass, and their scowling downcast looks betokened little satisfaction in the coming march. A one-eyed ancient, who had witnessed as many fights as the remaining locks upon his wrinkled head, was employed in grinding a notch from his long sweeping sword, whilst he ever and anon gave vent to his spleen and displeasure. "No good can ever come of intercourse with these unbelieving savages," growled the old man to a fellow gambler. "The skulking sons of the Débeni have been in close conference with the Ameer for the greater part of the day; and the youth Osmán is not the leader to conduct a party of the Faithful among the deserts and the hills of this parched land. Blood will flow from the veins of these hot-headed striplings, crimson as the cloth which flaunts above their head-gear. Aye, and the dream of the last night can be now easily interpreted. Listen to me," he muttered, in lower accents: "I dreamt of the pleasant lands of Saba, and saw the sparkling waters flowing over the bright green turf. The tribe of my fathers had assembled together, and the 'hail, welcome, may your arrival be happy,' came soothingly to my wearied ear; but an impassable gulf yawned at my feet, and the cold touch of the dread Azraïl startled me from my slumbers. Nevertheless if we be fated to perish by the hand of the savage, it shall never be said that old Kásim Ali was the man to oppose his destiny."

In good sooth the authorities had been sued for assistance by their friends the Wóema; and as immunities, and privileges, and certain percentage upon all slave caravans, were the inducements artfully held out by the sagacious tribe, the proffered alliance had been eagerly accepted. The Wóema deputation departed at sunset, after the ratification of the treaty; and a few of their scouts were alone left to serve as guides through a country hitherto untraversed by any Arab inhabitant of Zeyla.

Three quarters of the entire garrison were ordered for immediate duty. Gunpowder, balls, and coffee, had been handed out during the afternoon, together with a promise of arrears of pay on return; and as the moon raised her broad disk above the still expanse of the Indian Ocean, the party remained grouped as above related, awaiting in the market-place the arrival of their leader.

The impatient Osmán, accompanied by the Ameer and all the holy men of the town, shortly relieved them from suspense. His scarlet *abba* floated over his shoulders, and the gold of his headdress sparkled in the beams of the pale orb, as he placed himself at the head of the party to receive the "Salaam Aleikum" of his officers.

The young chief had lately arrived from the opposite coast to take the military command, but his proud and reserved bearing had gained neither the respect nor the good-will of his inferiors. Stories were whispered about that an evil star presided over his destiny, and that the settled gloom on his swarthy brow was caused by the continued tissue of ill luck which had hitherto blasted his every aspiration after fame.

His quick ear had caught the murmurings of the discontented. "Dread not events unknown," he exclaimed as he cast a withering glance over the group. "Be not down-hearted, for the fountain of the water of life is involved in obscurity. Defile not the spring of hope with the dust of despondency, for, praise be to God! the creator of the universe, if ye walk even into the dens of the lion or the pard, they will not tear you save on the destined day."

Then raising his voice Osmán shouted aloud, "*Seero*," move on in the name of the Prophet. "May Allah be with you! May Allah watch over you!" solemnly chanted the chief moola as he waved the holy book in the air. The troops poured through the gateway, and sweeping slowly, like a thick cloud, along the face of the plain, were soon lost in the darkness of the desert.

There be always some ardent spirits to raise the drooping mass; and in the commencement of a march, as in the beginning of life, even the most down-hearted feel a spark of hope as to the happy result. But after the first burst of enthusiasm was expended, and the troops were fairly launched into the lone waste, the loose discourse and the merry laugh gradually failed, and in sad and gloomy silence they trod on for hours, sinking in the deep hot sand, or stumbling among the black blocks of lava which were thickly strewed over this tract of fire.

The ominous bird of night flitted from left to right and hooted mournfully from a bare tree, as the gallant train swept past the last watering-place in the Wady of Takoosha; and many a *"wullah"* was poured forth, as the herds of antelope bounded along the same evil and portentous track, as if pursued by the exulting demon of destruction. "Man proposes but God disposes," muttered those whose secret misgivings were heightened by these prognostics: the heart of the bravest quailed under the accumulation of unlucky omens, and all felt for the moment, that they were doomed men.

Little order prevailed along the motley line. Mounted on his mule and wrapped in his own dark thoughts, Osmán led the van, and a group of light-limbed Wóema who clustered round the chief, pointed out the direction of march. No vestige was there of a pathway, and the dark ravine and the lone hill were passed in weary succession, as each camel, and mule, and man on foot, struggled along during many hours of the hot night. A few pools of standing water left by a providential shower of rain were at length selected as the first halting-place, and, worn out and dispirited, the sons of Yemen, piling their heavy fire-arms, sank to sleep upon the bare ground.

The tract of country extending from the coast to Ramudéle is a bare and joyless desert, where water is to be met with only at long intervals, where little food is to be procured either for man or beast, and where the heat is like the breath of the glass furnace. But Arabs are accustomed to the arid regions of their own stony land, and as they feed like famished wolves when food is to be obtained, they can, like those gaunt animals, endure the extremity of fasting. The morning sun roused the party to renovated strength; and as the news spread through the camp that the rich town of Aussa was the object of the enterprise, and that a large force of the Wóema had assembled to cooperate in the attack, no bounds were set upon the extravagant bravadoes uttered. Amru, as he strutted along with his turban placed jauntily upon his head, declared that even the gardens of Mocha and their rose-scented *houris* might be improved by a man of taste, if provided with the requisite means; whilst the grumbling old Kásim and his compeers, cheering up for the moment, commenced a calculation as to the probable gain to be derived from sundry captives, with which on their return they had resolved to fill the market.

But although a degree of hilarity had been thus restored throughout the host, the black cloud still hung over the brow of its leader. No friendly footing was established with his followers; no word of encouragement proceeded from his lips. Orders and arrangements were given in the cold, calm tone of desperation, and a feeling of coming evil shook each sturdy frame, as he strode in moody silence to his accustomed station in the line of march.

For seven weary days did they manfully toil through the blank dreary desert, where Nature had spread wide her plains of barrenness, and where the image of utter desolation was but seldom disturbed by the appearance either of man or of vegetation. The heat of the day caused the lips to peel. The poisonous wind dried the marrow in the bone; and at rare intervals indeed, some tiny encampment of the wandering *Buddoo* alone cheered the site of the stagnant pool. A few camels dotted the unbroken expanse of the forbidding plain, and here and there a withered acacia threw her thorny limbs wildly into the hot atmosphere.

The camp of the Wóema was pitched at Ramudéle, and fer on either hand as the eye could compass, stretched along the low belt of bushes which mark the course of the river Chekaïto. A confused mass of fragile mats, and animals, and human beings, lay huddled together. From the midst of the disorderly array arose a thick forest of broad-headed spears; and as the men clustered in hundreds to greet the arrival of their allies, the ferocity of their appearance elicited universal applause. The indomitable spirit of savage independence shone in their dark lustrous eyes, and their lank, but well-moulded figures were surmounted by the white ostrich feather drooping gracefully over the matted hair, the token of bloody prowess in the fight.

In barbarous profusion an ample entertainment stood ready prepared. Large messes of meat and dishes of melted ghee were smoking in every quarter of the camp; and after the welcome had been received from every hand, Osmán retired with the sheiks of the tribe to their temporary domicile, leaving the Arab host to resign themselves to enjoyment, and to rest after their long and weary march over the frightful Teháma.

Chapter Twenty Four
Massacre of the Five Hundred

Feasting and amusement wiled away the hours until the appointed day, when the necessary reinforcements having joined, the entire force moved hurriedly off towards the unsuspecting object of attack.

On the third morning of their march the hills of Dugódlee were crossed, and the smiling valley of Aussa was seen peacefully stretched at the feet of the invaders. Nothing could exceed the beauty of this oasis in the desert, so strangely expanded between two gigantic mountains; the crest of the one frowning black, broken, and abrupt, whilst the other rises in steep but gradual turfy acclivity to the very summit, whence rich indeed was the wide prospect displayed.

Green fields extended far as the eye could see. Flocks quietly ranged among the grassy nooks, and four lakes, unruffled by a breeze, reflected back the Iris rays of the morning sun upon the broken sides of the wooded lulls. Hemmed in by fantastic ranges, the river Háwash threaded the upper portion of the long valley like a cord of silver, and rushing into the broad expanse of Lake Hilloo, at length found rest for its troubled waters in the deep, mysterious basin, from which no visible stream adds its tribute to the blue ocean.

The city of Aussa was pleasantly situated on the upper extremity of the lake, and its low, conical, thatched roofs were half concealed among the towering verdure of the shadowy trees. As the host crowned the opposite hill, herds of beasts, and crowds of human beings, streamed from every side through the stout hedge of thorns that encircled the wall, and the voice of the muezzin rising faintly from the distant mosque, summoned the inhabitants to prayer in this most unlooked-for tribulation.

Confident of success, and exulting in their own numbers, and in the potent fire-arms of five hundred bearded allies, the savage host rushed whooping down the hill, their spears erect, and their souls hungry for the prey. But no shout responded from the silent town of the Mudaïto, and no weapon glittered in its defence. Already had the Wóema formed in serried lines, and already were the eyes and the shields of the warriors agitated by those portentous revolutions which are the prelude to the fatal rush, when a portion of the thorn fence was quietly drawn aside, and a band of aged men stepped upon the intermediate plain. A green branch waved in their unarmed hands, and their venerable white beards flowed nearly to their girdles. The sages of Aussa, whose wisdom was "as the depths of the sea," and who engrossed all the learning and holiness of the land, were there congregated together. The prejudice of the savage was aroused, and the presence of men acknowledged, to whom every dispute among the tribes had hitherto been referred, and whose decisions had been always most implicitly received. The cause of complaint, and the hope of plunder, were for the moment almost forgotten, and every spear sank to the ground as sheikhs and akils advanced to the front to receive the message from the beleaguered city.

Assuming the posture of earnest entreaty, the elders of the Mudaïto were not sparing of their oily words:—"All ancient differences should be fully adjusted, and the Wóema should depart to their own tents, loaded with the richest produce of Aussa as a free gift of its elders; but the great conference could not be held until the morrow; the chief, Yoosuf Ali, was absent, and a swift messenger could scarcely reach him before nightfall. Would the Wóema meanwhile destroy the seat of learning and of religion? Would the sons brandish the gory spear where their fathers were wont to fall prostrate in prayer? If camels had been stolen, the thieves should be delivered over to punishment, and every point of dispute should be most satisfactorily arranged."

The chiefs of the Wóema withdrew in order to deliberate apart, and divers were the opinions given in the ensuing discussion. The fiery Arab urged an immediate attack, now that the enemy were unprepared and fully given into the hand of the spoiler; but the words of mercy at length prevailed, and the terms having been acceded to, the wily elders, as they took their departure, displayed features lighted with a grim smile of inward satisfaction.

High raged the storm in the camp of the invading chiefs. Expressions of contempt were bandied back upon the term of coward, with which Osmán had taunted the Adel conclave. Swords and creeses were drawn, and stout adherents were not wanting with spear and matchlock to support their respective leaders. The veteran Sheïkh nevertheless contrived to still the troubled waters. Commanding his clan to draw back, and be at rest, he succeeded in convincing the Arab that *he* was not to be forgotten in the forthcoming division of the spoil. Finally the parties separated in sullen mood—the Wóema to ascend the hills of Hy Tunkóma, where they had resolved to rest among the rocky caverns, whereas the fearless sons of

Arabia remained upon the open plain on which the angry dispute had taken place.

Meanwhile the town was in a state of hot fermentation. The few warriors who were accidentally at home, inflamed by the speeches of their respected elders, prepared quietly for the most desperate resistance. Swift-footed messengers stole out ever and anon through various cuts and passages in the hedge, with orders to call to the rescue every member of the tribe; and the most fearful denunciations were prepared for any who should refuse aid in this the day of national distress. Onwards over hill and dale sped the untiring scout. At his warning voice the shepherd left his flock, and the hunter stayed his successful chase. Sheïkhs and akils seized spear and shield, and with all disposable force obeyed the hasty summons. Every encampment joined its quota to the fast swelling host, now streaming towards the valley of the deep waters; and long ere the moon raised her pale disk above the hills, full communication had been held with the city, and every arrangement was thoroughly matured for the attack.

Blinded by the feint of abject submission, the doomed body of Arabs had encamped upon the open plain. Little order or arrangement could be observed, and not a symptom was there of military vigilance. No watchful sentry paced his steady beat, nor had any disposition been attempted for safety or for defence. All had bivouacked on the spot where they happened to be standing, and after their appetites had been sufficiently appeased, the lazy partisans lay grouped together with their long pipes, talking over the pleasant hopes of the morrow, or uttering the scornful taunt on the coward folly of their infatuated allies. The song and the keen joke of their distant country occupied the first hours of the evening, and then the greater portion sank to rest upon the green sward.

But the slumbers of many were of a disturbed and fitful nature; and at midnight old Kásim Ali, whose advice, though ungraciously given, was generally attended to, repaired to the light pall under which reposed his leader. Osmán was still awake, and after listening to the words of the veteran, who predicted coming evil, the first orders were given. Guards having collected under arms, matches were lit, and some preparation attempted for defence. But the warning voice had come too late. The Mudaïto host, crouching warily upon the ground, had glided like serpents along the dark plain till they had gained the requisite distance for the onset; and as if starting from the very bowels of the earth, a countless array showed suddenly a bristling front, not one hundred yards from the encampment.

Short was the time allowed to awaken the drowsy soldiery. A hurried exclamation from the chief to stand like men, and a feeble cry from his followers in reply, was succeeded by the rush of the savages. Forward they came, carrying their broad spears erect, whilst their black ferocious eyes gleamed at the thoughts of blood, like the fiery orbs of the basilisk. A volley from the matchlocks only checked their progress for a moment; and as the firing ceased, there arose to heaven a wild unearthly yell, which was closely followed by the fierce shouts of men in contention, and by all the sounds of terror, confusion, and despair.

No walls or enclosures were there in that naked plain, or the sons of Ishmaël, who well understand their defence, might have fought on more equal terms; but overwhelmed by masses of the reckless foe, and hemmed in on every side by ten times their own number, the struggle was but the effort of individual desperation. Dropping shots had continued for some time in all quarters of the straggling encampment, and Mudaïto spear still clashed heavily upon Arab scimitar, when the war-cry of the Wóema rose pealing among the cliffs. As the tramp of their footsteps was heard descending to the plain, a short respite was allowed. The assailants withdrew from the murderous onslaught, and the fainting hearts of the survivors again bounded with hopes of life. But transient indeed were their expectations of succour and assistance. The wary eye of the Wóema had scanned, even in that uncertain light, the overpowering masses of the foe that crowded the plain; and suddenly wheeling round the shoulder of the hill, they disappeared like a wreath of the morning mist.

The Mudaïto meanwhile, like hungry wolves, hemming in the devoted party, awaited only the dawn of day to complete its destruction. But the remnant of the Arabs who had escaped now first found leisure to close their ranks; and, taking up a position at the foot of the isolated Jebel Gúrmah, they resolved to sell their lives as dearly as possible. Osmán, wounded and bleeding, was still alive; himself, with Kásim Ali and about fifty men, being all that survived of the gallant five hundred who had marched from Zeyla. The excruciating pangs of thirst were added to the tortures of creese and spear-wound: and in this, their last extremity, the solemn prayer arose to the Prophet of the Faithful, as of men whose hours were numbered.

As the day broke, Kásim volunteered to carry a message of capitulation to the savage army; and reposing full confidence in the white cloth waving in the hand of the veteran, each anxious eye was strained in the direction of his footsteps. Received in moody silence by the Mudaïto band, a ferocious savage was about to drive a spear-blade through his unflinching breast, when the son of the Sheikh bounded suddenly to his side, and warding off the descending shaft, seized the hand of the old man, kissed it with every reverence, and addressed a few words to the tribe. In days gone by the youth Boorhán had been saved under the creese by the son of Yemen, and gratitude, rarely found in the savage, now paid her outstanding debt.

The veteran's overtures of surrender having been received, he turned again towards his comrades, but a fearful sight fell on his sickening gaze. Two large bodies of the enemy had in the interim stolen round the hill, and clustering upon the very edge, were already swarming unseen to the last attack. Vain were his frantic gestures to direct the attention of his doomed comrades to the coming storm; he was seized and pinioned in the iron grasp of a multitude, and the succeeding rush was as the burst of the overcharged thunder-cloud.

And feeble was the defence made by men weary, and thirsty, and unprepared. With an appalling whoop, the triumphant savages soon joined the ranks of their sheïkh, and not one turbaned head remained visible above the wide plain. All had found a gory pillow in a far distant land. Creese and matchlock, mingled together, plentifully strewed the ground; and clutched in the cold hand of each grim warrior, lay the long Arab sword, dripping to the hilt in the blood of the assailant.

The acacia still throws her scanty shade over the bones that whiten on the scene of this conflict. Although of the same persuasion as the invaders, the men of Aussa could neither forgive their most unprovoked attack, nor consign to a quiet resting-place the remains of the true believers. The severe loss they too had sustained, still keeps the wound festering, for well indeed in that fatal night had been upheld the character of the sturdy children of Yemen. Taken by surprise and at every disadvantage, each had fought on fiercely to the last; and although broken matchlocks and rent shields dangle in the mosques as trophies of their defeat, many a Mudaïto mother long bewailed the loss of a beloved son, and many a bereaved widow mourned the absence of her liege lord, who returned not from the valley of the deep waters of Aussa.

Chapter Twenty Five
Fiálu, a Den of Thieves in the Wóema territories. Barurúdda and Killúlloo

After a march of three miles on the 22nd, over a stony table-land thickly strewed with the never-ending basaltic boulders, the caravan entered the territory of the Danákil tribe Wóema, under the uncle and father of Mohammad Ali. A desolate hollow passed on the way, which appeared in the rainy season to form an extensive pond, was enlivened by four bee-hive-shaped wigwams, placed as usual on the site where large hot stones were most abundant, and tenanted by goat-herds, whose numerous flocks were being driven forth to graze by the Bedouin females. Their supply of water is derived from a sequestered pool, occupying a deep narrow precipitous ravine, which abounds in the Hyrax, and boasts of a few trees not dissimilar from the Casuarina. Bearing the euphonous title of Korandúdda, this gully wound at the foot of the high terrace selected for the encampment—another right dreary plain, covered with volcanic pebbles, among which the dry yellow grass peeped out in scanty tufts.

No traveller through the bleak barren country of the Adaïel can fail to appreciate the simile of "the shadow of a rock in a weary land;" for a tree is indeed a rare phenomenon—and when a few leafless branches do greet the eye, they are studiously shunned, upon the same principle that induces the savage to eschew the immediate vicinity of water. A few straggling acacias occupied the valley of Fiáloo, half a mile to the southward, which is the usual encamping ground, and here were large herds of cattle, eccentrically marked and brindled, and glorying in superb horns raking gracefully from the brow. A fat ox was purchased without difficulty, together with a supply of fresh milk, which, if not improved by confinement in a greasy skin bag, proved nevertheless an extraordinary luxury.

One of the retainers of Mohammad Ali was now despatched to acquaint Ali Abi of the arrival of the káfilah. It had all along been promised that after entering the territories of the old Sheikh, every danger was to cease, but the goal now gained, the country proved to be a perfect nest of hornets. The thieving propensities of the Galeyla Mudaïto having been lately exercised upon the Wóema, it had been resolved to inflict summary chastisement, and rag-a-muffins were collecting from all quarters, preparatory to a "*goom.*" From morning till night the camp and tent were unceasingly thronged with scowling knaves, amongst whom were several of the Eesah—their heads decorated with white ostrich plumes in token of having recently slain an antagonist in single combat, or more probably murdered some sleeping victim.

Towards evening a gang of the Abli, whose chieftain is appropriately surnamed Jeróaa, or "the thief," made a desperate attempt to carry off the best horse, upon which they had strongly set their affections; but the rogues were fortunately observed by the lynx-eyed Kákoo, henchman to Mohammad Ali, just in time to admit of the animal being recovered. The war-cry caused all to fly to their arms; blows were exchanged without any blood being spilled, although one of the Wóema shields was perforated by a well-launched spear; and the ringleader of the horse-stealing gang, who had thus narrowly escaped a mortal feud, having been secured to a tree, was by his own tribe severely castigated on the spot.

A dense cloud of dust rolling along from the north-eastward, closed the day. Revolving within its own circumference, and advancing on a spiral axis, it burst in full force in the very centre of the camp. The tent fell on the first outpouring of its wrath, and the consistency being so dense as to render it impossible to keep the eyes open, the party were fain to take refuge beneath tarpaulins, and stretched upon the ground, to listen with quick and difficult respiration, until the whirlwind had expended its violence among chairs, tables, and bottles. A few drops of rain ushered in the night which was passed by a newly-entertained Bedouin guard in carousing upon the choice dates of the Embassy, a bag of which had been unceremoniously put in requisition by the Ras, "in order to keep the savages in good humour," or, in other words, to save them the trouble of stealing it; and the musket announcing relief of sentries was discontinued by request of the same authority, lest the smell of gunpowder might have a prejudicial effect upon the voracious appetites of the savages.

Before dawn the chief of the nomade tribe Hy Somauli arriving with a hungry and dissatisfied retinue, a halt was proclaimed, to the end that they also might be fed, pacified, and propitiated. The potentate was duly introduced by Izhák as a most particular friend, who had journeyed a long way for the express purpose of making the acquaintance of his English charge; and a deep sense of the honour conferred having been expressed, it was ascertained that the secondary object of the visit was to inquire by whose authority so formidable a party of foreigners were being smuggled through the country, and how it happened that they were suffered to build houses wheresoever they thought proper?—this last allusion having reference to the tent, which had again been pitched, and was very sapiently conjectured to be a permanent edifice.

The "Kafir Feringees" therefore continued to be objects of undiminished curiosity during the whole also of this sultry day; a greasy disorderly rabble, which occupied the tent from an early hour, being continually reinforced by parties weary of the debate held immediately outside, which lasted until the going down of the sun. Each new visitor, after staring sufficiently at the white faces, invariably exclaimed "Nubeeo," "Holy Prophet," a mark of undisguised disapprobation, which was further elicited by every occurrence that did not exactly coincide with his nice ideas of propriety, such as eating with a fork, keeping the head cool under a hat instead of under a pound of sheeps' tail fat, or blowing the nose with a handkerchief in lieu of with the fingers. Paws were nevertheless incessantly thrust in at every door, accompanied by reiterations of the Dankáli verb "to give," used in the imperative mood; the never-ending din of "Ba, Ba," being uncoupled with any noun designative of the commodity required—a proof that he who demanded was a ready recipient for any spare article that might be forthcoming.

A long and tedious palaver, in which voices occasionally ran extremely high, at length terminated in a general uprising of the senators. Izhák was seen curling his scanty side locks in token of victory. The chief had become satisfied of the temporary nature of the tenement inhabited by the "Christian dogs," after one or two of the savages had thrust a spear-blade through the canvass; and the malcontents having to a man been sufficiently crammed with dates, coffee, and tobacco, finally took their departure, chuckling at the success of the foray, and having ingeniously contrived to turn their time to account by stealing one of the mules.

Many significant glances had been exchanged over portions of the baggage that had unavoidably been exposed; but a night of redoubled vigilance was cut short by a summons to relinquish sleep and bedding at two in the morning, and a march of sixteen miles over a vast alluvial flat conducted past the Bedouin station of Ulwúlli to Barurúdda, on the plain of Kelláli. The road led along the base of the low range of Jebel Eesah, through abundance of coarse grass concealing lava pieces and volcanic detritus, the prospect being bounded by distant blue mountains towering to the peak of Kúffal Ali. A *korhaan* rose at intervals, wild and noisy as his chattering kindred in the south, but few other signs of animated nature enlivened the long sultry march. In the grey of the morning, a solitary Bedouin horseman ambled past with some message to the savages at Amádoo, and from him was obtained the disagreeable intelligence, which subsequently proved too true, that not a drop of water existed over the whole of the wide plain within a day's journey, and that the station beyond was thronged with tribes, collected with their flocks and herds from all the country round, at this, the oasis.

After a hot dusty day the sky was again overcast, and sufficient rain fell to render every one wet and uncomfortable, without filling the pools, or checking the dire persecutions of a host of cattle ticks, which covered every part of the ground. Absence of water led to another midnight march, and the moon affording little light, the road was for some time lost, though eventually recovered by the sagacity of a female slave of Mohammad Ali's, when all the lords of the creation were at fault. This damsel, who always led the foremost string of camels, was one of those frolicsome productions of Nature, which the wanton dame pawns on the world in her most laughing moods, and the appearance of her daughter could scarcely fail to elicit the mirth of the most sedate beholder. A small round bullet head, furnished with a well-greased mop, and a pair of moist brilliant eyes, formed the apex of a figure, which, in all other respects, was that of the concentrated amazon, exhibiting a system of globes both before and behind, agitated by a tremulous vibration as the short fat legs imparted progressive motion. A blue kerchief tied jauntily over the head—ponderous wooden ear-rings, fashioned on the model of Chubb's largest lock—a necklace of white beads, and a greasy leathern apron slung about the unwieldy hips without any remarkable regard to decency—set off the corpulent charms of the good-natured Hásseinee, the exhibition of whose monstrous eccentricities in Europe, must infallibly have ensured a fortune to the showman.

The road continued to skirt the low Eesah range for several miles (see Note 1) to the termination of the plain, which becomes gradually shut in by rounded hills enclosing a dell choked with low thorns, and tenanted by the *galla-fiela* (i.e. camel-goat), a strange species of antelope, having a long raking neck, which imparted the appearance of a lama in miniature. As the day broke, flocks and herds were observed advancing from every quarter towards a common focus, and on gaining the brow of the last hill overhanging the halting ground, a confused lowing of beeves and bleating of sheep arose from the deep ravine below, whilst the mountain sides were streaked with numberless white lines of cattle and goats descending towards the water.

Arriving at the Wady Killulloo, a most busy scene presented itself. Owing to the general want of water elsewhere throughout the country, vast numbers of flocks and herds had assembled from far and wide, and they were tended by picturesque members of all the principal tribes of Danákil composing the Débenik-Wóema, as well as from the Eesah, the Mudaïto, and their subordinate subdivisions. Dogs lay basking on the grassy bank beside their lounging masters; women, screaming to the utmost of their shrill voices, filled up their water-skins with an ink-black fluid stirred to the consistency of mire, and redolent of pollution; thousands of sheep, oxen, and goats, assembled in dense masses in and around the dark, deep, pools, were undergoing separation by their respective owners, before being driven to pasture; and, with the long files that ascended and descended the mountain side in every direction, imparted the bustling appearance of a great cattle fair.

The temporary mat huts of all these nomade visitors who boasted of habitations were erected at a distance on the table-land to the southwestward of this important wady, which occupies a rugged rocky chasm opening upon the Kellàli plain, and, receiving the drainage of all the southern portion of the Oobnoo range, disembogues during the rainy season into the lake at Aussa. Even during this, the hottest portion of the year, when the entire country elsewhere is dry, its rocky pools embedded in soft limestone, tainted with sulphuretted hydrogen, and abounding in rushes and crocodiles, afford an inexhaustible supply, without which the flocks and herds of the entire arid districts by which it is surrounded, could not exist.

To it the horses and mules of the Embassy were indebted for a new lease of life, short though it proved to many. Two of the former and eleven of the latter had already been left to the hyaenas, in addition to the animal feloniously abstracted by the Hy Somauli, of the recovery of which Mohammad Ali affected to be sanguine. But although the pleasure of another meeting with the robber chief, whereupon he rested his delusive hopes, was shortly realised, and brought with it a train of concomitant inconvenience, no mule was ever restored. Not one of these petty Adaïel tribes are subject to that abject despotism which controls the turbulent spirits of the more powerful African nations, and, bad as absolute power must ever be acknowledged, often tends to their ultimate improvement. The influence of a chieftain is here little more than nominal. All affairs are decided in council by a majority of voices; and, were it not for the fact, that, save during the existence of a common danger, no component member of his clan works for other than individual advantage, the wild and lawless community over whom he affects to preside, might in all respects be appropriately designated a republic.

> Note 1. The reader who may not feel thoroughly satiated with miles and furlongs, as embodied in this narrative, is referred to the Appendix, where they will be found detailed in a tabular form.

Chapter Twenty Six
Ominous Debates and Intolerable Delays at the Half-Way Stage

The second knot in the string of the tedious journey had been unloosed by arrival at Killulloo, which is considered exactly half-way from the sea-coast to the frontier of Abyssinia. But although the worst portion of the road was now behind, the Embassy was destined to waste many days of existence in this vile spot, amidst annoying debates and discussions, most trying to the patience, which threatened to terminate so unpleasantly as well nigh to result in the abandonment of the baggage, as affording the only prospect left of ever reaching the destination.

From the very first moment of arrival, Izhák, whose sole object ever appeared to be to render himself disagreeable, devoted his talents and energies to the establishment of a misunderstanding, upon the frivolous grounds of Mohammad Ali having been suffered to distribute a small quantity of tobacco, in order to get rid of some passing unpleasant visitors. "Who gave *that* man tobacco?" he captiously vociferated, bouncing into the tent as soon as it had been pitched; "this is a piece of interference with my prerogatives as Ras el Káfilah, which cannot be borne." And the explanation afforded not proving at all to his satisfaction, he roundly declared his determination of resenting the insult by throwing up the charge, and returning with all his paid retainers to Tajúra.

Mohammad Ali being now in the heart of his own country, and having rendered himself extremely useful on the road, whilst his venerable rival had been idle, seemed resolved to assert his claim to a share in the conduct of the caravan. Izhák as unflinchingly maintained his resolution, as brother to the Sultan of Tajúra—a point whereon he greatly piqued himself—to hold the reins exclusively in his own hands, or to decamp with the camels; and the Embassy, avowing themselves to be merely travellers through the country, desirous of conciliating all parties, and of interfering with none, maintained the strictest neutrality, and declined mixing at all in the dispute.

It was already dusk when a visit was received from the three principal persons of the countless multitudes assembled. These were Ibrahim ibn

Hámeido, Akil of the Hy Somauli, whose dominion extends from Ramudéle to Suggagédan; and the uncle and father of Mohammad Ali—to wit, Wáyess ibn Hagaïo, who divides with his brother Hagaïo Lád the government of the Derméla, the Wóema, the Rookhba, and the Midgan, collectively extending from Suggagédan to Waramilli—and Hajji Ali Mohammad, a hoary patriarch of most venerable appearance, commonly styled Ali Abi. As tokens of good-will they brought oxen, sheep, and bags of sour milk; but, owing to an obvious disinclination on the part of Izhák and his sulky colleagues to promote conversation, the interview was extremely stiff; and dates, coffee, and snuff having been duly handed round, the illustrious visitors, signifying an intention of discussing certain topics of importance which had yet to be adjusted, abruptly departed after the polished fashion of the country, without going through the ceremony of taking leave of their entertainers.

A vast concourse of armed natives, members of all the various tribes assembled, had in the meantime convened immediately on the outskirts of the camp, where they continued during the whole night in a violent altercation, which periodical supplies of dates and tobacco proved quite inadequate to allay. The discussion was shared by Izhák and by Mohammad Ali, with their respective partisans and retainers, and it continued during the whole of the next day; meanwhile the tent being perpetually thronged with thieves and idlers, who purloined whatever fell in their way, and contrived frequent broils amongst themselves which led to the drawing of creeses in the very centre of the encampment.

Throughout the whole of the ensuing night, and part of the day following, the wrangling among the tribes continued with little abatement or intermission, the litigants occasionally breaking into small parties, to hold private *kaláms*, and after much mysterious whispering, again resuming their seats in the general assembly. The question of precedence between the elders, already adverted to, and the propriety of suffering so large a party of armed Franks to proceed into Abyssinia, formed the principal subjects of discussion; and the prevailing opinion on the latter question was, that all ought to be compelled to return, if not to be put to death, as unbelievers whose presence boded evil.

But the opportunity was also taken of arbitrating old feuds and squabbles. Elopements were investigated and arranged, and all disputes and quarrels of a private nature fully dilated upon and digested. Hundreds of ruffians thus sate from the rising up of the sun to the going down of the same, and throughout the livelong night, formed in a wide circle; the chiefs and men of consequence in the centre, and the venerable Ali Abi, with thin floating snow-white locks, and highly ornamented weapons, seated as president of the council. During the lengthy discussion of each case, every spear stood erect in the hand of the warrior; and on the decision being promulgated, the bright blades were lowered with one accord, a portion of the Korán was repeated, and at the termination of every verse, a general hum succeeding, the concurrence of all parties was chanted in a deep stern *Ameen!*

Killulloo being the great mart between the Bedouin tribes and the passing caravans, where the produce of their flocks is bartered for blue calico and other imports in demand, the news of the arrival of so large a party caused an inpouring from every quarter, and each day presented at the rendezvous some new group of exacting chiefs to be propitiated, with a fresh train of thieving followers to be fed and kept in good humour. Every greasy scoundrel possessed a vote in the congress, together with the inclination to render himself obnoxious, and the ability to add his humble mite towards the irksome detention; and it therefore became requisite to court popularity, and to canvass public favour as sedulously as at a general election for a seat in parliament.

Ever and anon, a great noise and clamour, and the rushing, spear in hand, of all the idlers to one point, proclaimed a gentle passage of arms among the savages, of which, nine times out of ten, a woman was the subject—some gay Lothario having been recognised among the crowd by an injured husband. But no sooner had the cold steel fleshed from the scabbard, than the bullies were secured by the bystanders, and being perfectly *au fait* at the business, they were easily restrained from doing each other any grievous bodily harm. In one scuffle indeed, a hot-headed fool who had with singular want of discretion engaged in a quarrel at too great a distance from his companions, got his thick wig somewhat unpleasantly shaved to the skull a hand's breadth or more—a fortunate occurrence indeed as it turned out, since the sight of blood had the instantaneous effect of closing the senatorial proceedings of the great conclave, which had been all night sitting in deliberation, so that its members were yawning in a state of considerable exhaustion and owlish stupefaction. Tolo, the quarrelsome little warrior who thus suddenly adjourned the sessions, lost three of his front teeth by the hands of the husband whom he had injured in more ways than one—but he retained possession of the inconstant lady, and publicly pledged himself, that on his way back from Hábesh he would take measures which should set the matter at rest for ever.

The arrival from Shoa of a slave caravan in charge of the son of Abdool Rahmán Sowáhil, Kazi of Tajúra, added still further to the assembly in the persons of several hundred unfortunate children of all ages, who sought shelter from the fierce rays of the sun beneath the scanty trees which dotted the rugged basaltic valley of Killulloo, or lay huddled together beneath the hot shadow of an impending columnar rock. Each carried a small gourd as a water flagon, and, although generally in good spirits, some idea of the sufferings in store for these hapless beings could be formed by those who had just achieved the lower portion of the perilous and formidable road.

"Have all my children arrived in safety?" inquired a corpulent old slave-merchant who brought up the rear, tenderly accosting his mistress elect, and chucking her playfully under the chin, as she flew to hold the bridle of his mule; "are all my children well?" "*Humdu-lillah,*" was the reply of the coy damsel, a really beautiful Christian from Guráguê, with long raven tresses, and a very pensive expression, who had been compelled to profess Islamism. Honoured with the caresses of her flit and bigoted purchaser, the poor girl had been made responsible for a drove consisting of three score little sister slaves, all distinguished like herself by a tassel of green beads in the braided hair, and who were now about to be counted by their "father."

The son of the Kazi having brought letters from Abyssinia, was shortly introduced by Hajji Kásim, own cousin to Izhák, and by far the most reasonable of the Tajúra party. Being in the course of conversation quietly interrogated touching the cause of the Ras el Káfilah's continued irritation, he turned at once to his companion, and solemnly adjured him by the beard of the Prophet to answer conscientiously the following questions. "A head is ahead, is it not, all the world over?"

"Of course," responded the descendant of the chief justice, "there can be no disputing that fact."

"A tail, too, is a tail, or I am much mistaken," continued the logician, pursuing his thesis,—and this axiom was also unhesitatingly admitted as beyond all controversy. "Well, then," resumed Kásim, whose intellects had been sharpened by a pilgrimage to the shrine at Medina; "no Káfilah can possess two heads; and so long as Ali Mohammad, who is in fact the tail, continues these underhand attempts to usurp the authority vested in the brother of the Sultán of Tajúra, our acknowledged head, matters can never go on smoothly."

The old man was quietly reminded that the raw tobacco, which had given rise to so much heart-burning, bickering, and dispute, was the sole property of the British party, and that, with every deference to Izhák's supreme authority, some control might with propriety be conceded to the owners over their own wares; but that as to any interference in the quarrel for the Ras el Káfilah-ship, the thing was clearly impossible—the business having already been fully discussed and arranged with due Danákil patience, by the Sultán, in some twenty tedious conferences with the camel-owners and chiefs of Tajúra. Izhák, who had been listening to this conversation with a dark scowl upon his brow, now entered as if by accident, twirling his scanty locks, and beaming with smiles; proof of his restoration to good humour being immediately afforded in the extension of his right hand, not to perform the usual ceremony of reconciliation, but in view to the palm being filled with a sufficiency of Dr Ruddiman's Irish blackguard, to admit of indulgence in his favourite recreation.

Hopes were now reasonably entertained of an amicable adjustment, the real cause of dispute having meanwhile been traced to a jealousy respecting the reward which it was conjectured the leader of the caravan would receive at the hands of His Majesty of Shoa. Mohammad Ali had already been privately satisfied upon this point; and Izhák, in order to strengthen his own claim, falsely asserted himself to have received by the Kázi's son a letter from Sáhela Selássie, appointing the Sultán of Tajúra to the charge of all his European friends who might desire to visit Southern Abyssinia. But the congress still sat as usual. The dispute arranged to-night was renewed at morning's dawn, as though it had never formed the subject of deliberation; and at a period when the near approach of rain in the higher regions, and the consequent flooding of the Háwash, rendered every hour one of the utmost importance, not the slightest prospect of departure could be discovered, beyond the oft-repeated assurance, as often followed by disappointment— "Bád bokra Inshállah," "If it please God, the day after to-morrow."

Chapter Twenty Seven
Persecutions of the Gathered Clans—Parting Interview with the Avaricious Chieftains

Throughout this period of irksome detention, the thermometer stood daily at 112 degrees, and the temperature of the small tent, already sufficiently oppressive, was rendered doubly unbearable by the unceasing obtrusions of the wild, dirty, unmannerly rabble who filled the ravine. Imperiously demanding, not suing for snuff, beads, and tobacco, with paper whereon to write charms and spells for defence against evil spirits, swarms forced in their greasy persons from the first dawn of day to the mounting of the guard at night. Treating the pale-faced proprietors with the most marked insult and contumely, they spat upon the beds, excluded both air and light, and tainted the already close atmosphere with every abominable smell. Not one of the greasy crowd could be persuaded that the "cloth house," as the tent was denominated, had not been each day re-erected solely for his individual use and accommodation. Many attempted with their creeses to curtail the much coveted blue calico with which it was lined, and one lank ruffian, who was detected leisurely searching for a peg whereon to hang the skin and entrails of a newly killed he-goat, wrought himself into a positive fury on being civilly apprised that he must look for shambles elsewhere.

Neither on the part of those composing the caravan was much privacy allowed during the sultry day, when seclusion was so highly desirable. Here, as throughout the march, offensive camel-drivers obtruded themselves without any regard either to time or season; occupying the chairs, composing themselves to sleep in groups upon the beds or on the table; and, whilst they picked their ears and teeth with the pens, or employed the knives in the pleasing operation of paring their filthy talons, spitting without remorse wheresoever they listed. Hating and despising a Frank with all the zeal of the bigot, they yet insisted upon shaking hands, on each intrusion, with the most scrupulous attention to Danákil etiquette, and with unhesitating alacrity devoured the biscuits and swallowed the coffee of the "Christian dogs."

The despotic arrangements enforced by the Ras el Káfilah, although doubtless materially conducive to his own personal convenience, and to that of his unaccommodating followers, were moreover far from enhancing the comfort of the Embassy. Boxes and bales, after having been unceremoniously dashed upon the ground, in utter disregard of remonstrance or of the fragile nature of the contents, had on this occasion, as on the termination of each march, been piled in a circle, each component heap consisting of three sides of a square, which, with the addition of a few mats thrown over the top, formed a habitation fully as commodious as a Dankáli is ever accustomed to. Any attempt to disturb the economy of these tenements, by referring to the boxes employed in their construction, being regarded as an act of premeditated injury and insult, was stoutly resisted; and as no portion of the baggage once removed to the tent, was ever received again without a battle, the materials of comfort or occupation were very rarely obtainable. In the selection of his load at Tajúra, every self-willed driver had suited his individual inclinations, and as no persuasion could now induce him to deposit any portion in a spot where it might be under surveillance, the provisions, placed beyond the reach of their owners, but accessible to every hungry knave, were perpetually pilfered and purloined.

Universal somnolency on the part of the hired guard, had rendered two European sentries and an officer of the watch indispensable throughout the journey; and in such a nest of robbers as Killulloo, the precaution was more than ever requisite. In a fine climate, with a manly foe in front, a night watch is far from being a disagreeable duty. Here it was beyond all things annoying. Pacing up and down over the same re-trodden ground, to keep the heavy eyelids on the stretch, in order to prevent the prowling Bedouin from pilfering a bag of dates, or to detect the lurking assassin, who in the dark creeps like a wild beast to perpetrate his dastardly deed, is but a sorry business; and it was rendered more particularly hateful from the rank offensive steam, which arose thick and hot from the small circle in which the beds were spread. Stifling exudations from the fetid mouths of one hundred and seventy camels that fed on the most disgusting rubbish, filled the suffocating atmosphere, which was impregnated with atoms still more vile from the rancid sheep's-tail fat, wherewith every Dankáli is so liberally besmeared.

Among the motley races congregated at this crowded watering-place, were the endless tribes of Adaïel, with broad-headed spear and shield of high antiquity—the coast Somauli, armed with light lance and diminutive wrinkled buckler, scarcely larger than a biscuit—and his much-dreaded Eesah brother, carrying a long stout bow of the ancient form, with the double bend, and a quiver of poisoned arrows slung by a lion's tail. These latter were by far the most conspicuous, as well as the most agreeable figures. Their togas, although not less filthy than those of their neighbours, were thrown more gracefully over the brawny shoulder; their picturesque weapons were borne with an ease that habit can alone impart; and, notwithstanding that the white trophy floated over their raven locks in token of bloody deeds, nearly all boasted of laughing, intelligent, and far from unpleasing countenances—a delightful relief at all events from the scowling downcast look of the exacting, perverse, and impracticable Danákil.

The Wóema, deeming unlawful the use of the bow in their own persons, maintain upwards of one hundred Somauli archers, originally prisoners of war, who, although naturalised among their conquerors, retain their own language, and never intermarry. The hunting portion of the Eesah tribe, who are designated "Bone," usually carry a rude bamboo flute, the wild plaintive cadence of which is believed to charm the ostrich. Their hair, with the aid of suet, is often dressed in the figure of the "pudding" worn by children during their first lessons in the art of walking; and deeply graven on the forehead of each are to be seen the masonic square and compasses.

Universally skilled in woodcraft, the ferocious subjects of ibn Fára may be styled a nation of hunters, many being proprietors of trained ostriches, which graze during the day with the flocks in the open plain, and have their legs hobbled at night, to preclude wandering. These gigantic birds are employed with great success in stalking wild animals, a trained donkey being also in constant use—lashed below the belly of which, the archer is carried among the unsuspecting herd, when his arrows, poisoned with the milk of the *euphorbia antiquorum*, deal death on every side.

It is to the skill of these wild Nimrods that the Danákil are chiefly indebted for their shields, which are manufactured of the thick hide of the oryx, here styled the Baëza. Two bucklers of a foot or eighteen inches in diameter, fetching each four *tobes* of blue calico, value two dollars, are obtained from the animal's fore hand; and from the hind quarters are cut others of smaller dimensions, such as are in use among the pastoral Somauli. Ostrich feathers are also principally obtained from the Eesah; the unsullied plumes, when stripped from the fleet-footed bird, being deposited for the convenience of carriage, in portions of the gullet cut to the proper length. The process pursued by these children of the desert in the preparation of smaller fowls for the table, if not strictly in accordance with the directions of Dr Kitchener, can, at all events, claim ingenuity. From some superstitious motive, the feet are chopped off with the creese, and the carcase, undivested of the entrails, having been incased in wet clay, is thrust into a hot fire; on removal whence the feathers are left adhering to the paste, and in culinary phraseology, "the bird is done."

Crowds of Bedouin shepherdesses, and females belonging to all the various nomade tribes, were likewise assembled in the Killulloo ravine, and the cry of *"wúrkut, wúrkut!"* "paper, paper!" was incessant on the part of the softer sex, who, with a licence unknown and a freedom unenjoyed by the daughters of Eve in other Mohammadan countries, were unremitting in their attendance and flirtations, without exciting the jealousy of their lords. From the lips of these damsels, *"Mahissé, Mahisséni!"* *"Manína téni?"* "Good morrow!" "How do you do?" came not disagreeably; and trinkets such as they loved, being civilly solicited, instead of imperiously demanded, the applicants were rarely unsuccessful.

Amongst those who boasted of the most feminine and attractive appearance, were the fair partner and sister of Mohammad Ali—their wedded and single state being as usual distinguishable, from the coif of blue calico which marks the wife, and by the long uncovered plaited locks of the maid. Assembling with many of the frail sisterhood at the door of the tent, where numbers were usually lounging in careless attitudes, they one day demanded that the palm of beauty might be awarded. Unwilling to throw the apple of discord, the mirror was placed in their hands, that the coquettes might judge for themselves; and after each in succession had started involuntarily at the sight of her own greasy charms, and had defended the individual features whereof she was mistress, to the utmost of her eloquence and ability, the verdict was finally found in favour of the virgin daughter of the venerable old sheikh.

Although the majority of the slaves imported with the caravan from Abyssinia were of tender years, and many of them extremely pretty, they did not excite that interest which might have been anticipated. Children accustomed to sorry fare and to harsh treatment in their own country, they had very readily adapted themselves to the will of their new masters, whose obvious interest it was to keep them fat and in good spirits. With few exceptions, all were merry and light-hearted. Recovered from the fatigues of the long march, there was nothing but dancing, singing, and romping; and although many wore an air of melancholy, which forms a national characteristic, the little victims to a traffic so opposed to every principle of humanity, might rather have been conjectured to be proceeding on a party of pleasure, than bending their steps for ever from their native land.

A very limited number of Shankelas and a few natives of Zingero excepted, the whole consisted of Christians and Heathens from Guráguê, whence are obtained the "red Ethiopians" so much-prized in Arabia. Kidnapping has consequently been there carried to an extent so frightful as to impart the name of the unhappy province as a designation for slaves generally. Nearly all of both sexes, however, had already become passive converts to the Mohammadan faith, and under the encouraging eye of the bigoted drivers, oaths by the false Prophet resounded through the camp. Nine-tenths were females, varying in age from six to thirteen years, and all were clad alike in dirty cotton smocks of Abyssinian manufacture, adorned in some instances with cuffs of blue calico. Their long dark tresses, elaborately greased, were plaited into thin cords with tassels at the extremity, and interwoven about the head with a band of coloured thread, to which was suspended a distinguishing cluster of cowrie shells. Bead necklaces, pewter ear-rings, bracelets, and anklets, decorated the persons of the prettiest; and these ornaments, forming the stock in hand of the trader, are invariably resumed on each bargain effected, in order to be transferred to some victim hereafter to be purchased.

Each slave was provided with a cruse of water, and had walked the entire distance accomplished from the heart of Africa, with an endurance that in children especially of such tender years was truly surprising. A very few only, who had become weary or footsore, had been mounted on mules or camels, or provided with ox-hide sandals, which in some measure protected their tender feet against the sharp lava boulders. The males, chiefly boys, had been entrusted with the charge of camels, and required no compulsion to render themselves useful; and of the females, some, who boasted personal charms, occupied the position of temporary mistresses. Four large handfuls of parched grain, comprising a mixture of wheat, maize, millet, and gram, formed the daily food of each; and under the charge of the most intelligent, the respective droves slept huddled together on mats spread upon the ground. Some surly old drivers or wanton youths there were, who appeared to prefer the application of the whip to the more gentle persuasion of words; but in the trifling punishment inflicted there was nothing to remind the spectator of the horrors of slavery as witnessed in the western world.

Few caravans ever traverse the deadly Adel plains without losing some slaves at least by the sultriness of the climate, or by the wanton spear of the adjacent hordes. Three of the fat merchant's children had been murdered shortly after leaving Abyssinia, and at his instigation a foray was now concerting among the united warriors of the two caravans, having for its object the destruction of the neighbouring Wurbóro Galla, whose families were to be swept into captivity. In this unprovoked slave-hunt the Embassy were strongly urged to take part, but positively refusing the aid of British muskets in furtherance of any such object, the project was finally abandoned, more especially when a huge, brawny Shankela, the property of the Kázi's son, was one morning discovered to have effected his escape during the night, doubtless with the design of carrying to the unsuspecting tribe a timely intimation of the gathering storm.

Ominous *kaláms* meanwhile went on as usual, and fresh reinforcements arrived to take share therein. Villains of every degree continued to slide in as if hung upon wires, to stand cross-legged within the door of the tent until their curiosity was satisfied, and then to assume a seat in the congress. Hajji Abdállah and Elmi, the nephews of Ali Shermárki, listening by turns, brought hourly reports of the progress making towards final adjustment, and *"Bokra, Inshállah!"* "To-morrow, God willing!" the now undeviating reply to every interrogatory relative to departure, had become a perfect by-word in every mouth. At length, on the 28th, it was pompously announced by the Ras el Káfilah that every point at issue had *bonâ fide* been satisfactorily arranged—that the water-skins were to be filled in the evening before the flocks and herds should return from pasture to trouble the pools—and that the journey was positively to be resumed betimes on the morrow.

Upon this welcome assurance the three potent chieftains already named were again received, though with closed doors at their own request, in order that each might be invested with a turban and an honorary mantle of scarlet broad-cloth, as rewards of their villainy. A most difficult point of etiquette had now to be overcome. The Akil of the Hy Somauli, whose liege subjects had abstracted the mule from Fiáloo, was the bosom friend and partisan of Izhák, whilst the illustrious personages who sat in regal dignity on either side were near and dear relatives of Mohammad Ali; and the rivals respectively watching with jealous eye every act that could be construed into favour or partiality, would infallibly have fired at any preference shown in the presentation of these enviable distinctions from the British Government. The presents were therefore placed on a table immediately opposite to the respective parties, and thence simultaneously launched with the same arm into the laps of the confronted recipients; when each bundle, even to the envelope, being found the exact counterpart of the others, no grounds for jealousy or heart-burning could be devised.

Misfortune had during this interim overtaken the "Sahib el bayzah," the imp whose acquaintance was formed in the harbour of Tajúra. Detected in the mischievous dissemination of evil tales respecting his clansmen, and in circulating others of an equally discreditable tendency, purely the fruit of his own fertile invention, affecting the throng at Killulloo, he had been taken to task by Abroo ibn Aboo Bekr, upon whom he drew his creese without further ado. The bloodthirsty little savage, who had not numbered his fourteenth year, being seized, was tied to a tree, and most severely chastised. His passionate cries and shrieks under the lash had reached the tent during the interview now happily terminated, and no sooner was he taken down than he came blubbering to lodge his complaint. No satisfactory reply being elicited, the precocious youth unsheathed his knife, with which he viciously went through the form of disembowelling a prostrate foe. His feelings thus relieved, he dried his eyes, and, with a significant toss of the head, remarked as he walked away, "'Tis of no consequence, '*maphish*,' no importance whatever; but by the grace of God I shall cut the throat of that cousin of mine, before I am many days older!"

Chapter Twenty Eight
Renewal of Debates by Ibrahim Shehém Abli, surnamed "The Devil"— Final Escape to Waramilli

Affairs nevertheless began now to assume a more desperate appearance than ever. The night of this day of good tidings setting-in with a storm of dust, followed by a heavy fall of rain, a party of Bedouins scoured unperceived through the camp, and in spite of every precaution swept off many articles of trifling value. Amongst the booty was a tub of sugar-candy, which, on the hue and cry being raised, the rogues were fain to abandon, together with the bedding of one of the escort. An incessant bombardment of large stones was kept up during the whole night from the thick underwood in the vicinity, directed as well against the sentries on duty, who paced the same weary ground for the ten thousandth time, as against the position occupied by the sleepers, one of whom, having emerged for a moment from the tarpaulin which the rain had rendered indispensable, received a severe contusion.

Mohammad Ali, in a state of evident alarm, came as soon as the shower had abated to say that there existed no prospect of the march being resumed in accordance with the solemn promise of the Ras el Káfilah; and that feeling longer unable to answer for the lives of the party amongst such a congregation of lawless ruffians, he was desirous of conducting to Shoa on horseback all who felt so disposed, leaving the heavy baggage to be secured by his father as far as circumstances would admit. Should matters unfortunately reach the decided crisis which there seemed every reason to apprehend, the son of Ali Abi was clearly the staff whereon to rely, his intercourse with Europeans having rendered his manners more frank and ingenuous than those of his selfish and shuffling rivals; but although *kaláms* and altercations had again commenced, a sense of duty for the present precluded the adoption of his project.

Morning of the 29th dawned upon no preparations for departure, and a fresh source of detention was indeed found to have arisen from a new claim for precedence put in by Ibrahim Shehém, the litigious member of the tribe Abli, which ranks in the Danákil nation next to that of Adáli, to which the brother of the reigning Sultán belongs. Another tedious day of insult and debate ensued; but the question was at length disposed of by the congress, who decided the fiery little warrior to hold place second to Izhák in the conduct of the káfilah, to the exclusion of Mohammad Ali, through whose tribe the party were now to pass.

Again it was announced with due formality that all matters at issue were peaceably and satisfactorily arranged, and several bales of blue calico, with quantities of snuff, tobacco, and dates, having been distributed among the weary disputants, they were finally induced to disperse, each carrying his *tobe* folded in triangular form, and stuck, as if in triumph of his plunder, like a placard, at the end of a slit stick. Ibrahim ibn Hámeïdo, Akil of the Hy Somauli, left at his departure a clump of twenty bold spearmen to escort the Embassy to the banks of the Háwash; and, after shaking hands with each of the European party, to the benediction *"Fee amán illah,"* bade the whole *"Tarik is sulàma"* God speed upon the road.

Ibrahim Shehém Abli, appropriately surnamed by his compatriots "Shaytan," or "The Evil One," carried a great soul under a very diminutive person; and being a perfect Roostum in his own estimation, was one of those who honoured the humble tent of the Embassy with a much larger share of his presence than could have been desired. No sooner was it pitched than the consequential little man strutted in as if by previous invitation, and, with an air that left no doubt as to the side on which he considered the obligation to lay, spread his mat in the least convenient position that could have been selected to the lawful proprietors of the interior. By virtue of a claim which it had heretofore been difficult to understand, he considered himself entitled to the receipt of rations in addition to the handsome pecuniary remuneration extorted at Tajúra, and to keep him out of mischief, he had daily obtained in common with the Ras el Káfilah two large handfuls of rice.

Elated by his recent advancement, he this evening, after sleeping some hours on the table, suddenly bounced upon his legs, and assuming an attitude of mortal defiance, which his contemptible presence rendered truly diverting, exclaimed with the most exaggerated want of courtesy, "You Franks don't know who I am, or you would treat me with more respect. I am Ibrahim Shehém Abli, who slew the chief of the Mudaïto in single combat, and"—placing the hand of one of his audience in a frightful chasm of the skull, which afforded ample room for three fingers and a half—"here is the wound I received upon that occasion. Do you conceive that I can always consent to receive the paltry pittance of rice with which I have hitherto been put off? Double the quantity immediately, and see that I have my proper share of dates and coffee too, or by the head of the Prophet we shall not long continue on our present friendly terms."

An Arab of desperate fortunes, the ancestor of this pugnacious little hero, is said to have concealed himself, clothed in white robes, among the spreading branches of a tree; and his partisans having induced the simple-minded villagers to repair to the spot in the dusk of evening, the intruder, on being discovered, was accosted deferentially as a spirit. Revealing himself under the character of a great Arabian warrior, who had shun his thousands in the battle, the man of valour was entreated to descend, and become one of the tribe; but to this he would by no means consent until a pledge had been passed to recognise him as its chief, and assign as his own the whole extent of country visible from his elevated perch, which done, he was pleased to alight, and became the father of Braves. 'Tis well for his posterity that the experiment had not been made in a later day, or the cotton robe would have been stripped from the shoulder of the warrior, and a lifeless trunk been left beneath the tree to mark the interview.

Throughout the sojourn of the Embassy at Killulloo, Izhák had peremptorily insisted upon the tent being struck at sunset, lest the display of so much white and blue cloth might excite the cupidity of the Bedouins, and the preparations making to carry this despotic order into effect, may perhaps have been the means of ruffling the never very placid temper of his now second in command. The aversion of the Ras el Káfilah to any thing like a habitable structure being well understood, the unhoused party amused itself at his expense, by the erection of stone walls of considerable extent, as a shelter during the coming night of rain. "In the name of Allah," he exclaimed, blustering up to the spot, and kicking over a portion of the fabric with the pointed toe of the very sandal that had suffered so severely during the disagreeable debate at Ambábo, — "in the name of Allah and his Prophet, what is the meaning of all this? We shall have our throats cut to a man if you people persist in this folly: there will be no rain to-night!"

But the rain did fall in torrents, notwithstanding the assurance of the Ras; and although the ravine was now comparatively clear of ragamuffins, stones continued to rattle at intervals against the awning erected for the shelter of the European sentries. That portion of the party off duty, steamed, after an hour's drenching, under thick heavy tarpaulins, whilst the fluid glided unheeded over the sleeping persons of the paid escort, who were well-greased and oiled, like wild ducks prepared for a long flight.

On the last day of the month, after nearly a week's tedious detention in an insalubrious and soul-depressing spot, surrounded by black basaltic rocks, where little forage could be obtained, where water, although abundant, was extremely bad, and where the persecutions of prying savages, from whom there was no escape, were unceasing, the Embassy was again permitted to resume its march. Every hour had seemed an age, and *"Galla gassetoï,"* the well-known cry to load, had therefore never been listened to with more heartfelt delight. Until after the rear of the string of camels left the ground, and Izhák was fairly seated on his mule, it was scarcely possible to believe that some fresh cause of detention would not be discovered; but the debates were at last over, and the litigants, weary of raising new objections, suffered their victims to advance in peace.

The road wound up the Killulloo Wady, and thence over a barren rise strewed with obsidian, and with stones, the common pest of the country, to Waramilli. An interesting sight was presented in the line of march of a tribe proceeding in quest of water to the northward—a long line of dromedaries, horned cattle, oxen, sheep, and goats, interspersed by women and children, scantily clad in leathern petticoats, and laden with the rude date matting of portable wigwams, or the still ruder implements of household gear. Whilst the females thus bore heavy burdens slung across their breasts or led the files of camels, upon which rocked the long, raking, ship-like ribs of the dismantled cabin, the lazy lords sauntered ungallantly along, encumbered with naught save the equipment of spear and buckler, the ferocious aspect of all giving ample presage of the intentions entertained towards any party less formidable than themselves.

Total absence of water on the route usually pursued had determined the Ras el Káfilah, after much discussion and deliberation, to adopt the lower and shorter road, which, in consequence of the frequent forays of the Galla, had been for some years closed to caravans. But notwithstanding that so much invaluable time had been lost at Killulloo under such provoking circumstances, and that the march finally made thence fell short of seven miles, he again persisted in halting, thus affording to Hajji Ali Mohammad and Wáyess ibn Hagaïo an opportunity of rejoining with a party of troublesome Bedouins. The renewed discussions, which did not fail to follow this influx of savages, together with the artful assurances given of the danger to be apprehended on the road selected, had nearly prevailed upon the unstable Izhák to take the káfilah back to Killulloo, for the purpose of proceeding by the upper road; but Ibrahim Shehém Abli, stepping forward in his new capacity, drew his creese, and performing sundry not-to-be-mistaken gestures, swore vehemently upon the sacred Korán to rip up the belly of the very first blockhead who should attempt a retrograde step—his object doubtless being to thwart the views of Mohammad Ali, whose tribe, occupying the upper ground, would derive advantage from the transit of the Embassy by that quarter.

Waramilli is the usual encamping ground of a section of the Gibdósa Adaïel, but their place was fortunately empty. Completely environed by low hills, it proved insufferably hot; and no water was obtainable nearer than Wady Killulloo, now distant more than two miles from the bivouac; but the party were in some measure reconciled to detention in this spot by the arrival from Tajúra of a special messenger, bringing letters which bore very recent dates. Nevertheless the Dankáli to whose hands the packet had first been consigned had nearly perished from intense heat and want of water in his attempt to pass the Salt Lake; and being compelled to relinquish the journey, had returned to the sea-port nearer dead than alive.

Petty thefts without end were committed by the lawless rabble who had followed the caravan and located themselves in the immediate neighbourhood. Ibrahim Shehém Abli, totally regardless of the character due to his exaltation, was detected in the very act of drawing a cloth with his foot over a pair of pistols, whilst he cleverly held the proprietor in conversation. His design was to obtain a reward for their restitution,—a trick in common practice by the camel-drivers and hired escort; and this was by no means the first exhibition of his own knavery. But it was some consolation to perceive that, although the Franks were of course the principal sufferers, depredations were not altogether restricted to their property. Numerous shields and cloths were abstracted from too confident Danákil; the Ras el Káfilah's sandals were purloined; and at the going down of the sun, a proclamation went forth through Ibrahim Burhánto, the common camp-crier, that Wáyess ibn Hagaïo, Akil of the Wóema, having lost his spear, all parties possessing knowledge of the nefarious transaction were required to give information of the same to the proprietor, as they hoped to prosper!

Chapter Twenty Nine
Naga Koomi—Meinha-Tólli—
Madéra-Dubba, and Sultélli

Two windy nights, during which it blew a perfect hurricane, were passed in unabated vigilance, owing to the number of ruffians lurking about the broken ground, the waters whereof tumble in the rainy season into the rugged chasm of Killulloo. At an early hour on the 2nd of July, a voice went through the camp, summoning the slothful camel-drivers to bestir themselves; and the incessant growling of their disturbed beasts, which arose in various keys of dissatisfaction from every part of the circle, followed by drowsy Danákil imprecations, and by the merciless dismantling of huts, to the destruction of bales and boxes, presently announced that the work of loading had duly commenced.

A march of fifteen miles over a country more level than usual, though sufficiently rough and stony withal, led through the Doomi valley to Naga Koomi. An abutting prong of land, under which the road wound, was adorned with a cluster of bee-hive-shaped huts styled Koriddra, and at its base the *Balsamodendron Myrrha* grew abundantly, the aromatic branches famishing every savage in the caravan with a new tooth-brush, to be carried in the scabbard of the creese. The encampment occupied a wide, dreary plain, bounded by the high mountain range of Jebel Feeóh; and although water was said to exist in the neighbourhood, it proved too distant to be accessible.

The Ras el Káfilah, at whose hands the Franks experienced about the same amount of respect and tolerance as a rich Jew in the days of Coeur de Lion, here imperiously demanded daily rations of rice and dates for the band of spearmen left as an escort by the Akil of the Hy Somauli; and on being informed that this very unreasonable request could not be complied with, in consequence of the tedious delays on the road having reduced the supplies so low as to be barely sufficient to last to Abyssinia, his brow became suddenly overcast, he relapsed into his wonted ill-humour, rejected a tendered sheep with indignation, and flung out of the tent in a passion.

It rained heavily during the greater part of the night, and an early summons to rise found the party again drenched to the skin. The inclement weather had not by any means tended to restore Izhák to smiles; and his mats having proved quite insufficient to preserve him from full participation in the pleasures of the nocturnal bath, the effect upon his temper was but too manifest. "Don't whistle, don't whistle!" he exclaimed with a sneer to one of his charge, who was so amusing himself within hearing; "what are you whistling for? I have loaded the camels under a prayer from the sacred Korán, and you are doing your best to break the spell, and call up gins by your whistling. '*La illah illallah, wo Mohammad rasúl illah;*'" "there is no God but God, and Mohammad is the Prophet of God."

"*Fein teró?* In the name of the three kaliphs where are you going to?" again vociferated the testy old man, in a terrible passion, to the same luckless individual, who, with a loaded rifle in his hand, had now left the road in pursuit of an antelope. "'*Taal henna!*' 'Come back, will you!' *Wullah!* you'll be getting your throat cut presently by the Buddoos, and then I shall be asked what has become of you. Can't you keep the road? This ugly defile is named 'the place of lions,' and one of them will be eating you anon."

Another march of fifteen miles brought the caravan to Meinha-tólli, where some hollows had been filled by the recent heavy fall of rain; but large droves of horned cattle having soiled in them, the muddy water was so strongly tainted as to be barely drinkable under any disguise. The country throughout bears signs of violent volcanic eruption of later times, which has covered one portion with lava, and another with ashes and cinders. At the outset the road led over the usual basaltic ground, strewed with fragments of obsidian, but after crossing Arnoot, a deep ravine choked with refreshing green bushes, in which the exhausted beasts obtained a most welcome supply of muddy water, the stony valleys gave place to sandy plains, clothed with short yellow grass, and intersected by low ranges of hills.

One wide level expanse, termed Azóroo, stretching at the foot of the peaked mountain Aiúlloo, was pointed out in the distance as the scene of a signal victory gained about six years since by the Wóema over their predatory foes the Mudaïto. The bones of upwards of three thousand of the combatants which now whiten the sands, have caused the desertion of the best road by the superstitious Danákil. With the escort were many warriors who had taken part in this engagement, and they described the conflict, which commenced in a night attack, to have raged, spear to spear, and shield to shield, throughout the entire of the following day, towards the close of which the "red house" was routed.

As usual, in the evening we sent for a sheep from our flock, but the Ras el Káfilah stoutly asserted that the whole had been transferred to himself for consumption by the escort of Hy Somauli, and although eventually compelled to relinquish one, he did so with an extremely bad grace. Thunder and lightning, with severe squalls and heavy rain, again closed the day— and great confusion and discomfort was occasioned by a sudden whirl of wind, followed by the fall upon the party, of the saturated tent, from the wet folds of which escape was not easily effected. A dreary night succeeded. The watery moon shed but a dull and flitting light over the drenched camp; and the pacing officer of the watch, after an hour's exposure to the pitiless hurricane, calling up his relief, threw himself with aching bones upon the inundated bed.

"Did I not tell you what would be the consequence of your abominable whistling," grumbled old Izhák, the first thing in the morning; "old Ali Arab is too sick to be moved, and one of my best camels has strayed, Allah knows where." The rope with which the legs of the lost animal had been fettered, was meanwhile rolled betwixt his hands, and sundry cabalistic words having been muttered whilst the Devil was dislodged by the process of spitting upon the cord at the termination of each spell, it was finally delivered over to the Dankáli about to be sent on the quest, and he presently returned successful.

Ahmed Mohammad, the messenger who had been despatched from Tajúra with an Arabic letter for Sáhela Selássie, requesting assistance on the road, returned during this delay. He had passed the night in a Bedouin encampment, the proximity of which had been betrayed by the barking of dogs at each discharge of the musket when the sentinel was relieved. The courier brought advices to the Embassy, and native letters for Izhák and Mohammad Ali. Owing to the jealousy of the frontier officers of Efát, he had been subjected to many days of needless detention, during which the king had led a distant military expedition; and although compliments and assurances of welcome were not wanting, they were coupled with the unsatisfactory intelligence that the party must trust entirely to its own resources, as in the absence of His Majesty, no assistance whatever could be rendered.

The rainy season having now fairly set in, it was believed that the pools on the upper road would furnish a sufficient supply of water, and the course was accordingly shaped towards it. Emerging upon the extensive plain of Merihán, bounded to the westward by the lofty peaked range of Feéoh, the route skirted the Bundoora hills, thickly clothed with grass, and varying in height from six hundred to a thousand feet. Wáyess, the chief of the Wóema, formerly held his head-quarters in this neighbourhood, at

Hagaïo-dera-dubba; but the Eesah Somauli making frequent inroads, and at last sweeping off all the cattle of the tribe, it was abandoned. The hill ranges on both sides have sent lava streams almost to the middle of the plain, but generally it is covered with a fine light-coloured soil, strewn with volcanic ashes and small fragments of obsidian—the grass, improved by the recent showers, having partially acquired a greenish tint. A singular detached hill composed of fresh-water limestone, contained a few impressions of small spiral shells, whilst the surrounding rocks exhibit the usual cellular basalt.

No one could conceive that the rugged arid wastes whereon he trod, had ever in themselves been either productive or populous. Saving the labours of the termites, exhibited in endless mounds of vast dimensions, no monument of industry redeems the inhospitable landscape; yet these measureless plains, no less than the barren mountain ranges so lately traversed, did formerly, as now they might, afford hordes of hardy soldiers, that under a bold leader, such as the mighty Graan, who in the sixteenth century unfurled the banner of the impostor, and at the head of a countless army overran and nearly destroyed the Ethiopic empire, were admirably adapted to possess themselves of the more fertile plains and provinces adjoining. Whatever may have been the virtues and endowments of these olden warriors, their posterity, like the dwellings they inhabit, are sufficiently rude and degenerate.

Wady Bundoora, clothed in a thicket of verdant bushes, had been selected as the halting ground, and its appearance promised a copious supply of water; but every pool proved dry, and the march was therefore continued to Madéra-dubba—a second and similar ravine, which was confidently expected to afford the desired element. Disappointment was however again in store, and the rain not having extended thus far, the usual reservoirs were referred to in vain. Worse than all, information was here received that not a drop of water would be found at the next station; whilst, owing to the wear and tear of skins, added to the too confident anticipations indulged, barely a sufficient supply for even one day accompanied the káfilah.

It had been determined under these untoward circumstances, to move on at midnight; but after an insufferably hot day, rain again interfered. Unfortunately it did not fall in sufficient quantities to be of much utility; a few pints caught in tarpaulins, which, with all available utensils, were placed for the reception of the precious fluid, proving very inadequate to the wants of the thirsty party. At 3 a.m. the caravan advanced down the valley, with cool refreshing weather, and a fine moon shining brightly overhead. From the summit of a tumulus of black lava, marking the point where the undulations of the Bundoora hills trend towards the mountains of the Ittoo Galla, an extensive view was obtained with the dawning day, over a country bearing the most extraordinary volcanic character—huge craters on the one hand towering to the clouds, whilst on the other sank the wide valley of Kordeité, through which lay the high road to the desolate plains of Errur.

A few pools of muddy rain-water by the wayside were eagerly drained by the sinking cattle, but a deep ravine, bordered with green trees and bushes, was explored to no purpose; and after crossing the fine open plain of Eyrolúf, abounding in gazelles and swine, the road led round the base of a remarkable cone, styled Jebel Hélmund, which had long been in view. Isolated, and four hundred feet in height, with a crater opening to the north-eastward, which would seem at no very remote period to have discontinued its eruption, it is surrounded by a broad belt of lava, some three miles in diameter. This has formed towards the plain a black scarped wall, rising from fifteen to twenty feet, of which the wooded crevices teemed with quail, partridges, and guinea-fowl, and were said to be so many great dens of lions.

The sultry afternoon was already far advanced, when the weary eye was refreshed by a glimpse of the verdant plain of Sultélli, a perfectly level expanse, so ingeniously overgrown with pale green vegetation as to furnish an exact representation of a wide lake covered with floating duckweed, around which numerous camels were busily browsing on the rank herbage. During the greater part of the year, this plain presents one vast and delightful sheet of water; but the fairy form of the light-footed gazelle was presently seen bounding over the delusive surface, and although clothed throughout with the most tantalising verdure, it yet proved perfectly dry. The camels were milch females, capable of subsisting for days, and even for weeks together, without drinking, whilst their milk serves to quench the thirst of their unwashed Bedouin attendants. Beedur, the chief of a section of the Débeni, who resides in this spot during the rainy season, had long since decamped with his clan to more distant pastures.

Every hollow in the rich black soil abounding with shells, was vainly explored; and after a seventeen mile march, the party, weary and thirsty, were fain to encamp on the opposite side, and giving up the search as fruitless, to rest satisfied with the nauseous contents of water-skins filled at the putrid pools of Meinha-tólli—a second, and if possible, a worse edition of the impurities brewed at the Salt Lake. Both amongst men and cattle the utmost distress prevailed. A suffocating blast blew incessantly, heat the most intense was reflected from the adjacent black rocks; and nearly all of the horses and mules were so completely exhausted that there appeared no prospect of dragging them other sixteen miles to the nearest reservoir.

But towards midnight the beneficent flood-gates of Heaven were providentially opened, and a violent storm bursting over the camp, in less than half an hour filled every ravine and hollow to overflowing, and afforded a plentiful and truly seasonable, although transient, supply. Tearing up their pickets from the saturated soil, the dying animals thrust into the turbid stream that rolled through the encampment their hot noses, which for two entire days and nights had been strangers to moisture, and filled their sunken flanks almost to bursting. Cackling troops of guinea-fowl flocked to the pools from the adjacent heights. Embankments were thrown up, and wells excavated; and European, Danákil, and camp-follower—Christian, Moslem, and Hindoo—all drenched to the skin, falling together upon their knees in the posture of thanksgiving, sucked down the first copious draught of palatable water that had been enjoyed since leaving Fiáloo.

Chapter Thirty
Field of Extinct Volcanoes.
Oasis of Yoor Eraïn Mároo

Singular and interesting indeed is the wild scenery in the vicinity of the treacherous oasis of Sultélli. A field of extinct volcanic cones, vomited forth out of the entrails, of the earth, and encircled each by a black belt of vitrified lava, environs it on three sides; and of these, Mount Abida, three thousand feet in height, whose yawning cup, enveloped in clouds, stretches some two and half miles in diameter, would seem to be the parent. Beyond, the still loftier crater of Aiúlloo, the ancient landmark of the now decayed empire of Ethiopia, is visible in dim perspective; and looming hazily in the extreme distance, the great blue Abyssinian range towards which the steps of the toil-worn wayfarers were directed—now for the first time visible—arose in towering grandeur to the skies.

Overwhelmed by violent subterranean convulsion and commotion, which, reversing the order of things, has again and again altered the former appearance, the face of the country for miles around the base of the larger volcanoes, presents one sheet of lava. Activity would not appear to have extended much beyond the immediate neighbourhood of each; but there is a connection between the whole cluster visible in small lava streams and a vast quantity of volcanic débris, converted into humus, in the adjacent valleys. Yet it is by no means apparent that these alone have contributed to form the present surface, the south-eastern side of the field terminating in much older formation of wacke. Neither would any one of the craters appear to have very lately poured out the fiery stream. Ibrahim Shehém Abli indeed deposed with an oath to having seen Father Abida in flames about twelve years previously; but, on further investigation, there seemed reason to believe that the conflagration he witnessed must have been confined to the long grass with which portions of the steep sides are clothed.

The well-timed deluge of rain which fell during the night had been so eagerly drunk by the thirsty desert, that when the morning dawned the only traces of the storm were presented in numberless channels left by the torrent, with here and there a muddy pool, around which the guinea-fowl were still rallying in clamorous troops. Every portion of the road having been saturated, and rendered far too heavy for the jaded camels, advance was of necessity delayed until noon, by which time they had become sufficiently dry to admit of the resumption of the journey. A bare alluvial plain, skirting the base of the Kóomi range, led to a few acacia trees of larger growth than had heretofore been seen. They occupied a hollow styled Ras Mittur, which is the point of union of the two roads from Killulloo, and hence the caravan struck off across a grassy plain, abounding in herds of graceful *mhorr*. The course followed the eastern border of the field of truncated cones; and in the fresh green hue of the bushes with which the cindery tract is studded, was afforded abundant proof of the fertility of its decomposed lava.

Passing a cluster of Bedouin huts, whose inmates were watching their grazing herds of milch camels, the road next threaded a narrow belt of verdant jungle. This suddenly opened into the wide plain of Moolu, studded in every direction with flocks of sheep and goats, assembled from all parts of the country round; and in a deep hollow in the very centre lay the attraction—the oasis of Yoor Eraïn Mároo, a noble sheet of water surrounded by a belt of hillocks, and measuring during even this season of drought, a full mile in diameter. It was indeed a sight most refreshing to the eye. Troops of waterfowl of various plumage sailed over its glassy surface. Birds chattered amongst the autumnal branches of the numerous trees, whose tall stems, half immersed, rose thickly in the centre, and the cool waters of the basin afforded to the weary and travel-stained pilgrims the first unlimited supply of pure liquid that had been revelled in since bidding adieu to the shores of India.

In so sultry a land, where, throughout the desert and forbidding plain, Nature has dispensed the first necessary of life with a most niggard hand, those pools which have not a constant supply of running water soon become adulterated by various decompositions of organic and inorganic matter. Wacke cannot resist any long exposure, and hence fluid in contact with it imbibes oxide of iron and muriate of soda; whilst flocks and herds, corrupting the element in a still more offensive manner, not only impart a fetid taste and smell, but stir up the deposited mud, which emits a volume of sulphuretted hydrogen. Yoor Eraïn Mároo was free from all these impurities, and its reservoir affords a never-failing supply; but the surrounding country is said during the wet season to be extremely unhealthy, violent storms and incessant rain compelling the shepherds to abandon the plains and wadies, and retreat with their flocks to the neighbouring mountains.

From Waramilli to Moolu, the country is chiefly occupied by the sub-tribes of Débeni, under the chiefs Beedur and Boo Bekr Sumbhool, the latter of whom usually resides at Hamoosa, and the former at Doomi or

Sultélli. Although not always to be trusted, these wanderers appear under a friendly garb; but the lion-hearted guides and escort, with Izhák at their head, had, from the first moment of leaving Killulloo, been doing their utmost to impress upon the minds of their audience the extreme danger to be apprehended on this portion of the road, from the various wild hordes now adjacent, whom they painted as perfect dare-devils.

"The Galla are pagans," quoth Ibrahim Shehém Abli with a bigoted sneer, "and, uncircumcised knaves that they are, never heard either of Allah or the Holy Prophet; and as for the Mudaïto, although nominally Moslems, they have little more religion than their infidel neighbours. But wait until I get an opportunity," he added, with a caper and a sardonic grin, as he unsheathed his creese for the purpose of going through the figure of disembowelment, "only wait until I find an opportunity, and, *Inshállah*, we shall square accounts."

Many were the harrowing tales that had been called to mind by the first loom of the Abyssinian mountains, touching the toil-worn traveller, who, having surmounted all the perils and privations of the road, and arrived within sight of the promised land, had been cut off at the very last step towards the goal. Perpetual strife is waged betwixt the Galla and Mudaïto, and the plain of Moolu forming a sort of neutral ground between the countries inhabited by the rival clans, it proves one continual scene of foray and bloodshed. The heathen, watching like hawks from the tops of trees and eminences, pounce, whenever opportunity offers, upon the flocks and herds of the true believers: retaliation is not slow to follow, and thus the feud is well and incessantly sustained.

During the latter part of the march, the Ras el Káfilah was nearly thrown into hysterics by the sudden desertion of one of his charge, who, in defiance of the thraldom, which rendered all more like prisoners than freemen, had made up his mind to dine that night upon venison, and had accordingly taken up arms against the alluring herds of sleek and timid antelope that, with white discs on their cruppers, bounded in all directions before the advancing string of camels. Repeated interrogatories of *"Fein tóro?"* "whither are you going?" were launched in a commanding tone of voice after the truant, without eliciting the smallest attention or reply. A shot was fired — a fat buck fell — and the successful Nimrod, dismounting, proceeded to secure the spoils; an operation which brought from their occupation in the adjacent pasture, two ancient Bedouin crones in wrinkles and leathern aprons, to be spectators of the dissection.

Izhák was old and captious, and not seeing very clearly, the apparition was too much for his shattered nerves. "Allah, Allah!" he peevishly exclaimed, seizing his broad-headed spear from the hand of his henchman, and violently kicking the flanks of his jaded mule towards the spot; "merciful Providence, what childish folly is this? Is the commander a babe that he thus trifles with the safety of the caravan? I did fancy that he possessed some sense, but this is positively the act of a madman. Look at those Buddoos, they will cut his throat immediately, and then we shall have a pretty blood feud, involving the lives of half a dozen Danákil."

Despite of all the twaddling old blockhead could do to prevent it, the haunch was nevertheless brought in, and its appearance hailed with considerable delight. But it might almost as well have been abandoned to the vultures of the air, since the Persian cook, who had taken alarm at the menace extended to Quilp in the prosecution of his kennel duties, peremptorily refused to convert the venison into *kabábs*, upon the grounds that the knife of the true believer had not passed across the throat of the victim.

"Whose dog is Hajji Abdállah Kurmani?" he exclaimed in tones that might have been believed to issue from a dilapidated bagpipe; "whose dog is he, I repeat," throwing the haunch upon the ground, "that he should be invited to deal with any such abomination? Allah and his Prophet defend us, but the Hajji would as soon think of polluting himself with the touch of the unclean beast."

This spirited public declaration was by the Moslem audience received with the rapturous applause it claimed; and the worthy pilgrim, fairly carried away by the over-boiling of his virtuous indignation, was actually proceeding to wreak his last vengeance upon the venison, when arbitrary measures were adopted, which resulted in the imposition of twenty-four hours' fast in excess of the many inflicted by the apostle whose shrine he had visited at the holy city.

Now the Hajji bore a striking personal resemblance to Hudibras, and like that hero, regarded discretion as being the better part of valour. Since the melancholy disaster at Goongoonteh, he had encumbered himself with a musket and a modicum of cartridges; but even by his warmest admirers it must be confessed that there had never in his demeanour been observed the slightest indication of a design to throw himself away by rash exposure. Entertaining the highest respect for himself, the prudent son of Irán was rarely heard to speak of Hajji Abdállah save in the respectful third person singular. The words of Ibrahim Shehém had sunk deep into his soul, and after the affair of the venison, it was not a little diverting to hear him, in his wonted croaking accents, apostrophise the folly and the infatuation which had prompted him to brave the wilds of unexplored Africa.

"Hajji Abdállah was never taxed with lack of common sense," he exclaimed musingly in self-reproach. "Allah knows there be many greater blockheads in this sublunary world than his servant the Hajji. Is it not wonderful that the chief cook to Khwajah Mohammad Rahim Khan Shirázi, and master, too, of recipes for no fewer than nine-and-thirty piláos, should have proven himself such an ass, such a son of a burnt father, as voluntarily to get in the way of abuse for refusing to *kabáb* unhallowed meat which died without the knife or the Bismillah; and, worse still, in the way of having his own throat divided every minute of each day and night by these bloodthirsty infidels? '*La houl willah koowut illah billah ali ul-azeem,*' 'there is no power nor virtue save in God.' What true believer in the fair province of Kurmán would ever have suspected Hajji Abdállah of bringing his beard to so vile a market?"

Chapter Thirty One
Menace of the Dar Mudaïto.
Moolu Zughír, and Burdúdda

Boo Bekr Sumbhool and Datah Mohammad, co-chiefs of that section of the Débeni styled Sidi Hábroo, shortly sneaked into the camp at the head of an appropriate retinue of ruffians, and having been duly propitiated with tobacco and blue calico, deputed a son of the latter to represent the tribe, as an earnest of the black mail having been levied. Mohammad Ali proposed under these circumstances to halt a day, both in order to profit by the first opportunity enjoyed of purifying raiment, and, which was of still higher importance, to refresh the way-worn beasts. But the Ras was in such dire alarm of the Bedouins and Galla, that he had been with the utmost difficulty prevailed upon to encamp near the water, and no persuasion could now elicit his consent to tarry. Columns of smoke which arose high and dense from the country in advance, did not tend to diminish his apprehensions. A shadowy human figure stealing along the summit of the gloomy cliffs which overhung the camp, redoubled his mental perturbation; and anathematising Moolu as the most dangerous nest of thieves and cut-throats along the entire road, he would that minute have resumed the march in the dead of night, had not heavy rain compelled him to bite his nails until a late hour the following forenoon, by which time the camel furniture had become dry.

But the event proved that there were on this occasion some grounds for uneasiness. During the process of loading, three mounted Mudaïto scouts, wild-looking beings, rode into camp in a suspicious manner; and immediately after moving out of the bed of the hollow, whence the road led over an extensive plain covered with low shrubby undergrowth, the Ras el Káfilah, who momentarily waxed more fidgety and excited, called a general halt, and assumed his shield and brass-mounted spear.

"Look well to your weapons," he observed with a truly commander-in-chief-like delivery, "and let all the proprietors of fire-arms lead the van with myself. Two thousand of the Dar Mudaïto are out on a foray against the Galla of the neighbouring hills, and I have received certain intelligence that they purpose this day to fall upon the caravan. May Allah protect his servants in the coming strife!"

Suitable defensive preparations were made without delay, and the camels formed ten deep to admit of the whole line being enfiladed by rifle balls; whilst the Danákil and Hy Somauli escort, with loins girded for the fight, brought up the rear. Scarcely had these arrangements been completed, when a band of fifty warriors were descried advancing in a compact body over the brow of an adjacent eminence. Carrying their round bucklers on the left arm, and bristling their bright spears, they pressed rapidly towards the front of the line, "on hostile deeds intent." Out to meet them sprang the fiery little champion Ibrahim Shehém, who panted to flesh his creese in the body of another Mudaïto, and twenty stout warriors, casting off their upper garments to give freedom to their limbs, were not far behind him. The caravan remained motionless to watch the event, and the formidable line of rifles fronted the foe, who no sooner perceived the muzzles bearing directly on their phalanx, than they lowered their spears to demand a parley, and described themselves to be *en route* from Jebel Abida to join their clansmen, who were gathering at the waters of Mároo, preparatory to a *"goom"* or onslaught, upon their hereditary enemies, the Alla and Ittoo Galla.

The march was resumed immediately upon this banditti passing quietly to the rear, and Ibrahim Shehém Abli relapsed into his wonted composure; but the foot-prints of several other parties being shortly afterwards discovered, the beaten track was abandoned altogether, in order, if possible, to avoid meeting the marauders in number, when the plunder of so rich a caravan would doubtless have been essayed. An advance guard reconnoitred the country round from the summits of trees and termite cones, which alone admitted of an uninterrupted view over the thick verdant bushes that clothed the entire face of the plain. These were interspersed with rich yellow grass, swarming with antelope, hares, bustard, and florikin; whilst fine cedar-like camel-thorns stretched their long arms over troops of pintadoes, coveys of partridges, and spur-fowl. Not a trigger was suffered to be drawn, lest the report should attract to the spot the much-dreaded Mudaïto; but although hundreds of warriors might have been ambushed in the dense covert unperceived, it was safely traversed without further hostile demonstration; and the country becoming gradually more and more open, the view extended to the fine peaked range near Afrubba, inhabited by the Ittoo Galla—war-hawks of the mountains, who are distinguished for their sanguinary ferocity.

A cloud of dust in the extreme distance being believed to prognosticate a rush of these wild horsemen, the caravan was again halted ere it had proceeded far over the open plain; but the magnifying powers of a pocket telescope converting the objects of alarm into a troop of scudding ostriches, Izhák's confidence once more returned. The residue of the march lay over cracked and blackened soil, from which the vegetation had been burnt the preceding day, the embers still smouldering in various directions, although the columns of smoke had ceased to ascend.

Neither fuel nor water could be discovered at the ground selected for the bivouac, but a small supply of the latter requisite was obtained on the way, from a muddy brook trickling over the charred surface of the soil, and filling the gaping cracks and crevices on its progress towards the lower ground. This strange phenomenon arose from the wady at Moolu Zughír, near Afrubba, some miles to the southward, having been filled to overflowing by the recent heavy rain. Moolu Táni, or "the other Moolu," afforded a most alluring spot of bright green vegetation just sprouting from the rich soil which here abounds, and among it the cattle luxuriated until dark. Sundry invocations were now performed with horrid yells, to enable one of the savages to divine the coming of rain; but a night passed in vigilance by sentinels posted on ant-hills, which afforded an uninterrupted view over the surrounding plain, gave place to dawn without any molestation from thunder-storm, Galla, or Mudaïto.

Betimes in the morning the march was resumed across an alluvial plain, which a few days later in the season would probably have presented a swamp impassable to camels; but no difficulties were now experienced, and the caravan passed merrily on towards a conspicuous barn-shaped hill, which had been visible for many miles. At its base, among sundry other cairns, stood a mound of loose stones encircled by a thorn fence, and almost concealed under the forest of withered boughs that decked every part. Beneath this grotto reposed the sainted bones of Othmán, a celebrated Tukhaïel sheïkh of days long gone. Amidst prayers and ejaculations in honour of the departed, according to the custom still prevalent in the southern parts of continental Europe, each warrior of the Bedouin escort first in order, and then the drivers as they passed, having previously plucked from some adjacent tree a branch of verdant mistletoe, adorned the venerated pile; and long ere the arrival of the last camel, it had exchanged its sober autumnal garb for the bright green mantle of spring.

Picturesque clumps of magnificent camel-thorns of ancient growth here studded the face of the landscape, and, covered with golden blossoms, perfumed the entire atmosphere. The myrrh tree flourished on the hill-side, and the *"garsee"* was first found under a load of fruit resembling the *"leechee."* The bright crimson pulp possesses an agreeable acidity, and the kernel that it envelopes pleases the Danákil in a mess of sheep's-tail fat. No wood had hitherto been seen sufficiently dense to invite the elephant; but in this covert the giant evidently existed; and the oryx, appropriately styled *"Aboo el kuroon,"* "the father of horns," ranged in considerable numbers; the half-devoured carcase of one which had been slain the preceding night, attesting the presence also of the "king of beasts."

The agility of the Adaïel in reclaiming a refractory camel, although often witnessed with admiration, had never been more prominently exhibited than during this march. One of the most skittish and unmanageable animals of the whole hundred and seventy, had very judiciously been selected by Izhák for a large chest containing medical stores, and the halter was usually held by a gentle slave girl, whom it was the delight of the Sahib el Bayzah to cuff and maltreat. Taking a sudden whim into its head, the restive beast, after the performance of sundry preliminary plunges to ascertain if the load were firm, dashed off the road, galloped over the feeble maid, and, smashing her water-gourd into a thousand fragments, roaring and bellowing, pursued its headlong career across the stony plain. Phials and bottles were undergoing a most destructive discipline, when a fleet-footed savage, who was in hot pursuit, and had already twice turned the fugitive, darting across its orbit, abruptly terminated these gratuitous and uncouth gambols by a sudden twitch of the nose-rope, which brought owner, dromedary, and medicine-chest simultaneously to the earth, with a crash that sounded ominously enough, although not the slightest injury was sustained by either.

Meanwhile the caravan had reached Burdúdda, where a large pool of dirty rain-water extended strong inducements to encamp, and again led to a violent altercation between the authorities. Apprehensive of misunderstandings with the Bedouin shepherds in the vicinity, Izhák had sapiently resolved to proceed some miles further to a waterless station, whilst Mohammad Ali, insisting that the káfilah should halt, commenced the work of unloading. The camels of either party were for some time divided; but the Ras, after trying the stratagem of advance without shaking his rival's resolution, finally yielded up the point with a bad grace, and all set up their staff.

The outline of the highlands of Abyssinia, which had been first indistinctly visible from Sultélli, now stood out in bold relief; and to the southward the view was bounded by the lofty hills of the Afrubba, Farsa, and Azbóti Galla, where coffee grows wild in abundance. An intermediate extensive prospect is obtained over the thickly-wooded Moolu plain, stretching some thirty miles in the direction of Errur. This latter is the residence of the old sheikh Hajji Ali Mohammad, and the head-quarters of the Débeni, who take hereditary share in the waters of the valley with their brethren the Wóema. It forms, moreover, a place of resort for every wandering vagabond in the surrounding country who possesses a sheep, a goat, or an ox, or has the ability and the inclination to assert his privilege of erecting a temporary cabin; and thus the recurrence of each season of drought, compelling the abandonment of less favoured pastures, pours in its migratory swarm to swell the more permanent muster upon the sultry plains of Errur, and to create the strife inseparable from a gathering of these lawless hordes.

Chapter Thirty Two
A Tale of the Plains of Errur

Aylia was the comeliest of the dark-eyed daughters of the desert. Sixteen tropical summers had already ripened a form modelled in that exquisite perfection which nature is wont to bestow upon her wildest works, and the native symmetry of the sylph-like maid was yet unblemished by any of those barbarous improvements wherein her nation delight. Her sparkling eye, fringed with long silken lashes, in brilliancy eclipsed the pet gazelle that ever bounded by her side; and the graceful gambols of the sportive fawn would seem to have been inspired by the fairy footstep of its blooming mistress. Luxuriant hair fell in elf-like tresses over her ebon shoulder. Teeth of ivory whiteness were revealed by a radiant smile that ever played over her animated features; and few indeed of her virgin charms were veiled under the folds of the slender drapery that belongs to the Bedouin shepherdess.

> (Note 1. The following narrative, recounted by one of the Wóema escort, although necessarily enlarged, is as strictly literal as the embodiment of the subject would admit; and it will convey to the English reader a better picture of life in the desert than could be painted in a less connected form.)

The maid tended her father's flocks in the vale of Errur, which forms a constant scene of predatory incursion on the part of the ruthless savages that hover round the border. When least expected, the Galla war-hawks of the adjacent mountains were wont to stoop from their rocky fastnesses, and to sweep away the riches of the Wóema. The treacherous Eesah, although ready to extend the hand which should have denoted friendship, was nothing loath to the appropriation of other men's chattels; and throughout all the nomade Adel hordes, whose tents were erected during the more sultry months, the feud and the desultory skirmish favoured the inroads of the foe. Amongst the surrounding clans, even her own tribe was not notorious for its honesty, and by frequent depredations abroad, it invited the foray of reprisal. Thus the brawl and the mortal encounter would follow the stillness of indolent existence with a rapidity not less startling than frequent, and none knew what the next hour might bring forth.

But fear had no place in the breast of the daughter of old Ali. Nursed in the lap of strife, the Bedouin blood of her roving sire coursed through her young veins, and she pursued her Arcadian occupation beneath the spreading boughs of the venerable acacia, chanting to her gazelle the wild ditty that revealed the thraldom of her heart, or listening to the bleat of her black-faced lambs from the Hejáz. Often had the shrill war-whoop rung through the wild valley, and the rush of the gathering warriors who flew to answer the summons, arrested her plaintive song, but only lately had it caused her to spring to her feet with a bosom throbbing audibly; and now she would sigh as she sank again upon the smooth bank that formed her favourite seat, for the swain for whom her soft eyes had been strained across the flickering desert was not among the number of those that had swept past, and she knew not why, nor whither he had gone.

Many were the ardent suitors who had wooed the hand of the blooming Aylia, and often-times had she been sought from her avaricious father, who viewed the still expanding attractions of his daughter as a certain source of increase to his ill-gotten and idolised wealth. None, however, had yet been able to produce the price set upon the damsel's charms, neither had any possessed an advocate in her eloquence. Her heart had already been tacitly relinquished, but her hand she knew to be in the gift of her sire, and therefore not her own to bestow.

Ambeesa it was who had silently gained this ascendancy over the green affections of the maid. The milch goats of Irripa, his mother, were by her driven daily to pasture, and his wigwam was within spear's throw of her own. The twain had known each other from earliest infancy, for they came upon the world's stage in the self-same hour. They had feasted and they had played together as children; and now that their young hearts had become entwined, it was his wont to accompany the nymph into the vale, where they would hold converse the livelong day. The vapid language of the savage admits of but a limited embodiment of the softer passions; but the simple courtship of the uncultivated was ably sustained. Aylia felt the force of her charms when she saw the warrior grasp the spear and the shield, without which no Bedouin ever crosses the threshold of his cabin—in order that he might chase the fawn that she had coveted; or when he drew water from the well in her gourd, to replenish again and again the ox-hide that formed a drinking trough for her thirsty flock. And Ambeesa felt himself amply rewarded when the slender fingers of the blooming girl decked his hair with the aromatic herbs that she had plucked in the wild meadow, or she counted over the ewes that they were shortly to possess in common.

Ambeesa was ever in the foremost rank when the spear was thrown over the shoulder of the brave; and successful in every foray, he had won wealth as well as fame. None appeared more frequently in the many-tailed leopard spoils which form the garb of victory; and the white feather always floated above his raven locks. But his father having been treacherously murdered by the Eesah, a blood feud clung to the old man's sole descendant; and it formed to him a source of self-reproach, that although he had for years dogged the footsteps of the assassin, the opportunity had never yet occurred when he might wash out the stain! A skulker amongst his clansmen at a distant oasis, the cowardly savage had profited of his deep cunning to baffle the creese of the avenger; and he still vaunted his trophy of blood without any account of its acquisition having been required.

But the day of reckoning and of retribution was now nigh at hand. The mother of Ambeesa had counted out the dowry demanded of any who should espouse young Aylia, and had claimed the girl as her daughter-in-law elect. At the sight of the beeves and the fat rams and the trinkets and the trumpery cloths, the sole remaining eye of the old sheikh glistened with a lustre that it had not known for years; but his haughty soul could ill brook the thought of his daughter being wedded to one whose father's death thus rested unavenged. "Get thee hence, young man," he exclaimed sternly, shaking his silvered locks, after a short inward conflict with his avarice— "Get thee hence, nor show thy face again within my doors as a suitor until thou hast appeased the spirit of thy murdered sire. The blood of him to whom thou art indebted for existence crieth aloud to thee for vengeance; and *Wulláhi*, until the grave of Hássan shall have been soaked by thy hands, thou shalt not talk to Ali of his daughter."

Ambeesa sought not his dark mistress, but snatching the spear and buckler which had been carefully deposited in a corner of the cabin, stalked forth without uttering a syllable. Passing his own hut in mental abstraction, he took the road to the brook, and throwing himself upon his face, drew a deep draught to allay the fever that consumed him. Then whetting his brass-mounted creese to the keenest edge upon a smooth stone, he muttered a dread oath betwixt his clenched teeth, and strode moodily across the sandy plain.

The great annual fair had already assembled at the sea-port of Berbera, and tribes from all parts of the country were flocking thither with their motley wares. The curious stalls of the fat Banians from India were thronged from morning until night with barbarians from the adjacent districts, who brought peltries and drags to be exchanged; and the clamour of haggling and barter was hourly increased by the arrival of some new caravan of toil-worn pedlars from the more remote depths of the interior, each laden with an accession of rich merchandise to be converted into baubles and blue calico at a clear net profit to the specious Hindoo of two hundred per cent. Myrrh, ivory, and gum-arabic; civet, frankincense, and ostrich feathers, were piled in every corner of his booth; and the tearing of ells of Nile stuff and Surat cloth, and the counting out of porcelain beads, was incessant so long as the daylight lasted. Withered beldames, with cracked penny-trumpet voices, were meanwhile actively employed in the erection of new edifices; and more and more camels were ever pouring towards the scene of primitive commerce, loaded with the long elastic ribs, and the coarse date matting which form the skeleton and shell of the nomade's wigwam.

It was dusk when Ambeesa entered the long centre street of this busy scene. He had journeyed many days alone and on foot, and his mantle and his arms and his lofty brow were alike deeply stained with the disguising dust of the desert. A gang of *Bones*, with a stalking ostrich, driving before them sundry asses laden with the spoils of the chase, arrived at the same moment from the opposite direction. Rude parchment-covered quivers, well stocked with poisoned shafts, hung negligently by their side, suspended by the tufted tail of a lion, and with their classic bows over their wiry shoulders, the gypsey votaries of Diana advanced swearing and blaspheming towards the Eesah quarter of the straggling encampment.

The light which gleamed through the black goat-hair awning of a Guráguê slave-merchant, fell upon the features of the wild party as it passed; and Ambeesa's heart beat high with exultation when, in the person of one whose matted locks were decorated with a dirty ostrich plume, he fancied he could recognise the very foe of whom he was in search. The archer was in truth a most truculent-looking knave—one who, if his visage did not strangely belie him, might have been the perpetrator of any given atrocity. The tail fat of four Bérbera rams encrusted his head in a perfect helmet of tallow, and the putrid entrails of the antelope he had last slain, were slung in noisome coils about his neck, to the pollution of the atmosphere he breathed. His repulsive front displayed through the accumulated filth of forty years a perfect maze of mystic figures in tattooed relief, on which were imbedded amulets stitched in greasy leather; and the distended lobes of his enormous ears were so loaded with pewter rings, that not another could have been squeezed in. A gap, consequent upon the loss of five front teeth in a recent brawl, made room for a quid of no ordinary dimensions. Two small sunken blear eyes, which appeared to work upon a swivel, squinted alternately, as the inflamed balls were revealed by turns according to the employment of the wearer's sinister vision; and on his meagre sunken cheek yawned a seam five inches in length, which precisely corresponded with a gash known to have been inflicted by the youth's father during a certain moonless night at Errur, when a stab in the back had aroused the veteran from deep sleep to his mortal struggle.

"Stay you here, Moosa," quoth one of the bowmen, addressing this captivating hero, as they stopped before the doorway of an unfinished cabin at no great distance beyond the rover's pall,—"tarry you here, and *Inshállah*, we'll turn out these lazy wenches to unload the asses."

The name had not been lost upon Ambeesa, who, like all of his bigot creed, placed the firmest reliance in fate. He had sworn never to return until he should have given the body of Moosa to the wild beasts, where the vultures might pick out his eyes. The object of his weary journey was by the interference of destiny in his favour, already within his clutches. He who murdered his sire was assuredly alone with him in a dark lane, and Aylia was without doubt his own!

"*Wogérri maani, wogérri maani, wogérri maani*" repeated the Wóema coldly, as he extended his open hand towards the doomed victim in token of amity. "*Wogérri, wogérri, wogérri*," carelessly returned the savage thus accosted, at the same time passing his greasy fingers mechanically over the palm presented. The same triple salutation again reiterated, was thrice returned; and it gradually dwindled away to an assenting "*um hum*," in itself fully as frigid as the wearisome repetitions of inquiry had been deeply treacherous.

Moosa stooped to shake the pebbles from his dilapidated sandal. His bare back was towards the Wóema, for his garment had fallen from his brawny shoulder. It was enough. Muttering through his closed teeth an inaudible invocation to Allah, Ambeesa suddenly drew his creese, plunged the razor-edged blade to the very hilt into the yielding spine of his unsuspecting foe, tore the vaunting white feather from his greasy locks, spumed the prostrate carcase with his foot, spat upon the unseemly features now distorted in the agonies of death, and fled into the wilderness.

Months had elapsed, and the festive season had now returned at which the Bedouins annually celebrate their weddings. Many a dark-eyed damsel had been led by her happy swain to the nuptial wigwam, when a gayer procession than usual was to be seen passing up the centre street of the encampment at Gaïel. Eight wrinkled matrons led, brandishing swords and creeses with truly Amazonian gestures, whilst they danced to a wild song in which all joined chorus to the dissonant thumping of a kettle-drum. The charms of the maiden bride who followed, and had been long betrothed, were screened from vulgar gaze beneath a canopy of blue calico, home by a party of the village belles, splendid with porcelain jewellery and grease— their arms, like those of the sister Graces, entwining each other's waists; whilst every idle blackguard that could be mustered, swelled the nuptial train. At intervals, the music of the tambourine gave place to a shrill vocal solo, when the nymphs pirouetted in a mazy circle; and the procession, after thus parading through the hamlet, was preceded on its return by a party of dirty urchins bearing the dower in ornamented baskets woven of the wiry leaf of the palm. Massive ear-rings of brass and copper were amongst the treasures, and the much-prized, though far from becoming coif of blue calico which forms the badge of the wedded wife, had not been forgotten.

Aylia was still the fairest of all the daughters of her tribe, and Ambeesa ever the foremost when the spear was thrown over the shoulder of the warrior. Happiness and content reigned in the rude hut. No harsh word had ruffled the existence of the young pair, and the stranger never passed the door without the ready draught of milk being proffered, or the kind word exchanged. But in accordance with the barbarous usage of the Adel Bedouin, the wife was to remain an inmate of her father's dwelling, until she should have become the mother of three children.

'Twas mid-day in the sultry summer months, and the fiery sun poured his fiercest rays from his meridian throne. No human eye was able to endure the broad glare that pervaded the vast sandy plain of Errur, which at intervals was scoured by towering whirlwinds, imparting the aspect of a manufacturing town with its huge steam-engines at work. All animate nature shrank under the scorching heat, which had even curled the few scanty tufts of withered vegetation. The stillness of death pervaded a desolate scene over which floated the treacherous mirage. Not a creature moved, and no sound was heard save the roar of the angry whirlwind tearing every thing before it, as it swept in reckless wrath across the encampment, eliciting while it raged among the frail mat tenements of the location—unroofing some and filling others with dust and pebbles—a curse from the drowsy savage whose rest it had disturbed.

Suddenly a shrill cry arose in the distance, the well-known tocsin for the assembly of the men-at-arms. Electrical in its effect, every slumberer started to his feet, and each hut, which had for hours been silent as the tomb, poured forth its warrior, armed and ready for the fight. On the verge of the plain was descried a band of the Alla Galla driving off a troop of camels, and with the points of their spears goading the awkward animals to a grotesque gallop. Their remoteness, and the unnatural speed to which they had been urged, imparted, through the medium of the mirage, the appearance of dismembered animals flying in portions through the deceptive atmosphere. Now a head attached to a long neck was separated from the body, and elevated many feet above its proper place; and now animated legs of exaggerated length could alone be perceived flitting fast over the sultry desert. Unattached tails danced in the quivering vapour, and the entire distance was alive with fragments of men and dromedaries, which seemed to have been hurled through the air by the bursting of an exploded mine.

Galla and Wóema, pursuer and pursued, scoured for some hours over the sandy waste; and it was near sunset when the pagan marauders were overtaken on the confines of their own territories. A sharp conflict ensued; and two on each side having fallen, the booty was retaken, and the unbelievers put to flight by the sons of the Faithful.

From the door of her father's wigwam Aylia watched with inward misgivings the return of the victors; and as she saw the bodies of the fallen borne upon the shoulders of their comrades, her young heart throbbed audibly, for her newly-wedded husband was one of those who had gone forth. As her straining gaze fell upon the still gory corse of him she loved, a flood of hot tears dimmed her lustrous eyes, and uttering a piercing shriek, she sank senseless at the threshold. Roused again to life, the bereaved girl filled the hut with her doleful cries, and shriek succeeded shriek as she bewailed her fallen condition. Death would indeed have been almost preferable to the lot accorded by her destiny. The property brought at his marriage by the deceased was resumed by his grasping relatives, and the late light-hearted wife became once again a slave under the roof of her avaricious parent, there to lead a life of drudgery until another wealthy suitor should pay the dower fixed upon her charms. But the light elastic step was gone, by which Aylia had erst been distinguished above all the Wóema maidens. The full black orbs had lost their wonted lustre, and the radiant smile no longer beamed over her faded features. The orphan pledge of her first love clung to a widowed breast, and the heart that beat beneath was broken by the untimely fate of the brave youth Ambeesa.

Chapter Thirty Three
The One-Eyed Family. Háo, and
first Glimpse of the Háwash

The Arab chieftain of the Foudthli, of whom flying parties still infest the deserts of Aden, is renowned for the possession of two thumbs upon the dexter hand—a proud distinction by which his ancestors have been recognised from time immemorial. Sheïkh Oomer Buttoo ibn Ali, akil of the Tukhaïel, who occupy the country from the oasis of Yoor Eraïn Mároo to Háo, a few miles eastward of the Háwash, glories in the loss of the sinister eye; and he is reputed to have forfeited it by an hereditary visitation, which through every generation has disfigured his ancestors in like manner—no single head of the illustrious line having been known to possess two eyes! This venerable Polyphemus visited the camp after dark, attended by his hopeful son and heir, who has already qualified for the succession; and after receiving each a piece of blue calico in the clandestine manner which these savages prefer to a more orthodox public presentation, they slunk away, well satisfied with their booty.

A group of slatternly females belonging to the Ittoo Galla had sauntered carelessly into camp with ox-hides for sale, and tobacco, the produce of their own high lulls; and their abrupt departure as the evening shades drew on, had led to suspicions anent the object of their visit. At the going down of the sun therefore a caution was promulgated by the Ras, enjoining a vigilant look out for Galla and wild beasts; and his earnestness might almost have led to the anticipation of a rush of wild equestrians through the encampment, or a charge of hungry lions from the adjacent gloomy thicket, before the termination of the first watch. But the cry of "wolf!" had been too often dinned into every ear; and although both elders and escort had sworn that this night at least should be one of wakefulness, no surprise was elicited by the disappearance of their bushy heads, one after the other, beneath the mats—an example which was speedily followed by all the Europeans off duty, as the rain began again to tumble in torrents,

"Et veterem in limo ranae cecinere querelam."

The fear of attracting the "Buddoo," as the much-dreaded marauders of every class were generically designated, still invariably brought an order which there was no gainsaying, to strike and pack the tent before sunset, however threatening the aspect of the weather. But the despotism of the Ras was light in comparison with the tyranny exercised by his unaccommodating train. At whatever hour of the night the arbitrary mandate to load might be promulgated, it was required that the bedding of the whole party should forthwith be delivered at the quarters of the arrogant driver to whom it pertained, since he declined making his camel walk to the spot. Moreover the delay of a few minutes was sufficient to condemn it to be left on the ground, notwithstanding that preparations often occupied two hours, which might as well have been devoted to rest; and this wanton curtailment of sleep was doubly felt after the heavy nocturnal duty that devolved upon all.

The route on the 9th led across the flat of Halik-diggi Kabír, a continuation of the Moolu plain, extending from the Azbóti and Ittoo ranges to the mountains Aiúlloo and Abida. Twelve miles in breadth, it presents one monotonous alluvial level, treeless, but thickly covered with grass, interspersed with dwarf shrubs, and enlivened by herds of the elegant *mhorr*, amongst which the secretary bird occasionally strutted in native dignity. Baézas and zebras, too, were descried on the hills which bound the flat; and a luckless leopard being detected in the act of stealing across the expanse, the savage group pursued like demons from every quarter, and having presently hooted and hunted the terrified animal into a bush, transfixed his carcass incontinently with thirty spears.

The whole landscape was alive during this animated scene, which scarcely occupied a minute; and in due process of time the panting warriors rejoined the caravan, their necks, spears, and shields adorned with strips of the victim's tail, whilst he who by dint of superior wind and fleetness had drawn the first blood, was by his comrades publicly invested with the spotted spoils that he had won. The appearance of the party on their return, accompanied by a stray horseman who had fortuitously joined in the chase, gave birth in the bosom of the Ras to an apprehension that the Ittoo Galla were descending upon the caravan. The ranks were accordingly closed, and the Europeans again took post on the flank to be assailed, until a nearer approach revealed in the savage band the features of friends.

A descent of thirty feet over a narrow tongue of land, led into the valley of Halik-diggi Zúghir, styled by the Adaïel the Great Háwash—its breadth being about two and a half miles, and the bed a perfect level, covered with fine grass, on which grazed a troop of wild asses. Bounded throughout the serpentine progress by parallel banks of corresponding height and appearance, the hollow would seem to extend from the mountains of the

Ittoo Galla north to the Aiúlloo volcano. It wears the aspect of having been once the channel of a considerable stream—that of the Háwash perhaps, which river may not improbably have been diverted into its present course at the period when the extensive volcanic tract around Mount Abida was in a state of activity, and when subterranean influence must have caused extraordinary revolutions in the entire aspect of the country.

Here occurred the last specimen seen of the Kurbéta, the myrrh-bearing tree (Balsamodendron Myrrha), of which two varieties are found abundantly over all the barren hill-sides, from the Doomi valley to the borders of the Háwash. That producing the better description of the gum resin, is a dwarf shrub, with deeply serrated crisp leaves of a dull green; whereas the other, yielding a substance more like balm than myrrh, attains a height of ten feet, and has bright shining leaves. From any bruise or incision inflicted, the "*hofali*" flows copiously in the form of a milky juice, possessing a perceptible acidity, which either evaporates or becomes chemically changed when the gum forms. Left ungathered, it becomes hard with the loss of the volatile oil, and thus crumbles away; but if the wound be cleared frequently, a very large quantity may be collected during the seasons, which occur in January when the buds appear after the first rain, and again when the seeds are ripe, in March.

Three ounces of the finest myrrh and one of dross, may thus be obtained during the year, and the secreting vessels lying immediately under the epidermis, a very slight bend in a branch makes it flow freely. The wandering shepherds either tear off one of the lower limbs, or so bruise the stem with a heavy stone as to retard the growth of the tree; but every new sprout is spontaneously covered with gum, although in a somewhat more fluid state. Repeated injuries in the same spot lead to the formation of an ever-filling cavity, and

"The mirrhe sweete bleeding in the bitter wounde,"

is transferred by each passer-by to the hollow boss of his shield, to be exchanged for a handful of tobacco with the next slave-dealer met on the caravan road. But the Danákil are not altogether ignorant of the virtues of the drug, and invariably recommended it for those of the horses that were unable to proceed from heat and exhaustion.

It has been seen that from Yoor Eraïn Mároo, an accession to the escort was received in the person of the hopeful son of Datah Mohammad, co-chief of the Sidi Hábroo. This insatiable vagabond, a worthy scion of his stock, had received from the hand of Nature an aspect that could only have belonged to a finished cut-throat. Deeply scarred with the small-pox, his bloated half-shaven muzzle peered through a tangled web of grease-clotted hair, like a drowsy owl out of an ivy bush. He presented a truly striking picture of man in the natural state. Although never without a new quid in his mouth, and another half masticated behind either ear, he passed hours of each day in importuning for more "*timboo*" of which he was the most passionate admirer; and it was his undeviating rule never to pass a white face without repeating in an authoritative tone the trisyllable "*Irreboot*" in token of his determination to add still farther to his stock in hand of yam-needles, which already outnumbered the quills of the porcupine.

Firmly persuaded that every mule with the party had been purchased for his especial riding, and equally convinced that his presence was indispensable to the general safety, he appropriated the very first that came within his reach, changing it as often as he thought proper, and never leaving it without a galled back. If not a professor of equitation, he was at all events devoted to the science, and it was with a fiendish scowl indeed that while crossing Halik-diggi Zughír he received an order to dismount from a steed which he had selected out of the drove for the purpose of riding down an oryx. "*Tuwwaddee!*" "attend," he mumbled sulkily as he thrust away the animal with the butt of his spear,—"*Tuwwaddee!* I am a great man's son, and have no intention of walking. If I am not to have a horse, you may even settle as best you can with my father's Bedouins."

Mules, horses, and camels, in considerable numbers, were abandoned before the termination of this tedious and sultry march—fatigue, want of water, and lack of forage, having reduced all to such positive skeletons that they walked with difficulty. Ascending three successive terraces, each of fifty feet elevation, the road finally wound into the confined and waterless valley of Háo, famous for the number of parties that have at various times been surprised and cut up by the neighbouring Galla—

> "For, with hot rapine fir'd, ensuiguin'd man
> Is here become the lion of the plain,
> And worse."

Not a month had elapsed since three ill-starred individuals of a Tajúra caravan, impatient to satisfy burning thirst, hurrying in advance of the main body, were cut off by a band of Galla horsemen, who had lain concealed behind the rocks immediately above the present encamping ground, and who, after mutilating the bodies, bore off their barbarous trophies in triumph. The dale hard by had only two nights previously to the arrival of the present party, formed the scene of a skirmish between the Ittoo and the inhabitants of the plain, when the bodies of twenty of the former and nine of the latter were left to the vultures and hyaenas. Every hill and valley in this direction could, in fact, tell its individual tale of bloodshed and slaughter.

The wild barbarians keep a constant look out to pounce upon any wanderers weaker than themselves, and few are the natives to be seen who bear not on their persons some indelible mark of hand to hand combat.

Fatigued by the long march, the Danákil were all fast asleep within their temporary sheds, a few of the drivers excepted, who tended their browsing camels among the adjacent thorns. In an instant the whole valley rang with the cry to assemble at arms, and inconceivable was the confusion that ensued. Many of the escort, only half awake, in rushing forth overthrew portions of their dens upon others who were still inside. Warrior clashed against warrior, shield against shield. The rocky hill-side was presently a living mass of half-clad savages, panting up the steep acclivity, when a few Galla scouts, whose sudden appearance on the plain had caused the alarm, were perceived mounting their steeds; and, understanding themselves to be the objects of these warlike preparations, they precipitately sped their way.

From the summit of the height was obtained an exhilarating prospect over the dark lone valley of the long-looked-for Háwash. The course of the shining river was marked by a dense belt of trees and verdure, which stretches towards the base of the great mountain range, whereof the cloud-capped cone that frowns over the capital of Shoa forms the most conspicuous feature. Although still far distant, the ultimate destination of the Embassy seemed almost to have been gained; and none had an idea of the length of time that must elapse ere his foot should press the soil of Ankóber. A day of intense heat was as usual followed by a heavy fall of rain, which, owing to the unaccommodating arrangement again peremptorily exacted, of striking the tent at sunset, thoroughly drenched the whole party; but before finally drawing the mat over his sleepy head, the Ras el Káfilah mounted a cone which stood in the centre of the compact circle, and proclaimed in a loud voice to all, a night of light sleep and watchfulness.

Chapter Thirty Four
Passage of the Háwash

Numerous were the apprehensions now in agitation relative to the state of the formidable river in advance, whose shallow stream so easily forded during the season of drought, was not unreasonably conjectured to be swollen by the recent rains. Second of the rivers of Abyssinia, and rising in the very heart of Ethiopia, at an elevation of eight thousand feet above the sea, which it never reaches, the Háwash is fed at long intervals by niggard tributaries from the high bulwarks of Shoa and Efát, and flows like a great artery through the arid and inhospitable plains of the Adaïel, green and wooded throughout its long course, until finally absorbed in the lagoons at Aussa; and the canopy of fleecy clouds, which, as the day dawned, hung thick and heavy over the lofty blue peaks beyond, gave sad presage of the deluge that was pouring between the verdant banks from the higher regions of its source.

Passing along the face of the murderous hill, which is of wacke formation, the road descended by several sloping terraces, to the level valley through which the river winds. At first thinly wooded, the soil was covered with tall rank grass, which, in consequence of the perpetual incursions of the Galla, grew in all its native luxuriance, uncropped whether by flock or herd. But as the path wound on, gum-bearing acacias and other forest trees increased both in size and number—the jungle and undergrowth, teeming with guinea-fowl, which rose clamorously at every step, waxed thicker and thicker—groves of waving tamarisk, ringing to the voice of the bell-bird, flanked every open glade, whereon lay traces of recent inundation; and the noble trees which towered above them from the banks of the Háwash, gave evidence in their shattered branches of the presence of the most ponderous of terrestrial mammalia.

Vegetation having here assumed a luxuriance known to none of the joyless and unproductive regions hitherto traversed, it is with some difficulty that the pilgrim, anxious to behold the rare phenomenon of a running stream, forces his way through the dense thickets, which, until the foot touches the very brink of the precipitous bank, so completely screen the silent river from view, that its very existence might almost be questioned. But after a persevering struggle, further progress was at length arrested by a deep volume of turbid water, covered with drift-wood, which rolled at the rate of some three miles an hour, between steep clayey walls twenty-five feet in height, bounding a mere break through the mud and sand. The breadth of the channel fell short of sixty yards, and the flood was not yet at its maximum; but its depth and violence, added to the broad belt of tamarisk and acacia, interlaced by large creepers and parasites, which hems in both sides, promised to offer much difficulty and delay in the coming passage. Pensive willows that drooped mournfully over the troubled current were festooned with recent drift, hanging many feet above the level of the abrupt banks; and this appearance, no less than the rubbish scattered over the borders, fully proved the assertion of the natives that the water had recently been out, to the overflowing of the adjacent flat country for many miles.

The Háwash, here upwards of two thousand two hundred feet above the ocean, forms in this direction the nominal boundary of the dominions of the King of Shoa. Izhák was therefore strongly urged to despatch a courier in advance, who might apprise His Majesty of the near approach of the British Embassy. But from some latent and sinister motive of his own, the proposal was again negatived, as it had before frequently been, upon the grounds of the dangers to be apprehended on the road. These, according to his showing, rendered it impossible for a single messenger to venture on so rash an undertaking, notwithstanding that Ahmed Mohammad, the Dankáli who had been the bearer of the letter despatched to Shoa from Tajúra, and who was still with the caravan, had so recently passed twice in safety over this identical route.

As a measure of precaution against inundation, the camp was formed upon the summit of a small stony eminence, considerably above high water mark; and several armed Bedouins were presently lounging and prying about the tent, to the great annoyance and discomfiture of the Ras el Káfilah. "Those fellows call themselves Débeni," he remarked, "and will not commit murder wantonly, but the villains are thieves in grain, and will steal whatsoever they can lay their hands upon. They have no business here."

Many energetic remonstrances touching the impropriety of the obtrusion, produced not the smallest effect upon these obstinate savages; and finding that they continued to laugh him to scorn, and to set his boasted authority at defiance, the old man finally requested that a musket might be fired over their heads—a measure which quickly brought about the desired decampment. The smell of gunpowder is intolerable to every Dankáli. The bravest of the brave slide off with a growl and a sulky look, if a gun be but touched in their presence; and an unexpected discharge, as on this occasion, when a knot has collected, causes every man to start upon his feet, and, with a muttered curse, to bring his spear to the rest.

The residue of the day was devoted by the camel-drivers to the preparation of rafts for the transport of the baggage, and the working party was still at the river, when the Adaïel conch sounded to arms, and the shrill war-whoop again summoned all to the rescue. Great was the confusion that ensued, and light-footed warriors were to be seen scampering down every avenue, armed with spear and shield; but the cry proved to have been raised in consequence of a disaster that had befallen one of the camels. Too lazy to loosen the cord which fettered the fore legs of the animal, the stupid owner had driven it, thus crippled, down the steep slippery bank to the water's edge, when, as might have been anticipated, it was swept away by the strong current, without being able to make one struggle for extrication.

At sun-down the caravan was closely-packed within a stout thorn fence, serving as a partial protection against the wild beasts and plunderers with which the dense thicket is infested—its endless depths being so entangled and interwoven that no eye could penetrate the gloom. The moonless night was passed in extreme discomfort, owing to a deluge of rain which commenced early, and fell incessantly for many hours. Deafening thunder pealed in startling claps overhead, and broad sheets of fire lighting up the entire face of the landscape at short intervals, for a moment only disclosed the savage loneliness of the wild spot, which was the next instant shrouded in pitchy darkness.

With the dawning day, preparations were commenced for crossing the river on ten frail rafts which had already been launched—transverse layers of drift-wood rudely-lashed together, being rendered sufficiently buoyant by the addition of numerous inflated hides and water-skins, to support two camel loads. The sharp creeses of the Danákil had removed many of the overtopping boughs, interlaced with creepers, which impeded transit towards the point selected for the passage, and in the course of a few hours every portion of the baggage had been deposited at the water's edge.

Casting off his garments, Mohammad Ali, always the foremost in cases of difficulty and danger, now seized the end of a rope betwixt his teeth, and, plunging into the river, swam with it to the opposite bank, where it was belayed, upon the principle of the flying bridge, to an overhanging willow—a guy which connected it with each raft serving to counteract the violence of the stream, which, in spite of the heavy rain, had fallen upwards of a foot during the night. Raiment was now discarded by every Dankáli, and the work commenced in right earnest, but difficult and laborious indeed was the task before them. The water trickled over their greasy limbs until a late hour of the evening, and the utmost exertions only succeeded in accomplishing the transfer of the endless train to the western bank before nightfall, with the loss of three beasts of burden drowned, and sundry firelocks sunk to the bottom.

This latter disaster arose from the spontaneous going to pieces of one of the rudely-lashed rafts, when one of the clumsy followers became entangled in the wreck, and but for the exertions of the son of Ali Abi would inevitably have been lost. The fair Hásseinee was amongst those who were thus cast away in the middle of the deep waters; but hers was not the person to sink, and floating like a Naiad on the surface, with long raven locks streaming over her fat shoulders, the nymph appeared to be in her native element, and was soon shaking her wet petticoat on the opposite shore.

The baggage being of necessity divided, and the whole of the native escort as well as the camel-drivers employed in loading and navigating the rafts, it was deemed prudent, in addition to an ostentatious display of rifles on both sides, to make liberal disbursements of blue calico, in order to purchase the neutrality of the Bedouins, who infest the borders of the river. On the division of the party, some of the Adaïel females being separated from their lords, a characteristic trait of Ibrahim Shehém Abli was elicited by the proposal for solution of the old riddle of the three jealous husbands, with their wives, who found on the banks of a rapid stream which they were desirous of crossing, a boat that would contain only three persons, whereas each felt unwilling to abandon his fair partner to the mercy of the other. After puzzling for some time without being able to arrange the transit in a satisfactory manner, "*Murhabba!*" he exclaimed; "had I been one of that same party, I should soon have settled the difficulty by cutting the throats of the two jealous rascals, and taking all their women to myself."

The stream of the Háwash being exceedingly thick and troubled, from the distance it had rolled betwixt clayey banks, it was with much satisfaction that a pond of wholesome water, styled *Dubbélli*, was discovered, divided from the river by a narrow wooded neck of land, one hundred and fifty yards across. Steep shelving walls strewed with shells and the *reliquiae* of hippopotami, environed this singular basin, which appeared to be fathomless, and to measure a mile and a half in circumference. Lofty trees, in a wintry dress, cast their deep shadow over the brink; and whilst the stems of many were partially immersed, the leafless branches of some were loaded with storks' nests, and the shattered limbs of others presented tokens of the giant strength of the elephant, no less than of the terrible wrath of lightning and storm.

Corresponding tongues abutting from the opposite banks, divide the expanse into two equal bays. A group of wild Bedouins watered their camels on the shore, and in the centre Behemoth rolled his unwieldy carcase to the surface amid floating crocodiles—protruding his droll snout, which glistened in slimy ugliness, to blow ever and anon a snort that might be heard at the distance of a mile. A two-ounce ball, duly hardened with antimony, took effect in the skull of one of the boldest with a crash that was not to be mistaken; but although the monster went down, leaving a gallon of blood to denote the disaster that had befallen him, he had temporarily disappeared; and by the incredulous Danákil the assurance was received with a sneering shake of the head that his carcass must infallibly be found floating in the morning.

Much difficulty had been experienced in bringing the horses and mules across the river, and one obstinate donkey, but too well aware of its inability to swim, having pointedly refused to take the water, was towed over by main strength at the end of a rope. Inflated skins kept the animal afloat; but the stubborn head sinking below the surface, the poor beast landed with sides distended almost to bursting by too copious draughts of muddy water. His master, an aged washerman from Hindostan, loving Neddy as the apple of his eye, in the simplicity of his old heart, adopted the prescription of some wag who had facetiously recommended suspension by the heels, in order to try the ancient discipline of the Humane Society for the recovery of drowned mortals. A fit of apoplexy was the result, and the donkey expired under the lancet.

Followed by the lamentations of the disconsolate owner, the carcass was dragged some twenty yards beyond the limits of the encamping ground; and no sooner had the dark night thrown a shroud over it, than the foul scavengers of the forest assembled in numbers round the prey, and regardless of a blazing watch-fire that had been kindled to avert the visits of the monarch of the wilderness, commenced their revels with the demoniacal laugh indicative of a right happy mood. Whilst the rain descended in pitiless torrents, a continual chuckle of the highest merriment, which ran through all the various notes of a clear throat, resounded afar amid the crunching of bones and munching of flesh—a deeper growl from some larger beast of prey, now and then varying the infernal harmony, to be followed by another ringing laugh as of a whole legion of devils. Vivid flashes of lightning played over the scene of this midnight carnival; the violent snapping of branches in the adjacent forest proclaimed the nocturnal foray of the elephant and hippopotamus; the loud roar and the startling snort were neither wanting to complete the concert of the wild Háwash, and long ere the morning dawned, the place of the carcass knew it not, every vestige, even to the skull, having found a sepulchre in the maw of "the laughing hyaena."

Chapter Thirty Five
Wadi Azbóti. Arrival of a Spy from
the Abyssinian Mountains

"The Robi is *not* dead," was the first falsehood that greeted the ear when daylight had returned. To have told the truth on this occasion must have redounded to the personal advantage of the informant, but he had nobly upheld the national character at the sacrifice of a handful of his much-loved tobacco. Repairing to the margin of the lake, the freckled pink sides of a defunct hippopotamus were to be seen high above the surface, as the distended carcass floated like a monstrous buoy at anchor. It had become entangled among the tall tamarisks that rose through the shallow water near the brink, but hawsers were carried out with all diligence, and with the aid of the rudder-like tail, the Colossus was towed to shore, and landed among the mud under the acclamations of the assembled caravan.

"Where the carcase is, there shall the eagles be gathered together." A formidable band of "Bones" were already squatted at a respectful distance, to watch the progress of events, and no sooner had the teeth been hewn out than they laid aside their bows and quivers, and having stripped the thick hide from off the ribs, attacked the mountain of flesh with the vigour of a South African horde. Donkeys and women were laden with incredible despatch, and staggering under huge flaps of meat, the archers had soon left the scene of operations. Two reservoirs, each lying at the distance of a musket shot, had meanwhile been visited—the one a sulphuric basin of considerable extent, the other a vast sheet of water, embosomed in trees, dotted over with wood-clothed islets, and teeming with hippopotami. But this was neutral ground; and the fears of the Danákil conjuring into existence a host of lurking foes, the period allowed for investigation was brief.

Bidding adieu with light hearts to the muddy Háwash, the party resumed its march so soon as the camel furniture had become sufficiently dry; and skirting the Dubbélli lake, from the waters of which Behemoth blew a parting salute, passed the Bedouin hamlet of Mulku-kúyu in the Dófah district, to a fourth pond bearing the euphonous title of Ailabello.

Prettily situated in a secluded green hollow, and presenting about the same circumference as its neighbour, below which it is considerably depressed, this pool resembles a circular walled cistern, and is obviously the basin of an old crater. Its waters, alkaline, bitter, and strongly sulphureous even to the smell, receive constant accessions from a hot mineral well at the brink, and possessing the singular detergent property of bleaching the filthiest cloth, many of the Danákil were for once to be seen in flaunting white togas. Thence the road lay over a grassy plain, covered with volcanic sand and ashes, and shut in by cones of trivial altitude, forming another field of extinct craters, many very perfect, and each environed by its individual zone—whilst the circumjacent country, embracing a diameter of eight miles, exhibited through the superincumbent soil, tracts of jet black lava.

Apprehensions being entertained of the non-existence of pools at the station suited for the encampment, still some miles in advance, a détour was made from the main road to Ado, "the White Water," a very extensive lake, at which the skins were replenished and the thirst of the animals slaked. A belt of high acacia jungle embosomed this noble expanse, which exceeded two miles in diameter, the glassy surface in parts verdant with sheets of the lotus in full flower, and literally covered with aquatic fowls. Geese, mallard, whistling teal, herons, and flamingoes, with a new species of the *parra*, were screaming in all directions as they winged their flight from the point invaded, where a party of Bedouin shepherdesses deposed to having seen a troop of elephants bathing not half an hour before—the numerous prints of their colossal feet remaining in testimony, sunk fresh and heavy on the moist sands.

Prior to crossing the Háwash, the only sheep observed were the *Ovis aries laticaudata*, or Hejáz lamb, with sable head and neck, thick fatty tail, and fleece composed of hair instead of wool. This species had now, to the westward of the river, given place to the larger Abyssinian breed, with huge pendulous appendages of truly preposterous size, encumbered with fat, and vibrating to the animal's progress. Parti-coloured goats, armed with long wrinkled horns, still diversified the flocks, which were uniformly attended by small dogs with foxlike heads, spotted yellow and white, and evidently high in favour with their dark mistresses.

Several of these females wore around the neck large tinkling brazen bells, borrowed from the collar of an Abyssinian mule, and forming a very suitable accompaniment to the massive fabrications of pewter and copper which loaded their ears. Their long black tresses were braided into an infinity of streamers, each resembling the lash of a schoolboy's whip, and various most ingenious tattooed devices scarred their arms, temples, and bosoms. By the beaux of the caravan, unqualified homage was paid to certain coquettes, who carried milk jars curiously wrought of palm leaves, and studded with manifold cowrie shells. To the backs of sundry weird harridans were strapped skins containing sour curds, which attracted flies in the tens of millions usually seen around the molasses at a Banian's stall. No attempt was made to disturb those that clustered in their blear-inflamed eyes; and the swarms collected about the wrinkled comers of the mouth, were only put to flight when the hand was applied to second the wonted exclamation of surprise at the appearance of a white face, "*Nubbee Mohammadoo!*"

Numerous wigwams peeped through the extensive forest of aged camel-thorns, which borders on Lé Ado, and eventually debouches upon a succession of barren plains covered with herds of antelope. Two rough stone enclosures by the wayside were surmounted by poles, from which dangled the heads of as many lions, dilapidated by time, although still enveloped in the skin, and said to have been speared on this spot many years before by the Bedouins, who exalted these trophies in commemoration of the deed.

Immediately beyond this point lay the encamping ground at Wady Azbóti, where numerous shallow pools had been filled by the recent rain, but where the ill-starred cattle were compelled to content themselves with water only, not a vestige of grass or green herb remaining in the vicinity. It had, in feet, now become a proverb, that these two essential materials to existence could never be found in the Adel wilderness in one and the same place. Vast flights of locusts, which had assisted to lay the country bare, still carrying desolation in their progress, were shaping their destructive course towards Abyssinia. They quite darkened the air at the moment that the caravan halted; and a host of voracious adjutants wheeled high above the dense cloud, at one moment bursting with meteor-like velocity through the serried phalanx, and at the next stalking over the field to fill their capacious maws with the victims which their long scythe-fashioned pinions had swept incontinently from the sky.

The groves around Azbóti afforded a welcome supply of bustard, partridges, and guinea-fowl, together with the mhorr, and pigmy antelope; and on the return of the heavily-loaded Nimrods to the tent, infinite diversion was found in the horror depicted on the physiognomy of the warlike leader of the Hy Somauli band, whose old fashioned bob wig, quaint gait, and antiquated comicalities, had justly invested him with the sobriquet of "Doctor Syntax." The professor of natural history was as usual busily engaged in the preparation of cabinet specimens, when the old oddity advanced to see what was going on; and as the bodies of beetles and locusts were subjected to the process of toasting over the fire, his droll features were distorted by lines which revealed plainly enough an inward conviction entertained, that the operation was none other than culinary, and that the hideous insects were to be eaten.

But the war-whoop, without which few days ever drew to a close, had aroused the doctor from his cogitations; and at the head of his men he was presently in hot pursuit of a band of ruffians, who had cleverly contrived to drive off a camel pertaining to the káfilah. Returning with the booty after a long chase, the exploit was celebrated by the war-dance, which for an hour kept the camp in a fierce uproar. Formed in a circle, the excited warriors crouched low to the ground as they stomped *vis-à-vis*, and howled with the utmost fury. Then rising with one accord, they brandished their spears aloft, and vaulted frantically in the air through a maze of intricate figures. Next arrayed in line, a brave sprung ever and anon to the front, and striding up and down with mincing gait, went through strange gesticulations and contortions, as he recited the prowess of the dan, and urged it to future deeds of valour—the clash of spear and shield responding at every pause, whilst the wild chorus pealed along the ranks. Confusion now ensued: the band was engaged in a pantomimic conflict. Savage after savage, rolling his eyeballs, sprang panther-like across the loins of his nearest neighbour, and clinging fast with his beds, tightly clasped his erect opponent with the muscles of his legs. Creeses flashed brightly in the air; mock wounds were inflicted, and the form of dividing the windpipe having been duly gone through, long and loud arose, with the renewed dance, triumphant strains of "*Awey birooah! awey birooah!*" "I have slain my foe! I have slain my foe!"

Towards the close of the day, which was hot and muggy under the steam that arose from the saturated soil, a Bedouin rode consequentially into camp, and, after making his observations, departed even as he had come, without deigning an explanation of any sort. Attention was particularly attracted to this prying stranger, from the circumstance of his grey steed being branded on flank and wither with the Ethiopian sign of the cross. Delivering no message, although he was conjectured to be a retainer of Wulásma Mohammad, the Abogáz or *custos* of the frontier of Efát, whose post was now not distant more than twenty miles, the mysterious demeanour of this spy did not fail to strengthen a report, which had long been in circulation among the mischievous Danákil that at the court of Shoa, the British were far from being regarded in the light of welcome visitors, and further, that an armed party was in readiness to oppose entrance into the kingdom—a rumour which, however improbable, was unfortunately further supported by the extraordinary and unaccountable fact of no sort of recognition having, up to this period, been vouchsafed by His Most Gracious Majesty the King.

Rising tier above tier to the supremely soaring peak of Mamrat, "the Mother of Grace," with her domed head ever canopied in clouds, the lofty mountains which fortify the royal dominions now shot like giant castles from the sandy plain, the most conspicuous features in the landscape. Volcanic impediments, such as had beset the heretofore weary path, had at length finally ceased, but the glowing sulphur lulls of Sulláła reared their fantastic spires on the verge of the monotonous expanse; and high among the more venerable witnesses to the history of the troubled lowlands, the position of Ankóber was discernible to the naked eye, with the steep Cháka range stretching beyond at still greater elevation. The luxuriant verdure which clothed the rugged sides of the nearer slopes, whilst it contrasted strongly with the aridity of the barren tracts at their base, indicated the presence of the autumnal rains; and hereof further evidence was afforded in the low grumbling of frequent thunder, echoing like distant artillery among the serrated summits, as the heavy black clouds at intervals drew their smoky mantle across the scene, and veiled the monsters from sight.

The departure of the silent spy was followed by the arrival of a most boisterous visitor from the highlands. The hazy sun, shorn of his bright beams, and looming a dull fiery globe in the dense mist, had no sooner disappeared in wrath, than a furious whirlwind tore along the desert plain, and during the gloomy twilight, the storm, which had been cradled amid the mighty mountains, descended in desolation, like an angry giant from his keep.

Black masses of cloud, rolling impetuously along the steep acclivities, settled at length over the face of the waste, for a time shrouding the very earth in its dark dank embrace, only to render more striking the contrast to the dazzling light which in another moment had succeeded. Brilliant corruscations blazed and scintillated in every quarter of the fervid heavens, hissing and spluttering through the heavy fog, or darting like fiery serpents along the surface of the ground—at one instant awfully revealing the towering peaks that frowned far in the distance—at the next flashing in a hot sulphury flame through the centre of the encampment.

Meanwhile the deep roll of thunder continued without a moment's intermission, the prolonged growl of each startling clap varying ever as it receded in a fitful change of intonation; whilst the walling of the blast, accompanied by the sharp rattle of hail, and the impetuous descent of torrents of rain, completed the horrors of a tempest which, now at its height, careered madly over the unbroken plain. The soil had soon swallowed the deluge to overflowing. Muddy rivulets poured through every quarter of the flooded bivouac; and the heavy tarpaulins, which had afforded some temporary shelter, proving of little further avail, the shivering but still watchful party were exposed during many dismal hours that ensued to all the merciless fury of this unappeasable hurricane.

Chapter Thirty Six
Valley of Kokaï—Hostilities of
Wulásma Mohammad

A cool cloudy morning succeeding to this dreary, boisterous and uncomfortable night, the caravan was in motion before sunrise across the uninteresting plain of Azbóti, in parts completely swamped, and covered towards its borders with one interminable sheet of the aloë and *lilium*, growing beneath spreading acacias upon a gravelly soil. Then commenced a belt of hummocks, formed by prominences abutting from the high land of Abyssinia—a succession of hill and dale, thickly-wooded with a variety of timber, and still clothed with an undergrowth of the wild aloë, through which wary herds of Baéza threaded their way. The road soon entered the pebbly bed of a mountain stream, running easterly between precipitous basaltic cliffs towards the Háwash; but although such torrents of rain had fallen the preceding night, no water was discovered in the wooded wady of Kokaï, until reaching Dathára, nearly thirteen miles from the last encampment, where the party partook of the first crystal brook that had occurred during the entire weary journey from the sea-coast.

Three thousand feet above the ocean, with an invigorating, breeze and a cloudy sky, the climate of this principal pass into Southern Abyssinia, was that of a fine summer's day in England, rather than of the middle of July between the tropics. Here for the first time during the pilgrimage, the tent was erected under the shade of a wide-spreading tamarind, which, among many other trees of noble growth, graced the sequestered spot. Above the surrounding foliage the long white roofs of many of the royal magazines were visible, perched high on the blue mountain side. In the forked branches overhead were piled haystack-looking nests of gigantic dimensions, thatched with every attention to neatness and comfort—the small aperture left by the feathered architect turned in every instance to the eastward, and carefully secured from the weather; and perched on every twig, an assemblage of strange birds displayed their gay glittering plumage, or filled the cool air with melodious song.

But from the summit of an adjacent basaltic knoll, which was ascended towards the close of day, there burst upon the delighted gaze a prospect more than ever alluring of the Abyssinian Alps. Hill rose above hill, clothed in the most luxuriant and vigorous vegetation. Mountain towered over mountain in a smiling chaos of disorder; and the soaring peaks of the most remote range threw their hoary heads, sparkling with a white mantle of hail, far into the cold azure sky. Villages and hamlets embosomed in dark groves of evergreens were grouped in Arcadian repose. Rich fields of every hue chequered the deep lone valley; and the sun, bidding a diurnal farewell to his much-loved plains of the east, shot a last stream of golden light, varied as the hues of the Iris, over the mingled beauties of wild woodland scenery, and the labours of the Christian husbandman.

No delegate with greetings from the Negoos awaiting the British Embassy, and the frontier town of Fárri, where caravans are received by His Majesty's officers, being now only five miles distant, a letter was prepared, of which Mohammad Ali volunteered to be the bearer. In signifying gracious acquiescence to this arrangement, the Ras el Káfilah gravely intimated that the escort of Hy Somauli spearmen, famished at Killulloo by Ibrahim ibn Hámeïdo, declined permitting the departure of the son of Ali Abi, until they should have received the sum at which they were pleased to estimate their services. Little reason existing to be satisfied with the vigilance of this band of warriors, not one of the component members whereof, Doctor Syntax inclusive, had adopted the plan proposed by the poet for lengthening the days of existence by stealing a few hours from the night, compliance to the full extent of the exorbitant demand had previously been evaded. But as Izhák, in whom the truth was not, now falsely asserted and maintained that the Akil had taken his personal security for the sum, and as it was obviously of the last importance that arrival on the frontier should be timely reported, the money was reluctantly paid, and the courier set forth on his journey.

Rain was again ushering in the early hours of the night, when the unpleasant intelligence arrived that a certain Wulásma Mohammad was the delinquent, and that he had contrived effectually to thwart the intentions of his royal master. The king had commanded that his British visitors should be received on the western bank of the Háwash by an escort of honour. Under the commander-in-chief of the body-guard, three hundred matchlock-men had been for this purpose detached from the troops on service with His Majesty, and had actually reached Fárri, whence the jealous Moslem had dared to send them back upon the ridiculous pretext of being unable to obtain any tidings of the expected Franks.

This important functionary, in addition to his office of state-gaoler, is the hereditary Abogáz of the Mohammadan population of Argóbba on the east of Shoa, and the nature of his government exalts him in the eyes of all to the importance of a king. With the title of Wulásma—a word of uncertain derivation, known to Ludolf, the great historian of Abyssinia, who styles the dignitary "Pro rex of Efát"—he possesses unbounded influence over the frontier, his immediate duties being to preserve amicable relations with the Adaïel occupying the plain of the Háwash, and to protect káfilahs and merchants arriving from the independent principality of Hurrur, or from the coast of Tajúra. His functions as keeper of the state prison secure for him the respect of all. Christians as well as Islams, who have the fear of a dungeon before their eyes; and although numerous Abogásoch or Wulásmoch, governors of small detached provinces, share his power, the name and influence of all are dim under the light that glares from his loop-holed residence at Góncho.

It is the invariable policy of the haughty Abogáz to assume the great man to all travellers, since it is generally understood that through him alone foreigners can be received and forwarded, or if necessary presented to the Negoos. This arrangement involves not only trouble, but considerable expense. His despotic Majesty claiming the prerogative of franking every visitor through his territories, and a portion of the attendant outlay falling upon the functionary who may be honoured with the royal commands.

Openly opposed to European innovation, Mohammad particularly disliked the advent of the British Embassy, and was obviously doing his utmost to thwart the more liberal views of the crown, by treating the strangers with disrespect. The imperial order that an escort of matchlock-men should for the first time cross the hill frontier, and proceed into the plain of the Háwash, to do honour to the Christian guests, not only rankled in his Moslem breast, but was calculated to interfere with his resolution to preserve inviolate the avenues to the sea-coast. His intrigues had rendered abortive all attempts to communicate with the Court; and whilst the approach of the Embassy was not reported until its actual arrival at Dathára, his non-compliance with the order given had resulted most prejudicially, the Danákil guides being now more than ever unwilling to persuade themselves that the party would be welcome.

Preparations were making the following morning to continue the march to Fárri, when the burly functionary was seen pompously approaching with measured step, followed by a retinue of many hundred armed followers, whose shaven heads rose unturbaned above flowing white mantles. Far from announcing himself in the customary manner, he remained seated in portentous dignity, beneath the shade of a venerable tamarind by the road-side, until, every camel having been loaded, the caravan was moving off the ground. A peremptory message was then received through one of his myrmidons, to the effect that he stood strictly charged with the king's commands to suffer not one of the party to advance until the next day, and that he was prepared to enforce the interdiction. There seemed little reason to doubt of this being a premeditated falsehood, as it afterwards proved to be; but the Ras el Káfilah having heard the injunction repeated in presence of the Wulásma Suleïman Moosa, Abogáz of Chánnoo, as coming direct from His Majesty, timidly declined any infringement, and again threw down the loads.

Condescending at length in moody sullenness to approach with his host of retainers, the triumphant potentate, armed with the rosary, or chaplet of one hundred beads, which denoted his intolerant faith, squeezed his pursy figure into a chair, and composed himself with much apparent satisfaction at the success that had attended his scheme of opposition. A debauched, ill-favoured, bloated specimen of mortality, the lines of intemperance were deeply graven on his truculent visage, which was at once cunning, sinister, and forbidding. But the party were not long troubled with his obnoxious presence. The reception he experienced, although civil, was distant and studiously formal, and the sun, beating in a full blaze upon his bald crown, rendered his position so extremely untenable, that after stiffly murmuring replies to the customary inquiries anent the health and well-being of his august master, he rose unceremoniously, and abruptly withdrew.

Throughout this brief and very unbending interview, a brawny retainer stood behind the chair, denuded to the waist. In his right hand he ostentatiously displayed the chief gaoler's sword of state—a short heavy blade upon the model of the old Roman falchion, enclosed in a scabbard of massive silver; and his left arm supported a buckler of stiff bull's hide, elaborately emblazoned with crescents and brass studs. The benevolent and prepossessing aspect of the Wulásma Suleïman Moosa, who occupied a second seat, offered a striking contrast to the repulsive arrogance of his scowling colleague. On his right side, protruding upwards with the curve of a scorpion's tail, he wore a semicircular weapon, also denominated a sword, though in fact more nearly allied to a reaping-hook—a proud badge of office, with a fluted tulip-shaped termination to the silver scabbard, which, according to the wont of the despot, had been conferred on the occasion of his first installation in office, but which ludicrously interfered with comfort in an armchair.

During the residue of the day, the conduct of the state-gaoler was perfectly in unison with his character and previous hostile proceedings. He brought the white visitors neither presents nor supplies, according to the rules of Abyssinian hospitality; and although made fully aware that the camp was drained of provisions, prevented purchases by the undue exercise of his influence and authority. A pelting rain during the night, from which his sleek person was defended by naught save the pervious branches of a tamarind, had not tended to soften the asperities, or to alleviate the sourness of his aspect, when the day dawned; and it was only on finding the party prepared to advance at the hazard of forcible opposition, that he finally yielded the point, and betwixt his closed teeth muttered his grumbling consent to an arrangement which he felt longer unable with prudence to oppose. "The English are a great nation," whispered the nephew of Ali Shermárki, as he passed the haughty Abogáz, "and you had better take care to treat them civilly. *Wullahi!* one of their ships of war would carry this káfilah over the water, and you and all your host of followers into the bargain."

Chapter Thirty Seven
Dinómali. Greetings from the Negoos at Fárri, on the Frontier of his Dominions

Gradually ascending through a hilly and well-wooded country, still a positive garden of the wild aloe, the road now led through a succession of deep glades, which opened in turn upon verdant mountain scenery; and at on early hour, after the first signs of cultivation had been afforded in the truly grateful sight of ploughs turning up the soil, the tents were erected on the open plain of Dinómali.

At this, the frontier station of Argóbba, are levied the royal import duties of ten per cent; and a scene of noise, bustle, and confusion did not fail to ensue, such as is wont to attend the arrival of every caravan. In his character of collector-general of customs, the pompous Wulásma took seat below a tree in the centre, whilst his myrmidons, beleaguering every load the moment it was removed from the camel, prevented all access on the part of the owner until scrutinising search had been instituted by the secretary for the salt trade, and the imperial scribes had, by a tedious process denominated writing, completed an inventory of contents. From time immemorial it had been the law of the realm to regard the despotic ruler as the proprietor of every moveable in the land; and it was not without many looks of incredulity and amazement that the custom-house officers now received the astounding intimation that they would touch the baggage of the British Embassy at their peril.

Thus for the first time thwarted in their prerogative of forcing open boxes, and inspecting the wares they contained, Débtera Tekla Zion and his brother scribes were tempted to attribute the opposition offered to the truth of a vague report already current, that a foreign king was being smuggled into Abyssinia for evil. And they were still standing in mute astonishment, with idle ink-horns dangling from their hands, lost in conjecture of the probable consequences involved by the unprecedented interference exercised, when a message was received expressive of the compliments and best wishes of Sáhela Selássie. Still at a distance from Ankóber, His Majesty had resolved, in order to hasten the interview with his guests, to proceed at once to the capital, whither the English were invited to repair with all possible expedition.

The arrival of this unlooked-for salutation, which was coupled with an affirmative answer to a request previously made, that the presents in charge of the Embassy might neither be interfered with, nor subjected to the usual custom-house scrutiny when crossing the frontier, had the effect of bringing to his senses the overbearing Wulásma; and, in accordance with the king's instructions, oxen, sheep, bread, beer, and hydromel were liberally supplied without another moment's demur. But a fresh source of delay and annoyance forthwith arose on the part of the Ras el Káfilah, whose latent object being to transfer the charge of Danákil caravans from the hands of the corpulent and now civil gaoler to those of Wulásma Suleïman Moosa, made the acceptance of supplies at the hand of the former a pretext for throwing up his functions and setting out to Ankóber, exclaiming as he mounted his mule in a towering passion, for the avowed purpose of laying his complaint at the footstool of the throne, "Am not I the brother of the Sultán of Tajúra?"

But the furious elder had not proceeded far on his adventurous journey, ere his ears were saluted by repeated discharges of musketry, accompanied by martial music and a solemn vocal chorus. These served to announce the advent of Ayto Kátama, commander-in-chief of the imperial body-guard, with the escort of honour consisting of three hundred matchlock-men, who were to have received the Embassy on the banks of the Háwash. The arrival of this important personage, whose schoolboyish sallies ill became his years and high military functions, was speedily followed by the appearance of Ayto Wolda Hána, governor of Ankóber, and first nobleman in the realm, also fraught with congratulations. His presence had the effect of recalling the irritated Ras to a sense of duty; and no efficient carriage having been provided by the Abogáz, it was finally arranged, after many difficulties, objections, and disputes, that the baggage should be transported to Fárri, other two miles in advance, where Mohammadan porters could be obtained in sufficient numbers to convey it to its final destination—the mountains in every part being deemed quite inaccessible to the camel.

Although the distance from Fárri did not exceed a mile, the lateness of the hour at which this accommodation was vouchsafed, rendered it impossible to carry the measure into effect until the following day. The governor of Ankóber meanwhile politely insisted upon charging himself with the baggage, his officious zeal extending even to the effects of private individuals, whereby much inconvenience was entailed. But notwithstanding his garrulous protestations, and the presence of so large a body of the royal troops, everything was finally left unprotected; and, before his negligence was discovered, four of the remaining mules had been stolen from their pickets by the marauders who infest the neighbourhood.

Loaded for the thirty-fifth and last time with the baggage of the British Embassy, the caravan, escorted by the detachment of Ayto Kátama, with flutes playing and muskets echoing, and the heads of the warriors decorated with white plumes, in earnest of their bold exploits during the late expedition, advanced on the afternoon of the 16th of July, to Fárri, the frontier town of the kingdom of Efát. Clusters of conical-roofed houses, covering the sloping sides of twin hills which form a gorge wherein the royal dues are deposited, here presented the first permanent habitations that had greeted the eye since leaving the sea-coast; rude and ungainly, but right welcome signs of transition from depopulated wastes to the abodes of man.

As well from the steepness of the rugged mountains of Abyssinia, which towered overhead, as from the pinching climate of their wintry summits, the camel becomes useless as a beast of burthen; and none being ever taken beyond the frontier, many of the Wulásma's retinue now gazed at the ungainly quadrupeds for the first time. The "ship of the desert" has been created for the especial benefit of sultry, arid, and waterless plains, such as those now crossed, where no other domesticated animal could long exist, but where, even under the most scorching radiation of heat, when the skin peels from the parched lips of the pilgrim, and the horizon beams as with the fires of an hundred volcanoes, the soft lustrous eye of the patient dromedary loses not a jot of its wonted brilliancy. But numbers had been dreadfully wrung during the tedious march, those especially which carried tent-poles and other unmanageable burdens; and amongst others, two of the finest had sung under the weight of the galloper-gun. No sooner was the load now removed, than a swarm of parasitic birds, with brilliant golden eyes, here for the first time seen, swarmed around the galled part, and having dived into the gaping wounds, without causing perceptible annoyance to the sufferer, became so engrossed in the removal of ticks and maggots with their crimson bills, that several were made prisoner with the hand.

Boxes and bales as they arrived were deposited within a stone enclosure in the centre of the area; and the bloated Wulásma, again seated in regal dignity beneath an ancient acacia, which threw its slender shade over the heterogeneous pile, placing Ayto Wolda Hána upon his right hand, with the aid of the royal scribes and their ink-horns commenced an inventory *de novo*. Vigorous attempts to force open the cases were once more resisted, with complete success. Earnest expostulations tried in turn by the Moslem and the Christian, were alike unheeded; and amid noise, clamour, and confusion, such as could ill be described, the inquisitive functionaries were fain, as before, to content themselves with a list of packages in the gross. Rough conjectural estimates of the number of muskets contained in each matted roll were however clandestinely formed, by dint of squeezing and pinching; and these too were committed to writing, as though fears were entertained lest the king might now, in his own dominions, be defrauded of a portion of the investment transported in safety thither from a distant land.

Hajji Mohammad, a respectable old slave-dealer in the suite of the Abogáz, had during this interim obligingly undertaken to solve certain puzzling geographical questions proposed, and with a staff was methodically tracing on the sand, for the edification of his European audience, the position of the Háwash in its upper course. An insane old Hássóba, long resident at Fárri, whose head laboured under the effect of sundry wounds received in youth, had unfortunately become violently excited by too copious libations in honour of the safe arrival of his clansmen. To the annoyance of every one, he had been bawling incessantly for many hours, and he presently staggered up to ascertain if he could throw light upon the subject under discussion.

"What do you know about the Háwash?" he exclaimed, in a violent passion, as the name of the lone river fell upon his ear — "Pray where did you learn about the Háwash, or the Ittoo, or the Aroosi?" — and suiting the action to the word, his cudgel rattled heavily over the crown of the unoffending pilgrim to the shrine of the Prophet. Nettled at this unprovoked assault, the venerable man retorted with interest — blows pattered thick and fast, a crowd collected, creeses were drawn, and the friends of the respective parties felt themselves bound to interfere. The belligerent Hajji was held to prevent his committing murder; and the Adel geographer, as he walked reluctantly away, under a shower of stones, turning frequently to breathe defiance to the object of his ire, repeated with a sneer, "Here is the Háwash indeed: what the devil does that old donkey know about the Háwash?"

Meanwhile arrived a special messenger, bearing reiterated compliments from the Negoos, with a horse and a mule from the royal stud, attired in the peculiar trappings and colours which in Shoa pertain solely to Majesty. The bridles and breastplates glittered with studs and bosses of polished metal; gay embroidery in coloured worsted covered the saddle-cloth of the mule, and a collection of silver chains, jingles, and bells, encircled her neck. At sight hereof women and girls enveloped in blood-red shifts, who had thronged to the busy scene to stare at the white strangers, at once burst into a loud scream of acclamation. A group of hooded widows, occupying an adjacent public asylum, thrust their fingers into their ears, and joined in the clamour. Escort and camel-drivers, now at their journey's end, had placed no bounds to their hilarity. A fat ox that had been promised was turned loose among the spectators—pursued by fifty savages with gleaming creeses—and ham-strung by a dexterous blow, which threw it bellowing to the earth in the height of its mad career. The rival clans of lean curs, that are respectively quartered on the dung-heaps of the twin hills, and suffer no intrusion into each other's domains, rushed to the neutral ground, and forthwith commenced an indiscriminate engagement over the garbage; and whilst Débtera Tekla Zion, still counting and recounting, amended his long list with untiring perseverance, crowds of porters and lounging visitors added the mite of their united voices to the din, tumult, and intolerable uproar which continued until close of day.

Predatory incursions of the Galla upon the Argóbba frontier are frequent, and not many weeks had passed away since six of the king's liege subjects were murdered within the precincts of the encamping ground. In defiance of tempestuous weather, two European soldiers and an officer had been on guard without shelter during every night of the long and tedious march, and the sergeant of the escort had every hour personally relieved the sentries: but the exposed position of the baggage, added to the evil character borne by the spot, and the experience already gained at Dinómali, still precluded the discontinuance of watch and ward, whereof all were heartily weary.

In the dead of night an alarm caused all to spring from their couches on the hard ground, and to stand prepared for the reception of an unseen foe, whose approach was announced by the blast of some hideous war-horn. Halters had been broken, and mules and horses were charging over the tent ropes, nor was the real cause of the confusion discovered for some minutes. A thirsty dog, unacquainted with the artifice resorted to by the fox that needed water, had recklessly thrust his mangy head so deep into an earthen jar that he was unable to withdraw it, and rushing he knew not whither, was giving vent through his strange proboscis to fearful hollow groans, which might well have instilled terror into the breast of the superstitious, and did not fail to elicit ceaseless howls from the canine occupants of the dunghill.

The delinquent was shot, and order being at length restored, those who were entitled to slumber again proceeded to avail themselves of the privilege. After pacing his beat some hours beyond the wonted period of relief, the sentinel who mounted at midnight hailed the officer on duty. Receiving no reply to the challenge, he approached the door of the tent, and there, sad to relate, the first breach of discipline was detected on the part of the guardian of the camp, who, worn out by incessant vigils, was on this, his last watch, lying fast asleep upon his post, with a pistol in each hand!

Chapter Thirty Eight
A Parting Tribute of Gratitude
Inscribed to the People of Adel

Tradition asserts that prior to the invasion of Graan, "the mighty Adel monarch," who overran and dismembered once-powerful Ethiopia, the eastern limit of the empire was Jebel Aiúlloo, known to the Abyssinians as Mount Azulo. But although frequently invaded, no portion of the wide plain of the Háwash has been reconquered, whether by Sáhela Seléssie, or by his ancestors. The relatives of certain of those in authority have been made prisoners by treachery, and as hostages are held in close durance by the king, but the boasted influence of the Abogáz is principally supported by conciliation, and by the annual presentation of cloths and specie to the various chiefs and elders—a measure having for its object to preserve the avenues to the sea-coast and to the Bahr Assál, whereon Shoa and Efát are almost entirely dependant for foreign wares, and for salt, which the country does not produce.

The powerful independent chieftain of the principal section of Gibdósa, who occupy the detached hill of Rása, across the Róbi river, northward of Dinómali, is one of those in nominal alliance with the Negoos; but his wild Moslems make constant predatory inroads upon the frontier of Argóbba, slaying Christians and Mohammadans of either sex, without any compunction; and the policy of His Majesty prohibiting retaliation, however aggravated the outrage, Anbássa Ali, or "the Lion," who like Esau of old is said to be covered with hair from the crown of the head even unto the sole of the foot, not unfrequently makes hostile demonstrations in person, which require all the Wulásma's tact and diplomatic cunning to avert.

From Háo, on the eastern side of the Háwash, to Fárri, the intervening tract, under the nominal jurisdiction of Mohammad Abogáz, is in occupation of a mixed nomade population, not remarkable for their honesty, and composed from numerous subdivisions of the Danákil, but principally from the Burhánto or Adáli, under ibn Hámed deen Hássan. This latter, which takes Adaïel in the plural, is the clan of the reigning Sultán of Tajúra; and being in days of yore the most powerful and important tribe in the nation, its name has been imparted to the entire country, now corrupted into Adel.

In time of war with the adjacent Galla on the south, or when called upon to repel the predatory invasions of the Mudaïto, the tribes westward of the Háwash assemble with the Tukhaïel, the Débeni, the Derméla, the Rookhba, the Wóema, and the Hy Somauli, the extent of whose respective territories has already been defined. These, with the Abli or Dinsérra, under Mohammad Ali, surnamed Jeróa, or "the Thief," which is the tribe of Hámed Bunaïto, present wuzir and heir-apparent to the throne of Tajúra — the Adaneïto and Nakur, under Shehém Mulakoo — the Dondamétta, the Duttagóora, and the Hássóba, led respectively by Ahmed Kámil, Sheïkh Déeni, and Déeni ibn Ibrahim — collectively assume the title of Débenik-Wóema, *k* being the Dankáli conjunction.

Adalo bin Hámed, who leads a section of the Gibdósa encamped at Haódé and Dunné, occasionally unites with the Débenik-Wóema in the time of their need, but he is held virtually independent. The fourth and last section of the Débeni, under the authority of Mahmóodi, has its tents at the isolated volcanic mountain of Fantáli, southward of Dinómali, where reside also the united Adaïel clans Uluaïto, Muffa, and Eyrolásso, under the great "brave" Lamúllifan.

These tribes occupy the whole extent of country between Abyssinia and Mirsa Raheïta, near the entrance to the Red Sea, the head-quarters of Roofa Boorhán, sheïkh of a subdivision of the Duttagóora. Thence they stretch along the coast to the south-eastward, and from Góobut el Kharáb, between the parallels, bounded on the south by the Eesah and other Somauli tribes, and flanked on the north by the Mudaïto.

The Adaïel or Danákil population, which, including the Mudaïto, extends as far as Arkeeko, entitles itself Afer, and claims to be descended from Arab invaders, who, in the seventh century of the Christian era, overran and colonised the low tract which forms a zone between the Abyssinian Alps and the coast of the Red Sea. To a certain extent the northern tribes are subject to the Nayib of Arkeeko, whose authority is recognised in much the same proportion as that of the feeble Sultán of Tajúra by the southern clans; but although speaking the same language, they can hardly be said to constitute a nation, being so widely dispersed, that for many days together not a trace of man is to be discovered over the joyless deserts which form the lot of his inheritance, scorched by an ardent sun, and alive only with "moving pillars of sand."

From time immemorial every individual has been his own king. Each marauding community is marked by a wild independence; and the free spirit of the whole is to be traced in the rapine, discord, and bloodshed which universally prevails. Theirs is "an iron sky, and a soil of brass," where the clouds drop little rain, and the earth yields no vegetation. It is no "land of rivers of water," nor have the "lines fallen in pleasant places." The desert stretches far on every side, strewed with black boulders of heated lava, and enveloped by a glowing atmosphere. In this country of perfidy and vindictive ferocity, the proprietors of the barren land murder every stranger who shall intrude; and the common benefits of water are an object of perpetual contest. Reprisal and revenge form the guiding maxim of all. Monsters, not men, their savage propensities are portrayed in a dark and baleful eye, and the avenger of blood is closely dogging the footsteps of one half the population.

As laziness is the chief source of African misery at large, so is it with the Danákil in particular. They possess that "conceit in their misery" which induces them to despise the labours of the cultivator; and such is the characteristic want of water, that, excepting at Aussa, agriculture is unknown, even in its rudest form. A pastoral, itinerant, and belligerent people, divided into endless clans and ramifications, under divers independent chieftains, their mode of living entitles them to rank only one step in civilisation above the positive savage who depends for daily subsistence upon the chase and upon the spontaneous productions of nature.

Born to the spear, and bred in eternal strife with his predatory neighbours, each lawless member of the straggling community inherits the untameable spirit of the descendants of Ishmaël; and it is made subservient to all the worst vices and passions inherent in the semi-barbarian. In his very attitude and bearing there is that which proclaims him in his own opinion Lord of the Universe, entitled to enjoy, with a thankless heart, all that he is capable of enjoying. No favour claims his gratitude—nothing demands a thought beyond the present moment. Unlike the Arab Bedouin, he is too indolent and improvident during seasons of plenty, to convert the produce of his flocks and herds into a store against the coming day of drought and famine. Gorged to repletion, the residue is suffered to go to waste; and so long as his belly is full, his licentiousness gratified, and he has leisure to lounge about in listless idleness, the measure of his happiness is complete, and the sun may rise and set without his troubling his head as to the mode in which the day has been passed, or how the next meal is to be provided.

Many of the Adaïel are extensive owners of camels, and deal largely in slaves—a trade which yields three hundred per cent, with the least possible risk or trouble to the merchant; but when not upon the journey periodically undertaken to acquire the materials for this traffic, all lead a life of indolence and gross sensuality—eating, sleeping, and indulging in the baser passions, according to the bent of their vicious inclinations. Their delight is to be dirty and to be idle. They wear the same cloth without ablution until it fairly drops from the back; and abhorring honest labour, whether agricultural or handicraft, pass the day in drowsiness, or in the enjoyment of a quiet seat before the hamlet, where the scandal of the community is retailed. Basking in the sun, and arranging their curly locks with the point of the skewer, they here indulge in unlimited quantities of snuff, and mumble large rolls of tobacco and ashes, which are so thrust betwixt the under lip and the white teeth, as to impart the unseemly appearance of a growing wen, and if temporarily removed are invariably deposited behind the left ear. No race of men in the world stink more offensively; but whilst polluting the atmosphere with rancid tallow and putrid animal intestines, they never condescend to approach a Christian without holding their own noses!

Amongst the Danákil are to be found some of the most scowling, ill-favoured, and hideous-looking savages in the universe, but the features of the majority have an Arab cast which supports the legend of their origin; and notwithstanding the influence exerted upon the lineaments by passions uncontrolled, the expression of many is pleasing, and even occasionally intellectual. All are muscular and active, but singularly scraggy and loosely knit, and to an easy shuffling gait is added a national addiction to standing cross-legged. Young as well as old take infinite pains to disfigure the person, and thus to render it ferocious in appearance. Scars obtained in brawls and conflicts from stones and cold steel are esteemed the highest ornaments, and the breast and stomach are usually seamed with a mystic maze of rhombs and reticulated triangles, produced by scarification with a sharp fragment of obsidian, so as to resemble the plan of a fortified town of days gone by.

The upper lip is denuded with the creese, and the scanty beard suffered to flourish in curls along the cheeks and over the chin; whilst the hair, coarse and long, saturated with grease and mutton fat from infancy, and exposed during life to the fiercest sun, becomes crisped into a thick curly mop, like a counsellor's wig, which is shaved behind on a line between the ears, and constitutes the first great pride of the proprietor. The picking it out into a due spherical form affords employment during his ample leisure, and the contemplation of its wild perfection is the predominant object when the mirror is placed within his grasp. Baldness commences at an early age, and many of the ancient dandies seek protection from the solar influence under sheep-skin perukes of preposterous size, their artificial curls, in common with those that are natural, displaying an ornamented wooden spike or bodkin, which serves as a comb, and is often fancifully carved and provided with two or even three prongs.

The operation of greasing this wig without the aid of the barber is original. A lump of raw fat, cut from the overgrown tail of the Berbera sheep, having been some time masticated and mumbled, is expelled into the hands, betwixt the palms of which it is reduced by rubbing to a suitable consistency, and then transferred *en masse* to the crown. Exposure to the fierce rays of a tropical sun soon conveys the desired nourishment to the roots of the hair. A number of jets and brilliants, which first adorn the periwig, are presently fried into oily shreds, and the liquid tallow, adulterated with dirt, trickling in streams adown the swarthy visage and over the neck, exhales the most sickening of odours. All, however, cannot afford this luxury of the toilet, nor is it every one who can resist the temptation of swallowing the dainty morsel when once consigned to the mouth; and hence is seen many a poll of sun-burnt hair, in colour and consistency resembling the housemaid's cobweb broom which is quaintly denominated "the Pope's head."

The simple costume of the Bedouin consists of a piece of checked cloth wrapped loosely about the loins, and descending to the knees so as to resemble a kilt or short petticoat; whilst a cotton robe is thrown over the shoulder after the manner of the Roman toga. Miserly in disposition, few outward ornaments grace his person, save an occasional necklace of fat, and a few armlets and bracelets composed of potent passages from the Korán either stitched in leather, or enveloped in coloured thread. A thong adorned with a metal button girds to the right hip of old and young a creese two feet in length, the wooden hilt of which is decorated with a pewter stud, whilst the scabbard is ornamented with an aromatic sprig, employed as a tooth-brush, and masticated for hours together.

Three inches broad in the blade, and possessing a truly murderous crook in the centre, the creese is doubtless a most formidable weapon at close quarters. With it the Danákil builds his house; with it he slays the animal, and flays the carcase. It is his sword in battle, his knife at the table, his razor at the toilet, his hatchet, and his nail-parer. A savage desirous of illustrating the most approved exercise, after whetting the blade upon a stone, capers about describing a series of flourishes and cuts, both under and over the shield, stabbing and parrying to the right and to the left, until at length comes the last grand touch of disembowelment, when a ripping motion is accompanied by a bound into the air, and a howl of perfect satisfaction such as might be conjectured to issue from the jaws of the glutted vampire.

The spear, which is seldom out of the hand of the Danákil, is some seven feet in length, a shaft of tough close-grained wood called *"adepto"* being heavily poised with metal at the butt, and topped by a blade from ten to fifteen inches long, by three broad, reduced to as keen an edge as constant scouring with sand and grease can impart. Great aversion is entertained to this weapon being stepped over, and its fall to the ground, independently of the damage that might be sustained, is regarded as an evil omen, and believed to destroy its power over the flesh and blood of an enemy. The spear of a chief only is mounted with bands of brass and copper wire, but the points of all are graced alike with a lump of sheep's-tail fat. Although sometimes employed as a missive, the pike exercise is more usually resorted to—the warrior stealing onward in a crouching position, and springing suddenly with a yell and a cat-like bound to transfix the body of his foe. "None but a woman would retain the spear in the hour of battle," quoth one of the braves—"the creese is the hand to hand weapon!"

The shield, fashioned out of the stiff hide of the Báeza, or of the wild buffalo, is a perfect circle, of from one to two feet in diameter, with the rim turned outwards, and the centre convexed, for the purpose of checking the flight or launch of the missive. A button or boss which forms the apex is usually adorned with some proud trophy of the chase, in addition to the red beard of a he-goat, undeviatingly attached as a charm. A small bag, slung in the interior of the buckler, contains the portable wealth of the proprietor, and a forked stick is annexed to the hand strap, to admit of suspension to a tree. Engaged, the warrior keeps the shield in a continual revolving motion, in strict accordance with the movement of the eyes, which in fierce and violent frenzy are rolled in the sockets during the continuance of the conflict.

Cruel, bloodthirsty, and vindictive, the Danákil do not possess that spirit of individual enterprise or chivalry, or that reckless disregard of personal danger which, to certain races of men, imparts the stamp of military habits; but a season of scarcity dooms every neighbouring tribe whose pastures are more favoured than their own, to invasion, massacre, and pillage. A fiendish whoop is the signal for the gathering of the clan; and, obedient to the call, each man at arms, grasping spear and shield, abandons his wretched wigwam with truly savage alacrity. His fierce and untamed passions now riot uncontrolled, and those who during the foray are guilty of the greatest enormities, strut about on return amongst their fellows, bedecked with ostrich plumes, and other badges of distinction, reciting each to some wild tune, the tale of his bloody exploits.

Morose, and possessing little perception of the ridiculous, witticisms and hilarity in conversation are restricted to the ribald jest; but brawls are frequent, and the bivouac is often cheered by the wild chorus selected from a choice collection breathing in every line self-sufficiency and defiance to the foe. Accompanied by savage gestures and contortions—now menacing, now mincing, and now furious—these strains are chanted during the livelong night with clear and energetic throats, chiefly with the design of intimidating, by the noisy clamour, any hostile party that may be lurking in the vicinity of the encampment, intent either upon the requital of injuries done, or the acquisition of fame by aggressions unprovoked.

Superstitious to the last degree, the itinerant Bedouin takes the field arrayed in a panoply of amulets, designed as a defence against witchcraft, and to be thrown towards the enemy in the hour of battle. A verse from the Korán, sewn up in leather, and hung about the neck, secures him against all incorporeal enemies. No whirlwind ever sweeps across the path without being pursued by a dozen savages with drawn creeses, who stab into the centre of the dusty column in order to drive away the evil spirit that is believed to be riding on the blast. All have firm faith in the incarnation of the Devil, who is described as a monster with perpendicular eyes, capable of rolling along the ground with the rotatory motion of a ball; and Ibrahim Shehém Abli, a most unblushing liar, and no less notable a necromancer than warrior, confidently asserted his individual ability to raise seven hundred of these demons for evil, during any moonlight night of the entire year.

The mosque and the muezzin have no existence in the interior, where religion gradually shades away; and, unlike the people of Tajúra, there is here little external display of Islamism observable, save in the bigoted detestation evinced towards those of every other than the Mohammadan creed. But although prostrations are wanting, and rosaries are untold, the vagrants still preserve their knavish reputations unblemished. The white feather, which in Europe is the emblem of cowardice, is appropriately placed in the head of these midnight assassins, and the neighbouring tribes have not ill-portrayed the national character in the assertion, that "the tongues of the Adaïel are long for the express purpose of lying, that their arms are long but to admit of their pilfering the property of others, and that their legs are long in order that they may run away like poltroons in the day of danger and retribution."

Chapter Thirty Nine
The Gentle Adaïel, and Farewell to them

"Yet one kind kiss before we part,
Drop a tear, and bid adieu."

To be the wife of a true believer, in whatever state of society, from the most refined to the most barbarous, is to be cursed in the fullest acceptation of the word. But of the two extremes, many, if the choice were given, would doubtless prefer the drudgery that falls to the lot of the partner of the untaught savage, with all the manifold discomforts attending precarious subsistence, to the immolation and seclusion, which in civilised Mohammadan countries, is imposed upon the fairest of God's works. Taking no part with her lord in the concerns of this world—taught to expect no participation in the happiness of that which is to come—she is a prisoner kept to minister to the lusts of the flesh; and the higher the state of cultivation—the more exalted the rank of the captive—so much the more rigorous is the restraint imposed.

In the European acceptation of the term, small traces are here to be found of the sentiment of love; and jealousy, when it does exist, would seldom appear to arise from any regard for the object that has created the feeling. The Dankáli female has contrived to retain her natural right of liberty; and so long as the wife performs the labour required at her hands, she is at full liberty to flirt unreproved, to the full extent of her coquettish inclinations. Upon Baileela devolves the task of leading the foremost camel, or carrying the heavy burthen slung by a sharp rope which passes across her breast. She fetches water and wood, prepares the milk, and boils the meat. She it is who weaves mats of the date-leaf for the use of her listless and indolent lord; tends his flocks of sheep and goats, dismantles and erects his wigwam when migrations are undertaken to distant pools and pastures; and, seated at his feet, chases away the flies which disturb his repose beneath the shade of the palm. Here, however, the needle is monopolised by the male, and he is sometimes to be seen industriously stitching a new leathern petticoat for his hard-worked partner, who, conscious of the fleeting nature of her charms, makes the utmost of her short lease; and in the nature of her occupation finds ample opportunities for indulgence.

The features of the Bedouin damsel, although degenerate, resemble those of the Arabian mother, from whom she claims descent; and so close a similarity pervades the community at large, that one mould would appear to have been employed for every individual composing it. Nature being suffered to model her daughters according to her will, their figures during a brief period are graceful; but feminine symmetry is soon destroyed by the constant pressure of heavy loads against the chest, and under the fiery heat of her native sands, the nymph is presently transformed into the decrepit hag, with bent back and waddling gait. A short apron of bullock's hide, with frilled edges, is tied above the hips with a broad band, the sport of every wanton whirlwind; but from the waist upwards the person is unveiled. A coif of blue calico covers the head of those who have entered the conjugal state, whilst that of the virgin is unattired; but the hair of all is arranged in an infinity of elaborate plaits falling to the shoulders, and liberally greased. So are also sundry narrow bands of raw hide, which are usually tied above the ankles by way of charms to strengthen the legs, and which, contracting as they dry, sink deep below the surface of the part compressed.

A petalled sprig, appearing to grow out of the waistband, ascends on either side of the spine, in tattooed relief, resembling tambour work, and diverging across the ribs, finishes in fancy circles around the bosom according to the taste of the designer. This is a constant quantity, and the charms of many a belle are further heightened by scarification—an angle to break the evenness of the smooth forehead, or the arc of a circle to improve the dimple on the cheek, being favourite devices. From the ears of all who can afford personal ornament, depend two conical drops wrought of thick brass wire spirally coiled, resting on a curved iron base, and separated by two broad horizontal bands of pewter. When the wearer is in activity, the flapping of these cumbrous metallic appendages is ridiculous enough, and the rattle may be heard to a considerable distance as they come into violent collision with a necklace composed of a medley of beads, bones, cowrie shells, jingles, and amulets, strung in many rows upon a leathern collar embedded in dirt and grease, and terminating in a large rhomb of pewter. Bracelets and anklets of the same metal are usual, and the ornament of a squalling brat with inflamed weasel-like eyes slung over the back, is rarely wanting to complete the figure—a jerk to the right or to the left bringing it readily across the shoulder when occasion demands.

The Bedouin wigwam—a rectangle of eight feet in length by six broad, and five high—is constructed of a succession of branches in couples, curved before the fire, and lashed in the form of a lip-arch. A mat composed of date leaves forms the roof; and the whole fabric, wherein the hand of no master builder is visible, is thus readily transferred from place to place. "*Omnia mea mecum fero"* should form the motto of the wandering Dankáli, whose only furniture consists of a tressel hollowed at the top to serve as a pillow—a luxury restricted to the male sex. In the huts of the more wealthy, wooden platters and ladles sometimes form part of the household gear, together with closely-woven mat baskets to contain milk; but this beverage is more usually consigned to a bag of sheep or goat skin—sun-dried flesh, grease, grain, and water, being lodged also in similar receptacles.

Milk forms the principal diet of this Arcadian race; and they deride the dwellers in cities for eating birds or fowls, declaring that the flesh must have travelled upon four legs during life to be at all palatable. An ancient camel, a buck goat, or a bull calf, is occasionally slaughtered with a *Bismillah*, and the flesh not immediately consumed cut into long thin collops, and dried in the sun to be stuffed again into the skin for future use. Meat is broiled among the embers upon closely-packed pebbles, which prevents it coming into contact with the ashes; and the master of the house, taking his seat upon the ground beside a lump of raw liver, places a wedge-shaped stone under either heel, in order to impart a slight inclination to the body, and thus preserve the balance without personal exertion. Picking the bones one by one out of the fire, he seizes alternate mouthfuls of the grilled and the raw flesh between the teeth, and with an upward motion of the creese, divides them close to his nose.

It may be received as an axiom that no Bedouin will speak the truth, although the doing so might prove to his obvious advantage. He is not only a liar by the force of rooted habit and example, but also upon principle, and his oaths are simple matters of form. The name of God is invoked, and the Korán taken to witness, in falsehoods the most palpable; and to have sworn with the last solemnity is far from being regarded in the light of a binding obligation. A stone having been cast upon the earth, fire is quenched in water, and the adjuration repeated: "May this body become petrified, and may Allah thus extinguish me if I utter that which is not true!"

In conversation a portion of every sentence is invariably taken up by the person addressed—the last word being generally considered sufficient, or even an abbreviation to the final syllable. The salutation of the tribes, between whom little bond exists, beyond identity of language, is a cold forbidding touch of the fingers, fully indicative of the unfriendly sentiments of the heart. All prey upon each other, and every individual in whatever rank is by nature, as well as by habit and inclination, an assassin. None will hesitate to mutilate or barbarously put to death any member of another clan whom he may find at advantage, either sleeping or at a distance from succour—the appetite for plunder, and the thirst for blood, inherent in the breast, being quite sufficient to dictate every act of atrocity, and to impel every dastardly outrage, that a savage can devise or commit.

Dwelling in a scene of aridity, hostility, and bloodshed, traversed by barren chains bearing the impress of volcanic desolation, and cursed with a soil rarely susceptible of cultivation, but still more rarely cultivated, the hand of the roving Bedouin is against every man, and every man's hand is against him. The truth of the Scriptural prophecy respecting the untameable descendants of Ishmaël, here as elsewhere is well maintained; nor were the words of the poet ever more truly exemplified than in the hot weary wastes of the Adaïel—

> "Nothing save rapine, indolence, and guile,
> And woes on woes, a still revolving train.
> Whose horrid circle has made human life
> Than non-existence worse."

Arrogant, treacherous, and degraded barbarians, bound in the fetters of idleness and superstition—dissemblers, whose every word is a lie, and whose overbearing and unaccommodating disposition, grafted upon bigoted intolerance, was displayed on every occasion to the personal discomfort of those by whom they were paid and entertained—there was never throughout the long, tedious, and trying journey, either on the part of elders, escort, or camel-drivers, the slightest wish or effort, either to honour or oblige; and it was only on occasions when fire-arms, which they could not gainsay, might prove of service to themselves, that the blubber lip did not swell in scorn at the Christian Kafirs, who were sneered at even in conversation. And these, too, were savages who scarcely knew the use of bread, who rarely employed water for the ablution of their filthy persons, and who kept their heads and bodies floating in a perpetual sea of sheep's-tail fat. On taking leave of the tormenting fraternity at this the happy termination of a weary and perilous pilgrimage, which had been performed without once taking off the clothes, it may safely be averred that no member of the British Embassy had ever passed so long a period with so large a party, without desiring to make further acquaintance with at least one individual: but the last touch of the cold palm was for once received with heartfelt satisfaction, and each bade adieu to the whole community with an inward hope that it might never fall to his evil lot to see their scowling faces more.

Chapter Forty
Ascent of the Abyssinian Alps

Having thus happily shaken the Adel dust from off the feet, and taken affectionate leave of the greasy Danákil, it is not a little pleasant to bid adieu also to their scorching plains of unblessed sterility. Every change in the soil and climate of Africa is in extremes, and barrenness and unbounded fertility border on each other with a suddenness whereof the denizens of temperate climes can form no conception. As if by the touch of the magician's wand, the scene now passes in an instant from parched and arid wastes to the green and lovely highlands of Abyssinia, presenting one sheet of rich and thriving cultivation. Each fertile knoll is crowned with its peaceful hamlet— each rural vale traversed by its crystal brook, and teeming with herds and flocks. The cool mountain zephyr is redolent of eglantine and jasmine, and the soft green turf, spangled with clover, daisies, and buttercups, yields at every step the aromatic fragrance of the mint and thyme.

The baggage having at length been consigned to the shoulders of six hundred grumbling Moslem porters, assembled by the royal fiat from the adjacent villages, and who, now on the road, formed a line which extended upwards of a mile, the Embassy, on the morning of the 17th, commenced the ascent of the Abyssinian Alps. Hitherto every officious attendant functionary had exerted himself to the utmost to promote delay, confusion, and annoyance; and each now exhorted the respective members of the party to urge their jaded beasts to increased speed, and hasten onwards over a rugged path which, in the toil-worn condition of the majority, was not to be ascended without considerable difficulty. The king was waxing impatient to behold the delighting things that had been imported, an account of which, so far as the prying eyes of his servants had been able to discern, had been duly transmitted to the palace; and in order to celebrate the arrival of so great an accession of wealth. His Majesty's flutes once more poured out their melody, and his warriors again chanted their wild notes among the hills, until far out of hearing of the astonished population of Fárri.

It was a cool and lovely morning, and a fresh invigorating breeze played over the mountain side, on which, though less than ten degrees removed from the equator, flourished the vegetation of northern climes. The rough and stony road wound on by a steep ascent over hill and dale—now skirting the extreme verge of a precipitous cliff—now dipping into the basin of some verdant hollow, whence, after traversing the pebbly course of a murmuring brook, it suddenly emerged into a succession of shady lanes, bounded by flowering hedge-rows.

The wild rose, the fern, the lantana, and the honeysuckle, smiled around a succession of highly cultivated terraces, into which the entire range was broken by banks supporting the soil; and on every eminence stood a cluster of conically-thatched houses, environed by green hedges, and partially embowered amid dark trees. As the troop passed on, the peasant abandoned his occupation in the field to gaze at the novel procession; whilst merry groups of hooded women, decked in scarlet and crimson, summoned by the renewal of martial strains, left their avocations in the hut to welcome the king's guests with a shrill *ziroleet*, which rang from every hamlet. The leather petticoat of the wandering shepherdess was no longer to be seen. Birds warbled among the leafy groves, and throughout the rich landscape reigned an air of peace and plenty that could not fail to prove highly delightful after the recent weary pilgrimage across the hot desert.

At various turns of the road the prospect was rugged, wild, and beautiful. Aigibbi, the first Christian village of Efát, was soon revealed on the summit of a height, where, within an enclosure of thorns, rest the remains of a traveller, who not long before had closed his eyes on the threshold of the kingdom, a victim to the pestilential sky of the lowlands. Three principal ranges were next crossed in succession, severally intersected by rivulets which are all tributary to the Háwash, although the waters are for the most part absorbed before they reach that stream. Lastly, the view opened upon the wooded site of Ankóber, occupying a central position in a horse-shoe crescent of mountains, still high above, which enclose a magnificent amphitheatre of ten miles in diameter. This is clothed throughout with a splendidly varied and vigorous vegetation, and choked by minor abutments, converging towards its gorge on the confines of the Adel plains.

Here the journey was for the present to terminate, and, thanks to Abyssinian jealousy and suspicion, many days were yet to elapse ere the remaining height should be climbed to the capital of Shoa, now distant two hours' walk. Three thousand feet above the level of Fárri stands the market-town of Alio Amba, upon the crest of a scarped prong formed by the confluence of two mountain streams. A Mohammadan population, not exceeding one thousand souls, the inmates of two hundred and fifty straggling houses, is chiefly composed of Adaïel, Argóbba, and merchants from Aussa and Hurrur; and among this motley community it had been ordained that the Embassy should halt that night.

Ascending by a steep stony path to an open spot, on which the weekly market is held, the escort fired a desultory salute; and whilst crowds of both sexes flocked to behold the white strangers, forming a double line, they indulged in the performance of the war-dance. Relieved occasionally by some of the younger braves who had earned distinctions during the last campaign, a veteran capered before the ranks with a drawn sword grasped between his teeth; and for the edification of the bystanders the notes of a martial song were powerfully poured forth in chorus from three hundred Christian throats.

The cone occupied by Alio Amba is only one of the thousand precipitous eminences into which the entire mountain side is broken on its junction with the plain. Swollen and foaming, the intersecting torrents appeared from the pinnacle like small threads of silver, twining and gliding far below amid green bushes and verdant fields to the great outlet, whence they escape to be soon lost on the desert sand. Together with a boundless prospect over the inhospitable tract beneath, countless villages now met the eye upon the entire intervening mountain side, and wherever the slope admitted of the plough being held, there cultivation flourished. Wheat, barley, Indian corn, beans, peas, cotton, and oil plant, throve luxuriantly around every hamlet— the regularly marked fields mounting in terraces to the height of three or four thousand feet, and becoming in their boundaries gradually more and more indistinct, until totally lost on the shadowy green side of Mamrat, "The Mother of Grace."

This towering peak, still shrouded in clouds when all was sunshine below, is clothed with a dense forest of timber, and at an elevation of some thirteen thousand feet above the sea, affords secure shelter to the treasures of the monarch, which have been amassing since the re-establishment of the kingdom, one hundred and fifty years since. Loza forms the apex of the opposite side of the crescent, and perched on its wooded summit is a monastery forming the temporary abode of Halloo Mulakoot, heir-apparent to the throne of Shoa. But by far the most interesting feature in the stern landscape is a conical hill, conspicuous from its isolated position, and rising amid dark groves of pine-like juniper, from a lofty serrated ridge. Hereon stands the stronghold of Góncho, the residence of Wulásma Mohammad, constructed over the state dungeon keep, in which, loaded with galling fetters, the three younger brothers of a Christian king—victims to a barbarous statute—have found a living tomb since the present accession, a period of thirty years!

After much needless detention in the market-place, exposed to the impertinent comments and rude gaze of the thronging populace, Ayto Kálama Work, a tall raw-boned man with a loose scrambling gait and a dead yellow eye, introduced himself as governor of the town. He condescended in person to conduct the British guests of his royal master to a mansion which had once boasted of himself as a tenant, but was now in the occupation of a fat old Moslem dame and her three daughters, whose respective appellatives being duly translated, proved worthy the days of Prince Cherry and Fairstar. Eve, Sweet-limes, and Sunbeam, all clothed alike in scarlet habiliments, vacated the premises with the utmost alacrity, and many good-humoured smiles; but owing to the length and difficulty of the road, that portion of the baggage most in request did not arrive until midnight—when, through the officious interference of Ayto Wolda Hana, whose garrulity had increased rather than abated, a new inventory of effects in charge of each principal of a village was to be penned by the royal scribe, and thus neither bedding nor food could be obtained.

The edifice so ostentatiously allotted for the accommodation of the party by him of the unpromising exterior, was of an elliptical form, about thirty feet in length by eighteen in breadth, and surrounded on every side by those tall rank weeds that delight to luxuriate in filth. Two undressed stakes supported a tottering grass thatch. Windows there were none. A long narrow aperture did duty for a door, and the walls, which met the roof at a distance of ten feet from the ground, were of the very worst description of wattle and dab—the former an assemblage of rotten reeds, and the latter decayed by time in a sufficiency of places to admit the light indispensable to a full development of the dirt and misery within.

In the principal of two apartments, a circular excavation in the floor surrounded by a parapet of clay, served as a stove. Heavy slabs of stone embedded in high mud pedestals, and used for grinding grain, engrossed one corner, and in another were piled heaps of old bullock hides in various stages of decomposition. Very buggy-looking bedsteads, equipped with a web of narrow thongs in lieu of cotton tape, assumed that air of discomfort which a broken or ill-adapted leg is so prone to impart. The narrow necks of divers earthen urn-shaped vessels containing mead, beer, and water, were stuffed with bunches of green leaves. Larger mud receptacles were filled with wheat, barley, and beans; and huge lumps of raw beef, with sundry bullocks' heads, which were promiscuously strewed about, garnished the floor, the beds, and the walls, in every direction.

The inner chamber boasted the presence of mules and female slaves, who, if judgment might be formed from the evil odours exhaled, were revelling in the garbage of the shambles. Constructed on the slope of a hill, the floor of the edifice throughout was of the natural earth, and dipping at least one foot below the level of the threshold, had never known the presence of the housemaid's besom. Equalling the filthiest Irish hovel in dirt and discomfort, the cheerless abode could boast of no sleek little pig, and of no pond covered with fat ducks, both being alike held in abhorrence by the Jew-Christians of Shoa; and even the old hat was wanting wherewith to cram the gaps through which whistled the keen cutting blast of Alpine climes.

Fatigue soon closed the weary eyes; but the change in the atmosphere, consequent upon the great elevation attained, presently interfered with repose upon the damp bare floor. Rain then set in with extreme violence. The water came tumbling through the manifold apertures in the crazy walls and shattered roof, and having speedily flooded the sloping court, poured over the threshold to deluge the floor with standing pools. Although the smoke of sodden wood, unable to escape, proved an inconvenience scarcely to be borne, there was no dispensing with a fire; and troops of fleas and sanguinary bugs, coursing over the body, by their painful and poisonous attacks, might almost have caused a sigh for the execrated plains of the Adaïel, which, with all their discomforts of watch and ward, were at least free from the curse of vermin.

But the lingering day dawned at last, and with the tedious hours of a cold and sleepless night the rain had also disappeared. As the rising sun shone against the lofty and now cloudless peaks, preparations were made for continuing the journey to Ankóber, in accordance with the royal invitation; but Ayto Wolda Hana, whose presence ever betokened evil, after wading through the compliments of the morning, proceeded with unbending gravity to unfold the dismal tidings that the monarch had altered his resolves. His Majesty would tarry yet some days longer at Debra Berhán, and in consequence graciously extended the option of visiting the court there or resting at Alio Amba, pending his indefinite arrival at the capital.

The difficulty, not to say the impossibility, of transporting the mass of baggage to so great a distance, in such weather, and with very inadequate means at command, rendered imperative the adoption of the latter alternative. Aytos Wolda Hana and Kátama, with the whole of the escort, meanwhile took their departure, to report orally the important discoveries they had been able to make relative to the nature of the presents designed for the throne, together with the particulars of the quarrel betwixt Izhák and Mohammad Ali, and the respective pretension of the rivals to the honour of having conducted the British visitors into Abyssinia.

One of those mysterious boxes, the lading of which, unviolated by the scrutinising scribes, remained hermetically sealed to the inquisitive gaze of officious spies, had, before leaving Fárri, been broken open with the design of obtaining access to an indispensable portion of the contents. To this unfortunate necessity may possibly be ascribed the sudden and unlooked-for alteration in the royal intentions. In lieu of ingots of gold were revealed to the astounded sight the leathern buckets, linch-stocks, and tough ash staves pertaining to the galloper-guns. Words of derision burst from the mouth of every disappointed spectator. "These," exclaimed fifty vain-glorious lips at once, "be but a poor people. What is their nation when compared with the Amhára; for behold in this trash, specimens of the offerings brought from their boasted land to the footstool of the mightiest of monarchs!"

Chapter Forty One
Probation at Alio Amba

Slowly passed the days of fog, and the nights of dire discomfort, during the tedious detention which followed this unfortunate discovery. From the terrace commanding a boundless view over the desolate regions traversed, the overflowing channel of the Háwash, and the lakes Le Ado and Ailabello could each morning be perceived sparkling with increased lustre, as their fast-filling basins glittered like sheets of burnished silver under the rays of the rising sun. The industrious fleas continued their nocturnal persecutions, as if never to be sated with European blood; and a constant succession of clouds, which ascended the valley, drawing a grey cold curtain before the hoary head of Mamrat, proclaimed, amid prolonged peals of thunder, the commencement of the rainy season.

But each succeeding night and day brought no nearer prospect of release, and the change in the imperial resolves were scarcely less frequent than those which came over the towering face of the stronghold of his subterranean treasure. Remonstrances, penned with infinite labour and difficulty, were responded by endearing messages, garbled at the pleasure of those to whom they were confided; but the subtle excuse for the further delay of the desired audience was never wanting, and conjecture became exhausted in devising the true cause of the mortifying indifference displayed to the rich presents from "beyond the great sea."

A desire on the part, of the despot to preserve due respect in the eyes of his lieges, and perhaps also to imbue the minds of his foreign visitors with a befitting sense of his importance, were the most probable motives. Under the existing disappointment, it afforded some consolation to remember that embassies of old to Northern Abyssinia had experienced similar treatment, and to know that delegates to Shoa from the courts of Gondar and Tigré are never presented to the king until weeks after their arrival—a custom originating probably in the more kindly feeling of allowing rest to the way-worn traveller at the close of a long and perilous journey, but perpetuated for less worthy considerations.

At length there came a pressing invitation to visit the monarch at Debra Berhán, coupled with an assurance that the Master of the Horse should be in attendance to escort the party. But no Master of the Horse was forthcoming at the time appointed, and the following day brought a pathetic billet from the palace—a tiny parchment scroll, enveloped in a sheet of wax, breathing in its contents regret and disappointment. "Son of my house, my heart longed to behold you, and I believed that you would come. As you appeared not, I passed the day in distress, fearing lest the waters should have carried you away, or that the mule had fallen on the road. I commanded Melkoo to wait and receive you, and to conduct you to me; but when I hoped to see you arrive, you stayed out. The mule returned; and when I inquired whither you were gone, they told me that you were left. I have committed the fault, in that I gave not orders that they should go down, and bring you."

Meanwhile, the most vigorous attempts were made, on the part both of the Wulásma and of Ayto Wolda Hana, to exercise exclusive control over the baggage lodged at Alio Amba. Locks were placed upon the latches, and guards appointed over the doors of the houses wherein it was deposited— fully as much care being taken to preclude access on the part of those by whom it had been brought, as if His Christian Majesty had already become the *bonâ fide* proprietor. Repeated orders on the subject, obtained from the palace, were uniformly disregarded by the over-zealous functionaries, and it was only by force of arms that the repositories were finally burst open, and that charge of the contents could be resumed.

Neither were the persecutions of the gaunt governor of the town among the least of the evils to be endured, resulting as they did in consequences the most inconvenient. Specially appointed to entertain and provide for the wants of the guests, he supplied at the royal expense provisions alike inferior in quality and deficient in quantity, taking care at the same time that the king's munificence should be in no wise compromised by purchases, for these he clandestinely prevented. His conduct might be traced to the same jealous feelings that pervaded the breast of his colleagues in office. In the despotic kingdom of Shoa, the sovereign can alone purchase coloured cloth or choice goods; and Ayto Kálama Work, who is entitled to a certain percentage upon all imports, having formed a tolerably shrewd estimate of the contents of the bales and boxes, believed that these would effectually clog the market, and that his dues would be no longer forthcoming. Resolved to extend the most unequivocal proofs of his discontent, he was pleased to assign to the surviving horses and mules of the foreigners a tract destitute of pasturage—one mulberry coloured steed only being pampered, because from size, colour, and appearance, it was assumed that he must be intended for the king. The continued drenching rain at night during the later marches, with the intense heat and general absence of water and forage throughout the whole pilgrimage, had sadly reduced the original number. Many more had dropped on the ascent from Fárri, and of those whose strength had enabled them to climb the more favoured mountains of Abyssinia, the tails of one half were now presented as evidences of their fate.

Among the very few incidents that occurred to break the monotony of the probationary sojourn was the arrival of the "Lebáshi," the hereditary thief-catcher of the kingdom. For several hours the little town was in a state of confusion and dismay. Burglary had been committed—divers pieces of salt had been abstracted, and the appearance of the police-officer was not one whit more agreeable to the innocent than to the guilty.

A ring having been formed in the market-place by the crowded spectators, the diviner introduced his accomplice, a stolid-looking lad, who seated himself upon a bullock's hide with an air of deep resignation. An intoxicating drug was, under many incantations, extracted from a mysterious leathern scrip, and thrown into a horn filled with new milk; and this potation, aided by several hurried inhalations of a certain narcotic, had the instantaneous effect of rendering the recipient stupidly frantic. Springing upon his feet, he dashed, foaming at the mouth, among the rabble, and without any respect to age or sex, dealt vigorously about him, until at length secured by a cord about the loins, when he dragged his master round and round from street to street, snuffling through the nose like a bear in the dark recesses of every house, and leaving unscrutinised no hole or corner.

After scraping for a considerable time with his nails under the foundation of a hut, wherein he suspected the delinquent to lurk, the imp entered, sprang upon the back of the proprietor, and became totally insensible. The man was forthwith arraigned before a tribunal of justice, at which Ayto Kálama Work presided; and although no evidence could be adduced, and he swore repeatedly to his innocence by the life of the king, he was sentenced by the just judges to pay forty pieces of salt. This fine was exactly double the amount alleged to have been stolen, and one fourth became the perquisite of the Lebáshi.

The services of the hereditary thief-catcher are in universal requisition. Should the property lost consist of live instead of dead stock, it not unfrequently happens that the disciple remains torpid upon the ground; when all parties concerned feel perfectly satisfied that the animal has either strayed or been destroyed by wild beasts, and the expenses attending the divination must be paid by the owner. With the design of testing the skill of the magician, the Negoos once upon a time commanded his confidential page to secrete certain articles of wearing apparel pertaining to the royal wardrobe, and after an investigation of four days, the proper individual being selected with becoming formality, the professional reputation of "him who catches" acquired a lustre which has since remained untarnished.

Many a weary hour was passed in listening to tales of real or counterfeit maladies, which were daily recounted in the hovel at Alio Amba. Witchcraft and the influence of the evil eye have firm possession of the mind of every inhabitant, and sufficiently diverting were the complaints laid to their door by those who sought amulets and talismans at the hand of the foreigners. A young Moslem damsel, whose fickle swain had deserted her, could never gaze on the moon that her heart went not pit-a-pat, whilst the tears streamed from her dark eyes; and a hoary veteran with one foot in the grave sought the restoration of rhetorical powers, which had formed the boast of his youth, but which had been destroyed by the pernicious gaze of a rival. "Of yore," quoth he who introduced the patient, "this was a powerful orator; and when he lifted up his voice in the assembly, men marvelled as he spoke; but now, although his heart is still eloquent, his tongue is niggard of words."

Equally hopeless was the case of an unfortunate slave-dealer, who crawled in search of relief to the abode of the king's guests. A Galla of the Ittoo tribe had undertaken the removal of severe rheumatism, contracted on the road from Hurrur; to which end he administered a powerful narcotic, which rendered the patient insensible. Armed with a sharp creese he then proceeded to cut and slash in every direction, from the crown of the head to the sole of the foot; and when the mutilated victim awoke to a sense of his melancholy condition, the ruthless operator had disappeared. Scarred and seamed in every part of his body, he now presented the appearance of one who had been flayed alive, and the skin had so contracted over the gaps whence the flesh had been scooped, that, unless with extreme difficulty, he could neither eat, drink, nor speak. "My life is burdensome," groaned the miserable picture of human calamity; "and it were better that I should die. I have bathed in the hot springs at Korári without deriving the slightest relief. You white men know every thing: give me something to heal me, for the love of Allah!"

Chapter Forty Two
The Weekly Market

Surrounded by the myrmidons who collect the royal dues, Ayto Kálama Work was every Friday morning to be seen seated beneath the scanty shelter of an ancient acacia, which throws its withered arms over the centre of the market-place. On this day alone are purchases to be made, and the inhabitants of the adjacent villages pouring from all quarters to lay in their weekly supplies, a scene of unusual bustle and confusion animates this otherwise most quiet and uninteresting location.

Shortly after daybreak, wares of every description are displayed under the canopy of heaven, and crowds of both sexes flocking to the stall of the vendor, the din of human voices is presently at its height. Honey, cotton, grain, and other articles of consumption, the produce of the estate of the Amhára farmer, are exposed for sale or barter. The Dankáli merchant exhibits his gay assortment of beads, metals, coloured thread, and glass ware. The wild Galla squats beside the produce of his flocks, and the Moslem trader from the interior displays ostrich feathers, or some other article of curiosity from the distant tribe. Bales of cotton cloth, and bags of coffee from Cáffa and Enárea, are strewed in every direction. Horses and mules in numbers are shown off among the crowd to increase the turmoil; nor is even the wandering Hebrew wanting to complete the scene of traffic, haggling, and barter, which continues, without intermission, until a late hour in the afternoon, when the village relapses again into its wonted six days of quiet and repose.

Swathed and folded in dirty cotton cloth, behold in the cultivator of the soil the original of the Egyptian mummy. Greasy and offensive in person and in habits, he moves cringingly to pay his tax to the governor of the fair, who sits in conscious dignity upon a stone; and prostrating himself with shoulders bared among the mud, the serf hands forth the measure of grain from the leathern scrip, or scoops out the prescribed meed of butter from the jar—the vassal token of permission enjoyed to earn his bread by the unceasing hand of labour. No spark of intelligence illumines his dull features; not a trace of independence can be discovered in his slouching gait; and the cumbrous robe with which he is invested would indeed seem far better adapted for the quiet resting-place in the tomb, than for the bustling avocations of stirring life.

Here swaggers a valiant gun-man of the king's matchlock guard. The jealousy of the monarch forbids the removal of the primitive weapon from the royal presence, but the white *herkoom* feather floats in all the pride of blood over clotted tufts moist with the beloved grease; and the dark scowl and the lowering brow betoken the reckless cruelty which stains the character of the band. But the man is a poor slave, and his degraded state has entirely destroyed the few traits of humanity which might have smiled upon his nativity.

The surly Adaïel brushes past in insolent indifference to examine the female slaves in the wicker hut of the rover from the south. His murderous creese ensures from the bystanders a high respect, which frequent disasters in the low country has riveted on the heart of the Amhára; and men turn in wonder to gaze upon the mortal who entertaineth not a slavish adoration for the great monarch of Shoa.

Squatted beside his foreign wares and glittering beads, see the wily huckster of Hurrur, with his turban and blue-checked kilt. His dealings, it is true, are of no very extensive amount, and salt, not silver, is the medium of exchange; but there is still room for the exercise of his knavery. The countenance both of buyer and seller exhibits an anxious and business-like expression, and the same noise and confusion prevails regarding an extra twopence-halfpenny, as if the transaction involved a shower of golden guineas.

The Christian women flit through the busy fair with eggs and poultry, and other produce of the farm. Their ill-favoured features are not improved either by the eradication of the eyebrow, or by the bare shaven crown dripping with rancid butter; and the dirty persons of all are invariably shrouded in yet dirtier habiliments, from the tall masculine damsel of sixteen summers, to the decrepit and wrinkled hag who in cracked notes proclaims ever and anon, *"amole alliche bir,"* "salt to sell for silver."

The free and stately mien of the oriental female, and the light graceful garment of the east, are alike wanting. The heavy load is tied as upon the back of the pack-horse, and the bent and broken figure of the Amhára dame is debarred by the severe law of the despot from the decoration of finery or costly ornament. A huge bee-hive-shaped wig, elaborately curled and frosted, and massive pewter buttons thrust through the lobe of the ear, constitute her only pride; and nature, alas! has too often withheld even the smallest portion of those feminine attractions which in other climes form the charm of her sex.

The inhabitants of Argóbba or Efát, under the control of the sinister eye of the Wulásma, are followers of the false Prophet, and speak a distinct language. Little difference, however, is observable in the external appearance of the males from that of the Amhára subject of the empire; and it is not until the removal of the muffling cloth that the rosary of bright-spotted beads is displayed in lieu of the dark blue emblem of Christianity worn throughout Ethiopia. The women, on the other hand, are at once recognisable, no less by their Arab gypsy features, than by their long braided tresses streaming ever the shoulder, the ample smock of red cloth, dyed purple with accumulated lard, and the nunlike hood of the same material, buttoned close under the chin.

Fairer, more slender, and better favoured than their coarse Christian sisters of the more alpine regions, they are still scarcely less greasy and unattractive. Loaded with amulets and beads, their belief is proclaimed by the oft-repeated exclamation, "*Hamdu-lillah!*" "Praise be unto Allah!"—the courteous interrogatories of every passer-by, anent health, rest, and welfare, being by the burly and masculine ladies of Shoa, responded by the words "*Egzia behere maskin!*" "Thanks be unto God!" Unrestricted by harem law they fidget about in every direction, their great sparkling eyes peering through a mass of coal-black hair, half concealed by the crimson cowl, and the large shining necklace of amber reaching nearly to the waist. But the hideous sack chemise veils every feature of figure and personal beauty, and the naked hands and feet are alone exhibited, both rather misshapen from hard work and undue exposure to the climate.

The crowd makes way for a great Christian governor, probably from some distant province near the Nile. He is surrounded by a boisterous host of armed attendants, and, like them, paddles with unshod feet through the stiff black mire. The capacious stomach, and the bright silver sword with tulip scabbard, betoken high honour and command. An ambling mule tricked out in brass jingles and chains follows in his path; a long taper wand towers above his shoulder; and his portly figure is completely shrouded in the folds of a cotton robe, bedecked from end to end with broad crimson stripes. The garment might be improved by ablution; but repose upon the hide of a bullock is no aid to purity of apparel, and it is white in comparison with those of his unwashed retinue.

The arrangement of his hair has occupied the entire morning, and the steam of the fetid butter, which glistens among the minute curls, pervades the entire atmosphere. Muffled high above the chin, the eyes and nose of the functionary are alone submitted to the vulgar gaze, and as he halts for a moment to wonder at the unwonted sight of the Gyptzi strangers, the bloodshot eye betrays the midnight debauch, and the wrinkles of his turned-up nose, the scorn of the savage at the difference of costume and complexion. Approaching the acacia his shoulders are temporarily bared to the pompous dignitary presiding over the fair, who rising to receive him, returns the compliment, and there ensues a tissue of inquiries unknown even to the code of Chesterfield. Cantering over the tiny plain—a scanty level of an hundred yards—the wild Galla enters the scene of confusion, his long tresses streaming in the wind, and his garment blue with the grease of ages. A jar of honey, or a basket of butter, is lashed to the crupper of his high-peaked saddle; the steed is lean and shaggy as the rider, and the snort and the start from either proclaim undefined terror and amazement at the strange sights, and the rugged rocks and precipices, unknown to the boundless meadows of their own green land.

Dandies there are none, in aught of outward appearance, for the arrangement of the hair is the only latitude allowed to the invention of the would-be fop. The cotton cloth in every degree of impurity, floats over the swart shoulder both of noble and of serf. Bare heads and naked feet are the property of all, and the possession of the spear and shield alone marks the difference of rank. The chief scorns to carry a weapon except during the foray or the fight, whereas his followers never leave the threshold of their rude dwellings, without the lance in their hand, and buckler on their arm.

The terror and abhorrence in which the low country and its attendant dangers are held by the Abyssinian population, have placed nearly the entire trade of Alio Amba in the hands of the Danákil, who are treated by the monarch of Shoa with all deference and respect. Caravans arrive every month during the fair season from Aussa and Tajúra, and the traffic, considering the manifold drawbacks, may be said to be brisk and profitable. Numbers of foreign merchants, those of Hurrur especially, whilst disposing of their goods, hold their temporary residence at the market-town, the climate of which, many degrees warmer than the cold summit of the range which towers two thousand feet above, proves far more congenial to their taste and habits.

With the proceeds of foreign imported merchandise, human beings kidnapped in the interior countries of Africa are purchased in the adjacent slave mart of Abd el Russool. These wretched victims are then taken through the Amhára province of Giddem to the Wollo and Argóbba frontiers, some five days' journey to the north, and resold at a profit of fifty per cent,— the sums realised being there invested in *amoles*, or blocks of black salt, the size of a mower's whetstone. Obtained between Agámê and the country of the Dankáli, from a salt plain which not only supplies all the Abyssinian markets, but many also far in the interior of Africa, they pass as a currency, and, being bought on the frontier at the rate of twenty-five for a German crown, are retailed in Alio Amba at a profitable exchange. A large investment of slaves is finally purchased with the wealth thus laboriously amassed, and the merchant returns to his native country to traffic in human flesh at the sea-ports of Zeyla and Berbera, or on the opposite coast of Arabia—anon to revisit Shoa with a fresh invoice of marketable wares.

Ever ravaged by war and violence, the unexplored regions of the interior pour forth a continual supply of ill-starred victims of all ages to feed the demand, and the hebdomadal parade in the market-place under the ruthless Moslem monsters by whom they are imported, is sufficiently harrowing to those unaccustomed to such revolting spectacles. Examined like cattle by the purchaser, the sullen Shankala fetches a price proportioned to the muscular appearance of his giant frame; and the child of tender years is valued according to the promise of future development. Even the shamefaced and slenderly-clad maiden is subjected to every indignity, whilst the price of her charms is estimated according to the regularity of her features, the symmetry of her budding form, and the luxuriance of her braided locks; and when the silver has rung in confirmation of the bargain, the last tie is dissolved which could hold in any restraint the appetite of her savage possessor.

Chapter Forty Three
The Principality of Hurrur

Not many weeks had elapsed since certain substantial merchants of Hurrur, after visiting the shrine at Medina, and making a long and profitable sojourn in Alio Amba, had returned to their native land to enjoy the honours attaching to their religious pilgrimage. Slaves, ivory, and precious gums had been disposed of to great advantage in Arabia, and the proceeds invested in beads, berillés, and broad-cloth, with which the enterprising traders landed at the maritime town of Tajúra. Proceeding thence to Efát, they embarked their gains in slaves, mules, and cotton cloths; and designing to pass the residue of their days in ease and affluence, set out by way of Hurrur for the great annual fair at Berbera.

In advance of the time, however, these luckless individuals had ventured to speculate to their envious countrymen upon the advantage to be derived from foreign traffic and the presence of the white man. The incautious word had caught the ear of Abdel Yonag, the wily chief of the Hurrurhi, and letters were secretly despatched to his master the Ameer, representing the wealthy hajjis to be men of turbulent and ambitious views, who had devised dangerous innovations, and were plotting, with the Adaïel, the monopoly of the commerce in slaves. With hearts bounding at the sight of their native minarets, and utterly unconscious of the slander that had preceded them, the pilgrims entered the *Isma-deen* gate of the city; but ere return had been welcomed by wife or child, they were hurried by the soldiery to the presence of the despot, and, without even the mockery of a trial, were beaten to death with huge maces of iron.

The independent principality of Hurrur is a spot yet unvisited by any European, and is remarkable for its isolated position among the Pagan and Mohammadan Galla, against whose continual inroads it has hitherto contrived, with the aid of two hundred matchlock-men and a few archers, to maintain its integrity. The Alla, the Nooli, the Geeri, the Tarsoo, the Babili, the Bursoo, the Burteera, and the Gooti, compass it on every side, and making sudden descents, sweep the ripe crops from off the face of the smiling land; but their efforts against the town have uniformly proved unsuccessful, and caravans continue, in spite of hostilities, to carry on a very considerable traffic through the Ittoo and Aroosi tribes, with Shoa and the Somauli coast.

Originally founded and peopled by a colony of the sons of Yemen, the town is described to be situated in a pleasant and well-watered valley, surrounded by hills, and enjoying a cool and salubrious climate. A wall of mud and stone, six miles in circumference, with five fortified gates, affords security to the entire population, whose houses, many of them two-storied, are constructed of stone, whitewashed, and terraced. Mosques and minarets are conspicuous in every street. The matin voice of the muezzin is regularly heard, and the Jama el Musjid is believed to be the abode of guardian angels, who stretch the strong pinion of protection over the heads of the Faithful. "How could Hurrur have triumphed thus long over the unbelievers," inquire the devout citizens, "had Allah not extended his right arm to succour the followers of his Prophet?"

Aboo Bekr, the reigning Ameer, has wielded the sceptre during the last seven years, and pursuing the barbarous custom of Shoa, his brothers and family are permanent inmates of subterranean dungeons, which for better security are constructed immediately below the foundations of his own palace. Although cruel and vindictive, he is reputed a brave prince, heading the foray in person, and taking the front in the battle field; but suspicion of the stranger would seem to form the ruling feature of his character, nor is this to be wondered at, since bloodshed and aggression are known to have once marked the footstep of the intruder.

During the reign of Abd el Kurreem, uncle to the present Ameer, a large body of Arabs from Mocha, instigated by a disgraced member of the blood-royal, who had fled thither for safety, laid siege to the town, and assisted by guns of small calibre, which are now mounted on the walls, had nearly prevailed. Again the guardian angels stretched their white wings over the beleaguered city. The magazine blew up and destroyed numbers of the enemy, and their traitorous leader, who had induced the attack by representing his countrymen to be infidels and apostates from the true religion, falling into the hands of the garrison, had his head exalted on a pole in the market-place, after the brains had been dashed out with an iron club. Death is now the portion of every fool-hardy wanderer from the shores of Araby, and whilst the Galla is compelled to relinquish his arms at the gate, every precaution is taken to exclude from the land the foreigner of whatever nation.

In the features of the Hurrurhi is to be traced a strong resemblance to those of the parent stock. The costume consists of a checked kilt, a creese, and a cotton toga; the display of a turban being restricted to the Ameer, to the moolahs, and to those who have performed the pilgrimage to the shrine of the Prophet. Although distinct in itself, the language bears a singular affinity to that of the Amhára, but Arabic forms the written character. Barter is the most usual system of commerce, but the *mahaluk*, a small copper coin resembling the *dewáni* of Jiddah, is current in the realm. Twenty-two of these go to a nominal coin styled *ashrafi*, whereof forty are equivalent to the German crown. It bears on the reverse the name of the reigning Prince, and on the obverse the quotation from the Korán, "La *illah, illilah!*" "there is none other God but Allah."

Around Hurrur the soil is rich, and extensively cultivated, especially in coffee. Two thousand bales of the finest quality are annually exported into India and Arabia by the ports of Zeyla and Berbera, which are visited thrice during the year by large caravans laden with ivory, ostrich feathers, ghee, saffron, gums, and myrrh, which latter is produced in great abundance. Blue and white calico, Indian piece goods, English prints, silks, and shawls, red cotton yam, silk thread, beads, frankincense, copper wire, and zinc, are received in exchange, and a transit duty of one *frazil* of the latter metal is levied by the Ameer on every slave passing through his dominions from the cold hills of his brother of Shoa, where these commodities are bartered.

(The distance of Hurrur from Zeyla may be assumed at 150 miles south-south-west and from Ankóber, 190 miles East.)

Between Aboo Bekr and the Christian monarch the most friendly intercourse subsists. Letters continually pass and repass, and scarcely a month elapses without the arrival of a caravan. The chief of the Wurj or merchants of Hurrur, standing specially appointed by the Ameer, possesses absolute power to punish all offences, and adjust all disputes amongst his own countrymen, who are not less fond of drawing the creese than their Adaïel brethren. Tullah, an inferior description of beer, being brewed and swallowed in alarming quantities, brawls and scuffles too frequently terminate the debauch in blood. Should a Christian subject of Shoa be slain, the offence is passed over in politic silence, but when the reverse is the case, the worldly wealth of the sinning Abyssinian is confiscated by the crown, and his person handed over to the tender mercies of the Moslem savages.

The continual change of inhabitants, the excessive cheapness of provisions, and the prevalent custom of hand-fasting for the visit, tend little to improve the morality of the market-town. The chains of the convenient alliances formed, are by no means binding on either party, and the sum of twopence-halfpenny is perfectly sufficient to support during the week the trader and his temporary mate. One hundred pieces of salt are considered a large dowry; the nuptials are celebrated by feasting and routing alone, and whilst the utmost indifference prevails on the part of the husband, he loosens the matrimonial knot at pleasure, by carrying his partner before the kázi, and thrice repeating the words, "Woman, I thee divorce."

One fourth of the entire population of Alio Amba are Hurrurhi and Danákil. Of the worthies who accompanied the Embassy from Tajúra, the majority continued to reside at Fárri and Chánnoo for the convenience of foraging their camels, but flocking every Friday to the market, they never failed to confer the pleasure of their society for a few hours. Gubaïyo, the deputy-governor of the town, had been specially appointed to the service of the foreigners, and whilst discharging his office of spy with the most creditable diligence, he exercised with strict impartiality his functions as door-keeper, enforcing, greatly to the amazement of the independent Adaïel, the Abyssinian usage, which precludes the invasion of visitors unless duly introduced. The obnoxious red man, whose iniquities had well nigh cost the lives of the whole party at the Great Salt Lake, and who had now the impudence to seek a reward for his services on the road, was the first who came under the remorseless lash of the despotic bully; and it was a not less cheering and delightful sight to behold the warm-blooded little warrior, Ibrahim Shehém Abli, flying like a football down the steps leading from the court-yard into the muddy lane, before the propulsive impetus of a Christian toe, which presently sent the tyrannical Izhák bounding after his colleague, with many a severe thwack from the wand of office, ringing across his Moslem shoulders, as he vainly proclaimed himself own brother to the reigning Sultán of Tajúra.

Chapter Forty Four
Escape from the Market-Town

Abyssinian despots sully not their dignity by condescending to divulge even the smallest design to the most confidential of their courtiers. In elegant Amháric phraseology "the belly of the master is never known;" and thus it occurred that had any possessed the inclination to predict the probable period of detention, none could boast the ability. A fortnight rolled tardily away, and the burning curiosity of the savage having meanwhile overcome the scruples dictated by state policy, it became matter of public notoriety that the king had taken up his residence at the adjacent palace of Machal-wans, where preparations were actually in progress towards the long-desired audience.

The reappearance of the commander-in-chief of the body-guard, with the escort of honour, was the first welcome sign of approaching release from the vile market-town of Alio Amba; and the most illustrious peer of the realm, attended by a junto of scribes, and a host of reluctant porters, was not far behind him. Penmanship being so extremely tedious a process, it is not the court etiquette to endite letters when a verbal communication will answer the purpose; and the visitors were accordingly charged with abundant compliments, and with an invitation to behold the royal person on the ensuing Sabbath, which had been pronounced by the astrologers "a day of good omens."

"Tarry not by day, neither stay ye by night, for the heart of the father longeth to see his children. Hasten that he be not again disappointed."

But, unfortunately, the hour selected by the skill of "those who read the stars" did not find approval in the sight of the guests; and in order to gratify the royal impatience, it was therefore proposed that the interview should take place one day earlier. His Majesty, however, laboured under the effects of *cosso*, a drug resorted to by all who revel in raw diet; and feeling yet unequal to appear in public, it was finally arranged that audience should be deferred until the Monday following. A fresh inventory of boxes was immediately commenced; and, after much opposition, those intended for presentation to the throne were separated, and sent off to await arrival at a hamlet distant two miles from Machal-wans.

The next labour was to dismantle the structure of bales and packages which during the detention at Alio Amba had been piled in view to the economy of space, so as to admit of some of the party occupying the tier next the roof, whilst others had slept in cabins formed below, or upon, or underneath, the table. But no sooner had the king's baggage departed than the Wulásma came to announce that there were no more porters, and that if any thing still remained it must be left behind. Another battle followed, and a war of words, which lasted a full hour and a half, was again crowned with victory.

Ayto Kálama Work, who had been the chief instigator of this opposition, is charged with manifold affairs. Independent of his important duties at the seat of his authority, where he is responsible for all tribute in salt, in honey, and in specie, he is entrusted with the treasures lodged in Ankóber, Arámba, Debra Berhán, and Kondie, and is expected to be present on all state occasions at the palace. To assist in the discharge of these onerous and multifarious duties, he has many stewards and subordinates, of whom the chief, who superintends the *ghemdjia* house, or royal wardrobe, wherein the most costly manufactures are deposited, had already proceeded in advance to spread the carpets in the great reception hall. He was accompanied by Déftera Sena, the secretary, whose business it is to receive and register all transfers to the state revenues, and who had been for the last fortnight almost incessantly busied with his pen.

Liberated from irksome captivity, the utmost difficulty was next experienced in procuring mules—no steps to supply the place of those destroyed having been taken by the inimical functionaries whose express duty it was. The few survivors of the late numerous drove were mustered, but only one proved in a condition to proceed, and it was not until a messenger had actually set out with a complaint to the king, that measures were taken to supply the number required. A clamorous mob now assembled in order to witness the difficulties raised in the way of the foreigners; and it required the utmost exertion on the part of Gubaïyo, both with his long stick and still longer tongue, to keep the idle crowd at a respectful distance.

Mounted at length, the party turned their backs towards the market-place, and entered upon a circuitous path, winding, by abrupt declivities and steep ascents, over three mountain torrents, towards the village of Sallal Hoola, at which the night was to be passed. Kind nature had everywhere spread the ground with her gifts in inexhaustible profusion and variety, supplying all the more immediate wants of mankind, yet enforcing the doom of labour so wisely imposed upon her lazy children. Rich acres of corn by the wayside were interspersed with quiet hamlets, and with luxuriant meadows abounding in trefoil and a vast variety of red and white clover. Crystal brooks leapt in numerous cascades, and hedge-rows gay with endless flowers, the dog-rose and the fragrant jessamine, imparted to the rural landscape an aspect quite European.

Southern Abyssinia proper commences with Efát, at the foot of the first range of hills, which continue to increase both in altitude and fertility to the summit of the lofty barrier that stretches north and south to form the brink of the elevated table-land of Shoa. Violent storms of thunder and lightning, which usher in the rainy season, are attracted to this region as well by the great elevation of the mountain as by the highly ferruginous nature of the rocks. It is a land of hill and valley, smiling under the influence of the copious deluge; and so striking a contrast does it present to the general character and climate of the torrid zone, that at first sight the delighted traveller might believe himself transported by some fairy agency to his northern home.

Ayto Wolda Hana, although loquacious enough, had been somewhat subdued by the temperature of the low country, to which, as well as to every thing Mohammadan, he evinced an insuperable disrelish; but once again within the influence of the cold mountain breeze beyond the limits of the Wulásma's jurisdiction, and he was in his glory. Two running footmen kept pace with his gaily-caparisoned mule. Immediately behind him rode a confidential henchman carrying the emblazoned shield and decorated lances which denoted his position in society; and in the height of Highland anarchy the tail of the McGregor was seldom of longer dimensions than that of the pompous governor of Ankóber.

Suddenly leaving the party, the great man was observed to dive into a village by the road-side, whence in a few minutes he returned, issuing a variety of orders in a far from melodious tone of voice, which evidently had reference to the mulberry steed already mentioned as having been brought from Aden. The animal had not been seen for many days, and every application regarding it had been so dexterously evaded, that, although the tail had not been brought in, it was believed to have gone the way of all flesh. To the surprise of every one, the charger, prancing and neighing, was now led forth, in the best condition, by one of the King's grooms. So thoroughly had the worthy functionary been impressed with the erroneous conviction, that it formed a part of the present designed for his royal master, that the fortunate beast had been turned into clover, and duly fed with the choicest barley, whereas all its companions, although surrounded by plenty, had been suffered to starve.

At Sallal Hoola, another hovel had been provided by the royal bounty, smaller in dimensions, more dark, dirty, and dismal, and infinitely better garrisoned with vermin than the abode wherein the last fortnight had been passed. Environed by miry swamps and stagnant pools, it presented an appearance the most gloomy and wretched, whilst the materials for comfort were, as usual, denied by the officious functionaries, who had taken care to deposit the baggage most needed in quarters of the village where, at so late an hour, free access was impossible. The gloomy recesses of the veranda were crowded with female slaves, occupied in the various processes of preparing bread, which the population had been called upon to supply in large quantities to the palace against the approaching arrival of the foreigners. In one corner, two old women who alternately plied their pestles to a most monotonous ditty were pounding grain in a wooden mortar. In another a group of buxom lasses were rocking themselves to and fro over mills fashioned like the high-heeled slipper of the days of good Queen Bess, upon the inclined surface of which they contrived, with a stone and great personal labour, to convert the grain into a form something resembling flour. It trickled in a scanty stream into a vessel placed below the depressed plane for its reception, and was presently wrought into thick cakes, full a foot and a half in diameter. These were merely shown to the fire, and a crude substance was thus produced, which by a well-fed Indian elephant would certainly have been rejected with a severe admonition to his keeper.

In this dreary and soul-depressing spot, destitute of beds and not overburdened with food, were experienced the very opposite of the delights of the Salt Lake—cold, damp, and wet in perfection; but the glad prospect of an interview with His Majesty on the morrow buoyed up the spirits of all, and misery was disregarded. Ayto Kátama had proceeded in advance to Machal-wans to seek at the royal hands permission to fire a salute of twenty-one guns on the British Embassy reaching the royal lodge—a point previously urged, but without success. It had already been brought to the King's notice that the foreigners partook of food which had been prepared by Mohammadans—a proceeding which in Shoa is reckoned equivalent to a renunciation of Christianity. Ideas the most extravagant were, moreover, in circulation relative to the powers of the ordnance imported, the mere report of which was believed sufficient to set fire to the earth, to shiver rocks, and dismantle mountain fastnesses. Men were said to have arrived with "copper legs," whose duty it was to serve these tremendous and terrible engines; and in alarm for the safety of his palace, capital, and treasures, the suspicious monarch still peremptorily insisted upon withholding the desired licence, until he should have beheld the battery "with his own eyes."

Chapter Forty Five
Presentation at Court

It rained incessantly with the greatest violence throughout the entire night, and until the morning broke, when a great volume of white scud, rising from the deep valleys, and drifting like a scene-curtain across the stern summit of the giant Mamrat—now frowning immediately overhead— foretold the nature of the weather that might be anticipated during the important and long-looked-for day. The baggage having with considerable difficulty been collected from the various nooks and comers wherein the porters had deposited their loads, and no prospect of a brighter sky being in store, the circumjacent morasses were waded to the face of the hill which obscured Machal-wans. Too steep and slippery for mules, this was also ascended on foot, with the aid of long staves; and the rain, which had been dropping gently for some time, again setting-in with the most malicious steadiness, as if resolved to mar all attempt at display, the whole cavalcade was presently drenched to the skin.

An hour's toil over very heavy ground opened a sudden turn in the road, whence the escort, resting their cumbrous matchlocks over the rocks, commenced an indiscriminate fire—the reports of their heavily-loaded culverins, mingled with the answering note of welcome from the expectant crowd below, echoing long and loud among the broken glens. As the clouds of smoke floated slowly away on the dense atmosphere from the shoulder of the mountain, there burst upon the sight a lovely view of the stockaded palace at Machal-wans. Its conical white roofs were embosomed in a fair grove of juniper and cypress, which crested a beautifully wooded tumulus rising at the extreme verge of the valley from the very banks of a roaring torrent. A bright green meadow, spangled with flowers, lay stretched at its foot: the rose, the eglantine, and the humble violet, grew around in all the grace of native wildness, to recall recollections of happier lands, whilst the great Abyssinian range, which even here towered almost perpendicularly some two thousand feet overhead, and whose peaks were veiled in wreaths of white fog, formed a magnificent background to the picture. Isolated farm-houses were profusely scattered over the verdant landscape—rich fields glistened in various stages of maturity—and the rills, swollen by the recent storm, came thundering over the mountain side, in a succession of foaming cascades.

Another hour's wading through deep ploughed fields of beans and peas and standing corn, and across the rapid torrent brawling over a rocky bed, brought the draggled party to two time-worn awnings of black serge, which not five minutes before had been pitched for its accommodation in a swamp below the royal residence, and which admitted the rain through an infinity of apertures. This continued up to the last moment, thick and heavy; but the utmost efforts of the deluge had proven insufficient to cleanse the mud-stained garments; and now the tramp of six hundred porters, in addition to the vast crowd which had assembled to witness the long-looked-for arrival of the British Embassy, soon converting the ground into a positive quagmire, ankle-deep in black mud, seemed to render utterly hopeless any attempt at the exhibition of broad-cloth and gold lace on the approaching presentation at the Court of Shoa.

The governors of Ankóber and Alio Amba, whose special affair it was to provide food, and otherwise to render assistance needed, left the visitors to pitch their own tent, whilst they lounged in the palls, and contented themselves with urging the instant gratification of the royal curiosity, which was momentarily becoming more and more intense. Persecution on the part of the unruly and boisterous mob, to whom every object was new, meanwhile waxed greater and greater—thousands pressing forward to gaze as at wild beasts, and all contributing their mite to promote confusion and discomfort, now at the climax. Sally after sally was made by the uproused commander-in-chief of the body-guard, and many were the long sticks broken to small fragments over the backs and shoulders of the wild spectators in the course of his vigorous applications. But it was to no purpose. The ring was no sooner formed than broken, and the self-constituted clerk of the course, becoming at length weary of his occupation, he joined his idle colleagues in the tent, and left the multitude to their own devices.

A remonstrance to the King, touching the indignities to which the liege subjects of Great Britain were thus exposed at the hands of the Amhára rabble, on the very outskirts of the palace, was followed by a visit from

Birroo, the favourite page, bearing an apologetic message on the score of ignorance; and repeated messages through this shrewd little confidant of royalty, who possessed all the airs of a spoiled pet, elicited first permission to fire a single gun—then five—and lastly, the desired salute. With his assistance, moreover, the crowd was to a certain extent repelled, and the spacious tent having finally been erected, amid peals of savage wonder, the floor was strewed with heather and with branches lopped from the myrtles and from various aromatic shrubs that grew thickly around, and preparations were at length commenced for the interview, which, during the continuance of the tumult and uproar, had been by a succession of messages repeatedly and earnestly desired.

It was now noon, and the weather having temporarily cleared, the British party, radiant with plumes and gold embroidery, succeeded, after much fruitless opposition, in mounting their gaily-caparisoned steeds, and escorted by the governors, the commander-in-chief of the body-guard, and by a numerous and clamorous escort, proceeded in full uniform towards the palace. Many were the attempts made to enforce the etiquette which denies ascent in equestrian order; but as, on gaining the foot of the eminence, the roar of artillery burst from the centre of the encampment, and the deep valley, filling fast with a cloud of white smoke, began to echo back the salute at the rate of six discharges in a minute, no further interference was attempted, and an universal shout arose of "*Malifia Ungliz, melcom! melcom!*" "Wonderful English, well done! well done!"

Noise, bustle, and confusion, which in Abyssinia are reckoned highly honourable to the guest, were again at their climax on reaching the outer cricket, where the form of obtaining the royal permission to pass was to be observed ere entrance could be accorded by the state door-keepers. Further detention was experienced in the court-yard, at the hands of sundry officers of the privy chamber, whose visages were but ill-adapted to sustain the character of high official importance, and whose assumption of dignity proved singularly ludicrous. At length came a message expressive of His Majesty's unqualified surprise and satisfaction at the extraordinary celerity with which the guns were being served, and his desire to see the Embassy forthwith; but attempting to advance, opposition was again interposed, and it needed another message, and yet another command, before admission could be obtained to the royal presence.

The last peal of ordnance was rattling in broken echoes along the mountain chain, as the British Embassy stepped at length over the high threshold of the reception hall. Circular in form, and destitute of the wonted Abyssinian pillar in the centre, the massive and lofty clay walls of the chamber glittered with a profusion of silver ornaments, emblazoned shields, matchlocks, and double-barrelled guns. Persian carpets and rugs of all sizes, colours, and patterns, covered the floor, and crowds of Alakas, governors, chiefs, and principal officers of the court, arrayed in their holyday attire, stood around in a posture of respect, uncovered to the girdle. Two wide alcoves receded on either side, in one of which blazed a cheerful wood fire, engrossed by indolent cats, whilst in the other, on a flowered satin ottoman, surrounded by withered eunuchs and juvenile pages of honour, and supported by gay velvet cushions, reclined in Ethiopic state His Most Christian Majesty Sáhela Selássie. The *Dech Agafari*, or state door-keeper, as master of the ceremonies, stood with a rod of green rushes to preserve the exact distance of approach to royalty, and as the British guests entered the hall and made their bows to the throne, motioned them to be seated upon chairs that had previously been sent in—which done, it was commanded that all might be covered.

The King was attired in a silken Arab vest of green brocade, partially shrouded under the ample folds of a white cotton robe of Abyssinian manufacture, adorned with sundry broad crimson stripes and borders. Forty summers, whereof eight-and-twenty had been passed under the uneasy cares of the crown, had slightly furrowed his dark brow, and somewhat grizzled a full bushy head of hair, arranged in elaborate curls after the fashion of George the First; and although considerably disfigured by the loss of the left eye, the expression of his manly features, open, pleasing, and commanding, did not in their *tout ensemble* belie the character for impartial justice which the despot has obtained far and wide—even the Danákil comparing him to "a fine balance of gold."

All those manifold salutations and inquiries which overwrought politeness here enforces, duly concluded, the letters with which the Embassy had been charged—enveloped in flowered muslin and rich gold kimkhab— were presented in a sandal wood casket, minutely inlaid with ivory; and the contents having been read and expounded, the costly presents from the British government were introduced in succession, to be spread out before the glistening eyes of the Court. The rich Brussels carpet which completely covered the hall, together with Cachemire shawls and embroidered Delhi scarfs of resplendent hues, attracted universal attention, and some of the choicest specimens were from time to time handed to the alcove by the chief of the eunuchs. On the introduction of each new curiosity, the surprise of the King became more and more unfeigned. Bursts of merriment followed the magic revolutions of a group of Chinese dancing figures; and when the European escort in full uniform, with the sergeant at their head, marched into the centre of the hall—faced in front of the throne, and performed the manual and platoon exercises amidst jewellery glittering on the rugs, gay shawls and silver cloths which strewed the floor, ornamented clocks chiming, and musical boxes playing "God save the Queen," His Majesty appeared quite entranced, and declared that he possessed no words to express his gratitude. But many and bright were the smiles that lighted up the royal features, as three hundred muskets, with bayonets fixed, were piled in front of the footstool. A buzz of mingled wonder and applause, which half drowned the music, arose from the crowded courtiers; and the measure of the warlike monarch's satisfaction now filled to overflowing, "God will reward you," he exclaimed, "for I cannot."

But astonishment and admiration knew no bounds, as the populace next spread over the face of the hills to witness the artillery practice, which formed the sequel to the presentation of these princely gifts. A sheet was attached to the opposite face of the ravine. The green valley again rung to the unwonted roar of ordnance; and as the white cloth flew in shreds to the wind, under a rapid discharge of round shot, canister, and grape, amidst the crumbling of the rock, and the rush of the filling stones, the before despised sponge staves became a theme of eulogy to the monarch as well as to the gaping peasant. A shout rose long and loud over the pealing echoes which rattled from hill to hill; and far along the serrated chain was proclaimed the arrival of foreign guests, and the royal acquisition through their means of potent engines of war.

Compliments from the throne, and personal congratulations from the principal courtiers and officers of state, closed the evening of this unwonted display; and the introduction, by the hands of the favourite page, of a huge pepper pie, the produce of the royal kitchen, with a command that "the King's children might feast," was accompanied by the unheard-of honour of a visit from the dwarf father confessor, who might without difficulty have concealed his most diminutive person beneath the ample pastry. Enveloped in robes and turbans, and armed with silver cross and crosier, the deformed little priest, whose entire long life has been passed in doing good to his fellow-creatures, seating his hideous and Punch-like form in a chair placed for its reception, in squeaking accents delivered himself thus:—

"Forty years have rolled away since Asfa Woosen, on whose memory be peace, grandsire to our beloved monarch, saw in a dream that the red men were bringing into his kingdom curious and beautiful commodities from countries beyond the great sea. The astrologers, on being commanded to give an interpretation thereof, predicted with one accord that foreigners from the land of Egypt would come into Abyssinia during His Majesty's most illustrious reign, and that yet more and wealthier would follow in that of his son, and of his son's son, who should sit next upon the throne. Praise be unto God that the dream and its interpretation have now been fulfilled! Our eyes, though they be old, have never beheld wonders until this day, and during the reign over Shoa of seven successive kings, no such miracles as these have been wrought in Ethiopia."

Chapter Forty Six

By the passage of the polar star over the meridian, the magnetic variation at Ankóber was observed, with the aid of a well-regulated chronometer, to be 7 degrees westerly.

The longitude was determined both by a series of lunars, and by the eclipses of Jupiter's satellites, the mean of upwards of 150 observations having been taken.

Remarks on the Natural History of that Portion of the Adel Country Situated along the Route from the Sea-Coast to the Frontier of Efát.

From Tajúra to Killulloo

The advanced state of the season was unfavourable for observations in the department of natural history. Both animal and vegetable life were apparently in a state of torpor; the trees and shrubs were in general leafless; and no annual plant whatever was to be seen, even in the immediate vicinity of the watering-places. The few insects that were not in a state of chrysalis, seemed drowsily to procrastinate their existence until food for the new generation should be prepared by nature. Amphibia, Saurii, and Ophidii, which are generally not so dependent on a supply of water, existed in small numbers in their lurking-places, whilst birds and larger animals must at this season have migrated to more favoured countries.

Basaltic and trachytic hills, either isolated or in chains, rise at a distance of about half a mile from the sea-shore, which is winding and shelving. The hills are in general rounded, and marked by broad veins of similar composition, but containing more perfectly crystallised felspar, quartz, and zeolith. They have not the sharp peak, but are broken and cliffy, and have apparently been upheaved at different periods.

On leaving the shore, a most striking specimen of columnar basalt presented itself in the ravine of Galeylaféo, which, for nearly half a mile, runs through the heart of a huge mountain. In width it is about 200 yards, and the perpendicular pillars are 200 feet in height. It is evident that water could not have been the sole agent in producing such a huge cleft, although at present the ravine presents the appearance of a regular water-course. The surrounding hills consist of the same rock, but covered with loose boulders, which are much stained with oxide of iron.

Amongst the confusion of volcanic masses on the plain of Warelissán, excepting in some rare cases, when the true lava stream could be traced to its source, it was difficult to determine the exact site of the craters from whence they had been ejected. The hill which separates Báhr Assai from the sea, with its singular tops of limestone, slate, and creta, deserves a more minute examination than could be given at this season of withering heat. The western side is the most interesting, as being more open and disclosed; there is, however, as in all formations in the vicinity of volcanic countries, no uniform inclination of the layers. The range bordering the eastern shore of the lake is basalt and basaltic wacke; on the western, it is partly gypsum and limestone, but resting on basalt.

The great salt lake is a deep extensive basin, separated by an immense lava stream from the remainder of the bay, the head of which it once formed. Resembling the Dead Sea in the depression of its level, in the density and chemical constitution of the fluid, and in the loneliness, sterility, and desolation of its borders, it yet differs from it materially in the ways by which volcanic action has produced the strange phenomenon of the existence of shores so considerably below the level of the ocean. In the Dead Sea, the lake of Tiberias, and the valley of the Jordan between them, it has apparently been a distortion and crushing of immense masses which have subsided into subterranean caverns. In the Báhr Assai it has been produced by the erection of a new bank, serving as a dam or barrier across the head of a long narrow bay, by which a considerable body of sea-water was separated from the former common receptacle. As high as the level of the Arabian Gulf are to be found, in the basin of Báhr Assai, the salts and earthy (magnesian) precipitates of the salt water, which in the course of time was reduced to its present level by evaporation, the yearly supply of rain-water being but as a drop to the ocean. Huge heaps of lava, having been apparently in strife with the opposite element, are erected on the banks over wacke, or in other cases over a finely-grained soft mart. The latter, when clear of lava, presents a thin layer of gypsum, with numerous shells of Melania, Limnaeus, Physa, Planorbis, Cyclostoma, Unio, and Cycas, some of which are at present to be found in the distant fresh-water pools and rivulets.

The shallow water on the borders of the lake presents natural salt-pans, and a crust of fine salt, two inches thick and tolerably clean, covers nearly the whole of the surface. The supply would seem to be inexhaustible; for when cut out with a spaddle, a new crust is soon furnished from the waters beneath. Being visited by almost every tribe of the Adaïel and Somauli, and unhappily situated on the borders of the most lawless and savage of them, this remarkable spot is almost forbidden ground for the observer, not to speak of the obstacles thrown in the way by the destructive temperature and the general absence of the necessaries of life.

In the ravine of Goongoonteh, and during the continuation of the journey as far as Killulloo, slight variations of trap formation were met with. The wacke is of a fine grain, and its constituents are indistinctly mingled; it is traversed by empty holes and bubbles, and occasionally by druses of zeolith. Coarse quartz, sandstone, and conglomerates are sometimes found towards the surface. The country must have frequently been agitated by violent earthquakes, detaching huge masses of rocks from the hills; and, bereft alike of vegetation and animal life, it presents altogether a most monotonous appearance.

The lower classes of animals, of ephemeral existence, are found on every living or vegetating body.

Of *Coleoptera* were observed: two species of Pimelia (longipes), one of Cetonia, of Copris (Isidis), of Erodius (gibbus), several Staphylini and one Gyrinus.

Of *Orthoptera*: Locusts, Blattidae, Mantidae, Truxalidae.

Of *Hymenoptera*; several bees, especially at Killulloo, one of which, marked with light brown segments on the abdomen and bearing a long sting, was exceedingly annoying.

Of *Piezata*: many different ants.

Of *Diptera* and *Hemiptera*: several species.

Of *Lepidoptera*: two species of Papilio and several of moths; and it was a matter of great wonder whence these butterflies obtained food in a country where even one flower could not be discovered.

Of *Myriapoda*: one Iulus, and several Scolopendra.

Arachnida were in great numbers: Mygale, Epeira, Lycosa, and one small Androctenus.

Of *Crustaceae*: near the sea-shore a Pagurus existed in astonishing numbers, and in the sweet waters a Daphnia.

Vertebrata were still scarcer; and the *Reptilia* had their representatives in the three orders Saurii, Ophidii, and Batrachii. A small lizard, very agile, existed under stones; also serpents, Vipera and Coluber, and in moist places Bufo and Rana.

Amongst the Birds—

Of *Rapaces*: Perenopterus and Falco are numerous.

Of *Gallinacea*: Numida meleagris, and various partridges.

Of *Cursorii*: Struthio-camelus and Otis.

Of *Ciconidae*: Ciconia Marabu.

Of *Cantores*: Corvus, Loxia, Sylvia, Vidua.

Of *Mammalia*, three species of Antelope, one of Hyrax, one of Equus (Onager), one of Sus (Phacochaerus); and fresh holes in the sand indicated the presence of animals most probably of the order Rodentia.

The sheep of the country are the Hejáz lamb (Ovis aries laticaudata); white body and black head and neck, covered with hair, and having thick, short, fat tails; male without horns. The goats and cattle are generally small in stature, of all colours, and surmounted with very large horns. The shepherd dogs are small, and spotted with yellow and white; they have long pointed skulls like the fox.

With regard to the flora of this part of the country, the small quantity found in flower, belongs, with few exceptions, to the family of the *Leguminosae*, amongst which the order of *Mimoseae* is the most extensive both in species and specimens; they are however all stunted and shrubby, and seldom attain any size. Still the only fuel and shade found during the journey was supplied by this tribe. There exist also several *Capparideae*; Cadaba, Sodada, Capparis. Cadaba rotundifolia is the most common.

The *Asclepiadeae* are represented in the Stapelia pulvinata, which however was seldom found in blossom, and in the Pergularia tomentosa, with stately flowers and capsules.

The *Malvaceae* existed in Ruitzia and Abutilon; and the other families found by the wayside, Moringeae, Rutaceae, Tamariscineae, Chenopodeae, Amaranthaceae, Cruciferae, presented only solitary specimens.

Of the *Euphorbiaceae* there were but three; and of the Palm tribe there only appeared to be two species, the Phoenix dactylifera and Hyphaene crucifera, both of which gradually disappeared as the soil improved.

Nature has scattered the necessaries of existence with a niggard hand over these desert plains, and the supply of water is indeed scanty. In such a hot climate, those pools which are not fed by running streams soon become adulterated by the decomposition of organic and inorganic matter. The wacke cannot resist any long exposure, and thence the water imbibes oxide of iron and muriate of soda, discovered in the pools of Goongoonteh, Allooli, and Bedi Kuroof; and again the numerous flocks and cattle of the caravans which are driven into the pools taint and corrupt the liquid in a still more offensive manner. The fetid smell and taste of the waters of

Duwáylaka, Amádoo, Fiáloo, and Killulloo, is indeed so oppressive as to be subdued only by a considerable quantity of spirit; and moreover the deposited mud, when stirred up, emits a volume of sulphuretted hydrogen. During the wet season all the lower parts of the country are said to be exceedingly unhealthy, violent storms and incessant rain in the plains and wadies forcing the inhabitants to retreat to the mountains.

From Killulloo to the Foot of the Abyssinian Mountains

The desert of the Adaïel, spreading from the sea to the foot of the Shoan Alps, is not altogether a plain, as it has been most likely in remote ages, numerous wadies, with banks more or less high, now intersecting the greater part of it. These banks rise in some instances to hills of firm rock, generally wacke. They however consist of but lightly cemented conglomerates, or loose boulders. Towards the middle, as the ground rises, extinct volcanoes make their appearance, sometimes scattered and solitary, with indistinct cones and craters, completely covered with volcanic cinders, and sending off sheets of lava in all directions; or in whole clusters, with cones and craters complete, connected with each other, and environed by belts of their products. The extensive plain of Eyrolúf is a solid level of a dark, black, undecayed lava.

The tract of land between Killulloo and Dathára especially has been visited and overwhelmed by the action from below, which, having reversed the original disposition, has covered the surface with the effects of its violence. There is little to be seen of the under parts, although here and there some of the later formation, the residuum of the calcareous waters, has spread like a thin coat over the low grounds; but violent commotions have again and again altered and destroyed the first appearance, and it is now difficult to determine the centre pool from whence the fiery stream issued. In the absence of a main volcano and a main volcanic range, it may be concluded that, similar to some violent eruptions in South America, large mountains have been thrown up in the midst of former extensive plains, the fluid and half-fluid matter having burst forth wherever they were nearest to the surface.

Small extinct volcanoes were found on the plains of Sultélli and Eyrolúf. The road passes close to the isolated cone of one of these, called Jebel Hélmund. The walls are straight and black, covered with several smaller cones of ashes; the hill itself is about four hundred feet in height; the crater is on the eastern side, a little below the top; and the sides, which are steep and sloping, are clothed with shrubs towards the base.

On the road to Moo stands a similar volcano; but the influence of these craters does not seem to have extended far beyond the immediate neighbourhood, although there is a connexion between the whole cluster on the plain of Mittur, which may be seen in the small lava streams and débris of volcanic product on the adjoining plains of Sultélli and Eyrolúf. It is not, however, apparent that they alone have formed the present state of the surface, as the south-eastern side of the plains is terminated by a much older formation of wacke.

Between Meinha-tólli and Madéra-dubba, obsidian, pumice, clinkstone, and fresh-water limestone containing shells of Melania, were strewed about Excellent soil is found in all these situations, the low grounds being overflowed at some seasons, and, as in all volcanic countries, producing much vegetation. The extensive plains of Moolu and Burdúdda are thickly covered with grass, and intersected by small brooks and pools, terminating towards the Háwash in very broken, hilly ground, and the large plain on the eastern bank of the river bears every sign of being annually deluged.

The country of the Adaïel is throughout very sparingly watered. During spring and autumn the hills collect sufficient rain-water for numerous rivulets, which after a course of scarcely one mile are absorbed by the sands, and dry up altogether by the end of the rains, whilst the deep hollows and clefts in the firmer rock preserve small quantities for the dry months of the year. The Háwash itself, although receiving all the rivers of Efát, and of the eastern declivity of the Shoan mountains, does not reach the sea. The banks, thickly overgrown, are about thirty feet in height, and very abrupt. Its fall is scarcely perceptible, yet the rush of the water is very considerable.

On the western bank volcanic hills and sheets of water again appear, the latter being situated lower than the bed of the stream. One of these, impregnated with alkali, is evidently an old crater filled up, and supplied by a hot mineral spring. The water is much esteemed for washing clothes; it possesses an hydrothionic smell and a bitter taste, resembling that of the salt of magnesia; but the borders are verdant, and a species of Cyperus grows luxuriantly in the water.

This portion of the country, though still sparingly supplied with the means of subsistence, is more favourable for specimens of zoology than the burning tract between Tajúra and Killulloo.

Of *Beetles* the family *Coprophaga* had many representatives: Scarabaeus, Copris, Ateuchus, Onitis, Aphodius, Trox; Melolontha; four species of Cetonia (on the Aloe); one Silpha, Hister, Abax, Graphipterus, Anthia, Staphylinus, Elater, Cantharis, Erodius, Moluria, Pimelia, Mylabria, Chrysomela.

Of *Orthoptera*, large flights of Gryllus migratorius were observed near Azbóti. Acrydium and Gryllotalpa very common throughout. Also many Neuroptera, and termite cone studding the face of the country.

Of *Acephala* only one, Unio, was found near the Háwash.

A few frogs were seen in the waters, but no fish; and although lizards abounded on the land, there were no serpents. One large-sized tortoise was picked up.

Birds of all descriptions inhabit the plains and enliven the scanty woods: the ostrich, Otis arabs, the partridge, ducks, adjutant, Charadrius spinosus, Psittacus, Lampromis, Tanagra erythrorhyncha, Pyrrhocorax. Of beasts, the giant in creation, the elephant, and his rival in hugeness, the hippopotamus, abound in the plain of the Háwash; and rapacious animals, the lion, the leopard, and the hyaena, prowling about the camp during the night, render indispensable the protection of a stout thorn fence.

Of the order *Rodentia* the porcupine is common; also a variety of rats.

Of *Ruminantia*: a few antelopes.

Of *Fissungula*: Hyrax.

Of *Setigera*; Phacochaerus abyssinicus; and of *Lemures*: Galago.

The flora, so dependent upon the nature of the ground, offers little variety throughout this tract, although a few new plants were found in the favoured plain of Sultélli. Four *Compositae* (one Santolina), three *Leguminosae* (one Cassia, resembling Senna), one *Euphorbia* (rotundifolia), one *Solanum*, one *Cucurbitacea* (Cucumis africanus), one *Crucifera* (Farsetia linearis), three *Malvaceae* (Hibiscus urens, Althaea spec.), one *Tiliacea* (Grewia spec.), one *Cistinea* (Helianthemum spec.), one *Acanthacea* (Acanthus carduifolius), four *Gramineae*, one *Cyperacea*.

There were, however, no large timber trees, though edible berries of a sub-acid taste were supplied from a Helianthemum and a Grewia. Between Waramilli and Naga Koomi the shrubs of the Balsamodendron myrrha were first discovered, and these continued as far as the Háwash. Grass too is met with on the wide plains. Large camel-thorn acacias, and a strange tree of the family Capparidea, at intervals interrupt the uniform desert waste; but even the luxuriant vegetation which prevails on the banks of the Háwash contains little besides the Tamarix africana.

A high jungle of Acacia extends near the plain of Azbóti, supplying an abundance of sweet gum-arabic, and the last stage to Dathára is encumbered with the Aloe soccotrina. There are also many fine forest trees in the valley of Kokaï, amongst which the Tamarindus indica stands conspicuous; but no cultivation whatsoever is to be seen during the entire progress of upwards of three hundred miles from the sea-coast to the green hills of Abyssinia.

Description of the Frankincense Tree, as Found near Cape Guardufoi, on the Somauli Coast, by Captain C.B. Kempthorne, Indian Navy, Commanding the Hon. Company's Sloop of War "Clive."

At Bunder Cassim, about one hundred miles to the eastward of Berbera, the mountains come close down to the coast. There is a pass and road over them, and a few hours' walking will, it is said, lead to a fine climate, and to a beautifully fertile country, abounding in the elephant, the rhinoceros, and the lion, and thickly populated by pastoral tribes. Several rivers take their source in the high land, and, flowing to the southward and eastward, fall into the Indian Ocean, 4 degrees or 5 degrees north of the equator.

The chief town of the Miggertheyn Somauli is at Bunder Maryah, which lies twenty miles south-west of Ras Feeluk. The range is here about 5000 feet in altitude, and three miles from the shore. Ascending 1000 feet, a wide plain presents itself, bounded on every side by precipitous mountains studded with the frankincense and gum acacia trees, but looking bare and naked from the total absence of underwood.

The frankincense assumes the most singular aspect, from the fact of its invariably growing from the bare and smooth sides of the white marble rocks of which these bills are composed, without any soil whatever to nourish it. Many of the trees have even attached themselves to the huge masses that have rolled down into the valley, and now lie scattered over the stony surface. From the base of the trunk, and about treble its diameter, a very round thick substance is protruded, of a nature between bark and wood. This adheres most firmly to the stone, and at a distance resembles a mixture of mortar and lime. From the centre of the mass the stem, having first taken a bend or curve outwards of several inches, rises straight up to a height of forty feet. It throws from the top short branches covered with a very bright green foliage, the leaves being narrow and rounded at the end, five or six inches in length by one broad, crimped like the frill of a shirt; or rather bearing a stronger resemblance to that beautiful species of sea-weed found along the coast of England, and styléd by urchins "the old gentleman's ruffles."

From a foot to eighteen inches is the usual girth of the stem, and it tapers gradually away to the summit. The bark is perfectly smooth, and consists of four distinct layers. The outermost of all is very thin, and similar to that of the beech. The two next are of a singularly fine texture, resembling oiled letter-paper, perfectly transparent, and of a beautiful amber colour. It is used by the Somaulis to write upon. The inner bark of all is about an inch thick, of a dull-reddish hue, tough, and not unlike leather, but yielding a strong aromatic perfume. The wood is white and soft, and might be applied to many useful purposes. By making a deep incision into the inner rind, the gum exudes profusely, of the colour and consistency of milk, but hardening into a mass by exposure to the atmosphere.

The whole mountain range from Bunder Maryah to Cape Guardufoi is composed of limestone and marble, and near the latter place especially the marble is so white and pure that it approaches to alabaster. Pink and greyish black are also common colours, and in parts it might be mistaken for sandstone, until chipped off with the hammer. On the plain visited the frankincense is nowhere to be found resting upon the ground, or upon any sort of soil, and the purer the marble to which it adheres the finer the growth of the tree. It would seem that this singular production of the vegetable world derives its sole nourishment from carbonate of lime. The young trees produce the best and most valuable gum, the older merely yielding a clear glutinous fluid resembling copal varnish, and exhaling a strong resinous odour.

During the south-west monsoon the pastoral tribes in the neighbourhood of Ras Feeluk collect large quantities of frankincense, which they barter to the Banians, of whom a few reside at the villages along the Abyssinian coast. Boats from Maculla, and from other ports on the opposite Arabian shore, also come across during the fine season and carry away the gums that have been accumulated, and which are exchanged for a coarse kind of cotton cloth worn by the Somauli.